SCHOOL OF ADVANCED STUDY UNIVER'
Institute of Languages, Cultur

Mapping Post-War Italian Literature
Boom and Aftermath (1956–1979)

imlr books

This series (formerly known as igrs books) aims to bring to the public monographs and collections of essays in the field of modern foreign languages. Proposals for publication are selected by the Institute's editorial board, which is advised by a peer review committee of some fifty senior academics in the field. To make titles as accessible as possible to an English-speaking and multi-lingual readership, volumes are written in English and quotations given in English translation.

For further details, visit:
https://ilcs.sas.ac.uk/search-publications/imlr-books

Editorial Board

imlr books Volume 18

Volume Editor
Dr Anne Simon

Mapping Post-War Italian Literature
Boom and Aftermath (1956–1979)

Giulia Brecciaroli

SCHOOL OF ADVANCED STUDY UNIVERSITY OF LONDON

Institute of Languages, Cultures and Societies

2024

Published by the

Institute of Languages, Cultures and Societies
School of Advanced Study, University of London
Senate House, Malet Street, London WC1E 7HU
https://ilcs.sas.ac.uk

This title is published in association with the University of London Press
https://www.london.ac.uk/about-us/how-university-run/university-london-press

Cover image
View from Milan Cathedral over the Palazzo Reale with the
Velasca Tower in the background
Detail from photograph by PHOTOCREO Michal Bednarek
Shutterstock ID 117911920

First published 2024

ISBN 978 0 85457 284 7
ISSN 2632-9573 (Print)
ISBN 978-0-85457-285-4 (.pdf)
ISBN 978-1-915249-67-8 (.epub)
DOI https://doi.org/10.14296/wxvs7011

To the memory of my grandparents Aldo, Delia, Leonella and Luigi.
With gratitude and love.

Contents

Acknowledgements

This book has developed over nearly a decade and has benefitted from the help and support of many friends and colleagues. I am grateful to all of them. I am particularly indebted to my doctoral supervisor Jennifer Burns for her expert and perceptive guidance and for the support she has provided whenever (often) doubts and issues arose during my years as a doctoral student. I should also thank my viva examiners, Mila Milani and Silvia Ross, whose comments and observations have helped to sharpen the analysis in this book. Charles Burdett, Director of the Institute of Languages, Cultures and Societies at the University of London, has been an invaluable mentor. Without his critical insights and outstanding inspirational skills, my thesis would probably not have made it into book form. The entire team at the Institute of Languages, Cultures and Societies have been incredibly helpful and supportive. I am extremely grateful to Jane Lewin and Anne Simon for guiding me through the publication process with great professionalism and for their essential copyediting and proofreading work on the text. Sincere thanks are also due to the anonymous reviewers of the ILCS.

Furthermore, I also wish to express my gratitude to the University of Warwick for generously funding my doctoral research and to the Modern Humanities Research Association, whose Research Scholarship enabled me to write a further chapter and put together my application for the series 'imlr books'. My thanks also go to Graham for helping me to translate the quotations from the novels and for polishing my English on many an occasion.

Having lost my last grandmother this year, I would like to dedicate this book to my grandparents, loving figures of a childhood of which I shall always retain very happy memories. My grandfather Aldo, who passed away when I was still little, once told me that he regretted he would not be able to witness my school years as he thought I would do well. To this day, I am not sure I deserve the kind faith he had in me, but it makes all my efforts more worthwhile.

Note to the Reader

Throughout this book reference is made to both the original Italian editions and their published English translations. In quotations and the Bibliography the Italian text comes first and the English translation follows. Where no published English translation is given, the translations are by the author. In references to frequently cited primary sources the following abbreviations have been used:

FI   Alberto Arbasino, *Fratelli d'Italia* (Milan: Feltrinelli, 1963)
I   Luciano Bianciardi, *L'integrazione* (Milan: Feltrinelli, 2014 [1960])
VA   Luciano Bianciardi, *La vita agra* (Milan: Rizzoli, 1993 [1962])
HL   Luciano Bianciardi, *La vita agra; or, It's a Hard Life*, trans. by Eric Mosbacher (London: Hodder & Stoughton, 1965)
DD   Carlo Fruttero and Franco Lucentini, *La donna della domenica* (Milan: Mondadori, 1972)
SW   Carlo Fruttero and Franco Lucentini, *The Sunday Woman*, trans. by William Weaver (London: Collins, 1974)
PN   Carlo Fruttero and Franco Lucentini, *A che punto è la notte* (Milan: Mondadori, 1987 [1979])
VS   Natalia Ginzburg, *Le voci della sera*, in *Opere*, 2 vols (Milan: Mondadori, 1986), I, 667–777
VE   Natalia Ginzburg, *Voices in the Evening*, trans. by D. M. Low (London: The Hogarth Press, 1963)
LS   Anna Maria Ortese, *La lente scura. Scritti di viaggio*, ed. by Luca Clerici (Milan: Adelphi, 2004 [1991])
VI   Guido Piovene, *Viaggio in Italia* (Milan: Mondadori, 1958)
TT   Giorgio Scerbanenco, *Traditori di tutti* (Milan: Garzanti, 1999 [1966])
DM   Giorgio Scerbanenco, *Duca and the Milan Murders*, trans. by Eileen Ellenbogen (London: Cassell, 1972)

VP   Giorgio Scerbanenco, *Venere privata* (Milan: Garzanti, 1999 [1966])

M   Paolo Volponi, *Memoriale* (Milan: Garzanti, 1991 [1962])

MM   Paolo Volponi, *The Memorandum*, trans. by Belén Sevareid (London: Calder & Boyars, 1967)

MC   Paolo Volponi, *Le mosche del capitale* (Turin: Einaudi, 1991 [1989])

Introduction

The Economic Boom as Problematic Transition

In Italy the years after World War II brought about dramatic changes in lifestyle and in social and economic structures, one continuing symptom being the fact that the period of extraordinary growth which followed the reconstruction of the immediate post-war years is still remembered as the 'miracle' or the 'boom'.[1] When thinking of those years, what comes to mind first are glittering images of good-looking young people speeding by in their brand-new Fiat Cinquecento cars and on Lambretta motor scooters, or of beaming housewives who have had their lives transformed by the new electrical home appliances which have conquered the market. These associations have sedimented in the collective imagination thanks to the many advertisements, photographs and video clips of the time and have become the iconographic symbols of the allegedly carefree prosperity and unprecedented mobility of the post-war years. In public opinion the economic boom is also associated with the golden era of Italian TV and cinema.[2] It is not rare for Italians today to compare the issues

---

1   It is significant, for example, that two of the key texts examined more closely in the course of this study use the term 'miracle' in their title: Guido Crainz, *Storia del miracolo italiano. Culture, identità, trasformazioni fra anni cinquanta e sessanta* (Rome: Donzelli, 2003 [1996]); and John Foot, *Milan since the Miracle: City, Culture and Identity* (Oxford: Berg, 2001).

2   Such views can be found, for example, in the documentaries of the Archivio Luce, whose rhetoric describes a glittering, prosperous, carefree period. This idea persists to the present day and is reinforced through the contrast to current socio-economic issues in Italy. An example of the enduring fascination with the boom as a golden era, in contrast to other phases in contemporary Italian history, is a recent novel by Giuseppe Lupo which gives a largely positive portrait of post-war Italian society: Giuseppe Lupo, *Gli anni del nostro incanto* (Venice: Marsilio, 2017).

that beset present-day Italian society with the post-war period, when things were allegedly 'going well'. Nevertheless, historians and scholars of contemporary Italy have increasingly pointed out the contradictions that marked the process of economic development in the 1950s and 1960s.

In the course of a handful of years, on the cusp between those two decades, Italian society was transformed dramatically. After twenty years of Fascist dictatorship, the disastrous outcome of the Second World War and the efforts of the reconstruction period, in the early 1960s Italy experienced a phase of extraordinary economic development, turning from a traditionally agrarian, impoverished country into one of Europe's largest industrial producers, especially in the automotive sector and electrical appliances industry.[3] The boom did not happen overnight. It was enabled by a particular set of circumstances, such as the development of international trade from the 1950s to the 1970s; the influx of American capital, machinery and 'know-how' through the Marshal Plan deployed in Italy after the Second World War; the discovery of new sources of energy (particularly gas and hydrocarbons in the Val Padana); and the low cost of labour, which made Italian industry competitive on the international market.[4] That having been said, economic recovery still proceeded at a slow pace in the aftermath of the war and the reconstruction years. The concentration and intensity of the subsequent growth period, the boom being conventionally dated from 1958 to 1963, are, therefore, especially remarkable, even against the backdrop of Europe-wide economic development.[5]

The fact that growth occurred in such an extraordinarily short period of time and was followed by a downward trend in the global economy only a decade later certainly affected the course of action of Italian governments and their ability to tackle the major socio-political tensions of those years.[6] The international oil crisis of 1973 put an end to the positive economic phase. Guido Crainz's definition of 'paese

---

3 Paul Ginsborg, *A History of Contemporary Italy: Society and Politics 1943–1988* (London: Penguin, 1990), pp. 213–15.

4 Ginsborg, *A History of Contemporary Italy*, pp. 212–14.

5 Michael Caesar and Peter Hainsworth, for instance, have observed that in post-war Italy the transformations 'occurred more rapidly and in more concentrated a form probably than in any other European nation' (Michael Caesar and Peter Hainsworth, 'The Transformation of Post-War Italy', in *Writers and Society in Contemporary Italy: A Collection of Essays*, ed. by Michael Caesar and Peter Hainsworth (Leamington Spa: Berg, 1984), pp. 1–34 (p. 2)).

6 Ginsborg, *A History of Contemporary Italy*, p. 351.

mancato' [a country that never realized its full potential] conveys the idea of the missed opportunity for Italian post-war governments to deal with long-standing social issues by implementing structural reforms and building a robust collective dimension.[7] This failure fostered attitudes of individualism and economic gain[8] and may help to shed light on later phases of Italian society, in particular the conflicts of 1968, the mid-1970s and the 1980s.[9] It can be argued that the post-war period contained the germ of some of the later developments in Italian society and was somehow a testing ground in which models and attitudes that persisted in the following decades were generated. The controversial legacy of the boom may be detected in Italy's socio-political instability in the following decades, as well as in the widespread corruption of the Italian political and administrative systems, which was brought to public attention by the Tangentopoli scandal of the early 1990s.[10]

There is no doubt that the boom also brought advancements in Italian society, not only in terms of the increased wealth of the expanding middle class, but also in terms of a certain secularization of culture and society. Nevertheless, the fact that the boom was essentially unregulated and governed by the free play of the market accounts for many of the inconsistencies and discrepancies that marked the process of economic development.[11] Some of Italy's existing inequalities and territorial imbalances became deeper, this being especially the case with the long-standing gap between the North and South, the latter

7   Guido Crainz, *Il paese mancato. Dal miracolo economico agli anni Ottanta* (Rome: Donzelli, 2003), pp. 21–30.

8   Ginsborg observes that the boom lacked 'the dimension of collective responsibility' and therefore reinforced individualistic attitudes that were already present in Italian society (Ginsborg, *A History of Contemporary Italy*, p. 240).

9   Crainz, *Storia del miracolo italiano*, p. xiii.

10   As Crainz puts it, 'la radice dei processi e dei conflitti successivi (e forse del loro esito) sta insomma in larga misura nell'interazione di quegli elementi che appaiono chiaramente nello snodo del 1963–4: processi contraddittori ma potenti di modernizzazione; squilibri persistenti della società italiana, permanere di arretratezze culturali che improntano largamente le istituzioni del paese; fallimento di una politica riformatrice' [the root of subsequent processes and conflicts (and perhaps their outcome) lies to a large extent in the interaction of those elements that first appear clearly in the years 1963–4: contradictory but powerful processes of modernization; persistent imbalances in Italian society; the incalcitrance of a cultural backwardness that to a great extent characterized the country's institutions; the failure of a reforming policy] (Crainz, *Paese mancato*, p. 30).

11   Ginsborg, *A History of Contemporary Italy*, p. 216.

historically the more deprived half of the country. After the war the leading Italian industries were overwhelmingly based in the North, while the Southern economy still depended primarily on agriculture and other traditional activities.[12] The boom also accentuated the discrepancy between private and public patterns of consumption due to insufficient public funding allocated to the social service sectors such as health and education.[13] The picture, however, was multifaceted and reflected a society which, like all societies, was of course neither static nor homogeneous and reacted accordingly to the transformations underway. Guido Crainz suggests that it is more appropriate to speak of 'plural Italies' ('diverse Italie') rather than one monolithic, single Italy that underwent economic development.[14] Dichotomies such as North–South are more nuanced than commonly assumed, as was the situation within specific areas of the country. Such complexity is mirrored in this book by the diverse literary voices and genres that explore different places within the national territory: the industrial cities of the North, the small-town environment of the provinces and the changing perception of the national territory.

While the boom unfolded in just a handful of years, the period on which this book focuses extends to embrace the 1970s as well, in order better to emphasize the impact of spatial changes and the fact that they continued to inspire the imagination of Italian writers in the following decades. The long-term perspective does not intend to negate the significance of the boom as an abrupt transition, nor to underestimate the swift changes that were brought about in the lifestyle and aspirations of the Italian people. On the contrary, the fact that radical transformations were concentrated in a short period of time, a peculiarity of the Italian boom as opposed to similar growth trajectories in other Western countries, is key to the understanding of the main themes and threads in this book, such as Italy's controversial relationship to its own authoritarian history and a widespread sense of disorientation arising as the result of rapid transformation from the late 1950s onwards. The diffusion of more progressive ways of life gradually loosened Italians' traditional reliance on the institutions of the family and Church, historically essential points of reference, and hence contributed to feelings of uncertainty.[15]

12   Ginsborg, *A History of Contemporary Italy*, pp. 216–17.

13   Ginsborg, *A History of Contemporary Italy*, p. 216.

14   Crainz, *Storia del miracolo italiano*, p. viii.

15   Jennifer Burns, 'Founding Fathers: Giorgio Scerbanenco', in *Italian Crime Fiction*, ed. by Giuliana Pieri (Cardiff: University of Wales Press, 2011), pp. 27–47 (p. 35).

Italy's economic boom was an ambiguous transition, marked by the co-existence of sheer innovation and aspects of continuity with the past, the latter especially visible in the machinery of state and administrative structures, which passed practically unchanged into the Republic.[16] If economic growth inaugurated a new phase in Italian history, it also soon enough became clear that in the post-war Republic renewal went hand-in-hand with the survival of elements from the pre-war years. In the 1950s the state could still use repressive Fascist laws against its opponents.[17] The persistence of practices of repression and intimidation, aimed especially at members of the Communist Party and left-wing activists, found a new justification in the climate of the Cold War and in the context of the anti-Communist alliance between the countries of the Western Bloc.[18] Historians generally agree in their interpretation of a collective forgetting of Italy's totalitarian past to suit the needs of the reconstruction process at the end of the war. As Mirco Dondi puts it, in post-war Italian society 'forgetfulness and prosperity seemed to go together'.[19] Giuliana Minghelli has labelled this attitude the 'amnesiac culture of *benessere* [economic wellbeing]'.[20] Italy's unresolved relationship with its past and the implications of its collective forgetfulness cast a shadow over Italian society in the boom years and beyond.

16   Christopher Duggan, 'Italy in the Cold War Years and the Legacy of Fascism', in *Italy in the Cold War: Politics, Culture and Society, 1948–58*, ed. by Christopher Duggan and Christopher Wagstaff (Oxford: Berg, 1995), pp. 1–24 (p. 3). Claudio Pavone has made a seminal contribution to research on the continuity of the State. See, e.g., Claudio Pavone, 'La continuità dello stato. Istituzioni e uomini', in *Italia 1945–48. Le origini della Repubblica*, ed. by Enzo Piscitelli and others (Turin: Giappichelli, 1974), pp. 137–289.

17   Duggan, 'Italy in the Cold War Years', pp. 5–6.

18   Crainz claims: 'La "democrazia congelata" degli anni della guerra fredda si realizza tramite apparati e uomini formatisi negli anni venti e trenta; si traduce in meccanismi continui di controllo e di "esclusione"; vede i diritti formalmente riconosciuti al cittadino messi costantemente in mora da pratiche di discriminazione' [The 'frozen democracy' of the Cold War years is achieved through apparatuses and men trained in the Twenties and Thirties; it translates into continuous mechanisms of control and 'exclusion'; sees the rights formally granted to the citizen constantly nullified by practices of discrimination] (Crainz, *Storia del miracolo italiano*, p. viii).

19   Mirco Dondi, 'The Fascist Mentality after Fascism', in *Italian Fascism: History, Memory and Representation*, ed. by R. J. B. Bosworth and Patrizia Dogliani (Basingstoke: MacMillan, 1999), pp. 141–60 (p. 151).

20   Giuliana Minghelli, 'Icons of Remorse: Photography, Anthropology and the Erasure of History in 1950s Italy', *Modern Italy*, 21 (2016), 383–407 (p. 386).

A Literary Perspective

The crucial shift in modern Italian history is addressed here through a literary perspective and, more specifically, through the analysis of the representation of post-war Italy's changing geography in the works of several Italian authors, spanning a range of literary genres and written over the course of roughly twenty years, from the end of the 1950s to the end of the 1970s. Literature is a powerful tool for studying the changes occurring in society, thanks to its ability to disclose multiple layers of interpretation and meaning and to transport readers into the lived experience of subjects whose point of view may otherwise be inaccessible to them. The texts examined in this book are no exception. On the one hand, they provide original insights into post-war Italy's urban renewal and, on the other, they challenge clichéd representations of the Italian territory and national identity, problematizing long-standing commonplaces and narratives. Literary works are not inert objects: the tension they generate reverberates through the diversified positioning of readers, sparking debate and encouraging further discussion – all the more so in the era of mass communication.[21]

The texts discussed in this book capture the dual nature of space as factual and symbolic by portraying concrete cityscapes and landscapes and by steering the imagination associated with them, which in turn shapes these places both discursively and tangibly. In this sense, the genres analysed in this book may be regarded as discursive constructions of reality. The views that the authors express inevitably reflect 'collectively organized' interpretations of society, which are internalized and embedded within their writings.[22] It also goes to show that the dialectical relationship between literature, imagination and space is rich and fecund.[23] Literary representations of space prove especially fruitful for investigating the complexities

---

21   As Ann Hallamore Caesar and Michael Caesar put it, writers and 'literary objects' are 'active agents' in their society (Ann Hallamore Caesar and Michael Caesar, *Modern Italian Literature*, Cultural History of Literature (Cambridge: Polity, 2007), p. 8).

22   Charles Burdett, 'Nomos, Identity and Otherness: Ciro Poggiali's *Diario AOI 1936–1937* and the Representation of the Italian Colonial World', *Papers of the British School at Rome*, 79 (2011), 329–49 (p. 332).

23   Francesco Fiorentino argues that 'lo spazio che consideriamo reale si produce sempre da questa tensione, da questa dialettica tra l'esperienza dei luoghi del mondo e le loro rappresentazioni' [the space that we consider real is always produced by this tension, by this dialectic between the experience

of post-war Italian society, for they illuminate the interconnection of socio-political, economic and cultural changes, as well as the direct relation to the interiority of individuals. The question of the subject's interaction with the environment is at the core of humanist geography and its definitions of place and space.[24] As Silvia Ross puts it, 'the human experiential element of a given geography is [...] as important as the inanimate surroundings'.[25] In this study the interplay between these two poles is illuminated and centrality assigned to the writers' experience of space by examining their interiorization of spatial changes through the lens of different genres. These include crime fiction and travel literature, which have traditionally been seen as less important, have received limited scholarly attention in Italy (but whose renewed popularity, starting from the 1960s onwards, documents the redefinition of genre normativity in those years) and which therefore allow original perspectives on space and identity. By examining quite diverse authorial perspectives and forms of writing, the ambiguity and intensity of feeling in the period under scrutiny emerge more starkly, along with some of the underlying patterns of post-war Italian society.

The chapters that follow look at the rapid growth of Milan and Turin, the main industrial centres of the richer North, from the boom years onwards. They do so through a series of novels by Luciano Bianciardi and Paolo Volponi (Chapter 1); and the crime novels by

---

of places in the world and their representations]; and that 'i luoghi esistono – prevalentemente forse – in forza dell'immaginario che essi producono e da cui poi sono ri-prodotti. Lo studio delle topografie letterarie è in buona parte studio di questo scambio incessante tra la scrittura letteraria e lo spazio geografico che agisce sui testi e dentro i testi in cui è incluso o anche escluso, taciuto o descritto, sognato, meditato' [places exist – mainly perhaps – by virtue of the imaginary that they produce and from which are re-produced. The study of literary topographies is largely a study of this incessant exchange between literary writing and the geographical space that acts on the texts and within the texts in which it is included or even excluded, silenced or described, dreamt, meditated upon] (Francesco Fiorentino, 'Verso una geostoria della letteratura', in *Letteratura e geografia. Atlanti, modelli, letture*, ed. by Francesco Fiorentino and Carla Solivetti (Macerata: Quodlibet, 2012), pp. 13–44 (pp. 15, 16)).

24 Silvia Ross observes that 'what does emerge in the diverse theoretical understandings of place and space is an increasing acknowledgement that these concepts must perforce be analysed in relation to subjectivity [...]. Thus, when interpreting space, it becomes necessary to ask questions such as: Who perceives? How do the actions of the subject produce space? How does the subject experience space?' (Silvia Ross, *Tuscan Spaces: Literary Constructions of Place*, Toronto Italian Studies (Toronto: Toronto University Press, 2010), p. 10).

25 Ross, *Tuscan Spaces*, p. 11.

Giorgio Scerbanenco and the writing pair of Carlo Fruttero & Franco Lucentini (Chapter 2). Specifically, the works examined here include Bianciardi's *L'integrazione* [*Integration*] (1960) and *La vita agra* [*The Bitter Life*] (1962); Volponi's *Memoriale* [*Memorandum*] (1962) and *Le mosche del capitale* [*The Flies of Capital*] (1989); Giorgio Scerbanenco's 'Lamberti novels' *Venere privata* [*A Private Venus*] (1966), *Traditori di tutti* [*Traitors to All*] (1966), *I ragazzi del massacro* [*The Massacre Kids*] (1968) and *I milanesi ammazzano al sabato* [*Milanese Kill on Saturdays*] (1969); and Fruttero and Lucentini's *La donna della domenica* [*The Sunday Woman*] (1972) and *A che punto è la notte* [*At What Point is the Night*] (1979). Chapter 3 then goes on to explore the representation of the small-town environment of the northern provinces, where the changes are perhaps less dramatic but still significant, in Natalia Ginzburg's *Le voci della sera* [*Voices in the Evening*] (1961). Finally, the fourth chapter considers the transformations in the socio-cultural landscape of the country through three examples of Italian domestic travel writing. It focuses specifically on Anna Maria Ortese's collection of travel writings, which appeared in various newspapers between the end of the 1930s and the mid-1960s and were later collected in *La lente scura* [*The Dark Lens*] (1991). It also takes into account Guido Piovene's *Viaggio in Italia* [*Journey through Italy*] (1957) and Alberto Arbasino's *Fratelli d'Italia* [*Brothers of Italy*] (1963). Italy's physical territory and the perception of distances within the country were transformed by widely improved road and railway infrastructures connecting places that had appeared distant and almost irreducibly different from one another, as well as by the mass production of automobiles and motor scooters by companies such as Fiat and Piaggio. Christopher Duggan reports that the number of private cars circulating in Italy increased from 342,000 in the 1950s to nearly five million in the mid-1960s.[26]

The selection of literary texts and the emphasis on their representation of the changing geography of post-war Italy challenge narrations of the time frame under scrutiny as chiefly a period of achieved prosperity and growing optimism; and instead expose the less desirable consequences of modernization. Feelings of anxiety and unease that run through the texts may be related, on the one hand, to a rapid social change which is difficult to accommodate and, on the other, to the failure of Italian society to incorporate a moral confrontation with the past into its social and economic changes. This is not to deny that the post-war years also coincided with innovations

---

26 Duggan, 'Italy in the Cold War Years', p. 14.

in all aspects of Italian life, increasing wealth for larger sectors of the Italian population and cultural ferment. As Crainz puts it:

> Le potenzialità che si dispiegano in quel torno di tempo non suscitano solo frenesie acquisitive: alimentano anche fermenti, aspirazioni, ansie e progetti riformatori, in un pullulare di energie intellettuali di straordinaria vivacità.[27]

> [The potentialities that unfold in that lapse of time do not only arouse acquisitive frenzies: they also feed ferments, aspirations, anxieties and reform projects, in a teeming of intellectual energies of extraordinary vivacity.]

The intellectual energies evoked by Crainz are the same ones mobilized by the writers analysed here as they engage with the transformations underway. Anxiety may, therefore, also be a creative force that enables the authors to question established modes of representation, especially in relation to space and identity. By encouraging alternative ways of seeing and imagining society, literature once again has something specific and valuable to contribute in this context.

The authors examined here are both well-known figures and less frequently discussed writers of the period under scrutiny who offer an insightful experience of how change in those years was perceived. Existing literary criticism has generally privileged a formal and philological type of analysis.[28] The work of defining literary and intellectual figures from the period, such as Alberto Moravia and Natalia Ginzburg, has been approached by modern scholarship in ways that privilege existential themes and distinctive literary styles.

---

27   Crainz, *Storia del miracolo italiano*, p. xiii.

28   Examples of this general tendency in Italian literary criticism may be found in relation to all the writers examined in this study. An example of the tendency to analyse different literary genres separately is Salvatore Ritrovato and Donatella Marchi (eds), *Pianeta Volponi. Saggi interventi testimonianze* (Pesaro: Metauro, 2007). The chapters have been grouped into three thematic sections dedicated to poetry, the novel and the theatre respectively. The two former are the genres which Volponi employed most during his career, while the section on theatre offers a 'theatrical reading' of Volponi's *Il pianeta irritabile* [*The Irritable Planet*] (1978) by drawing on the fact that theatre was an integral part of Volponi's education and training as a writer. Another example is offered by the studies on Arbasino's *Fratelli d'Italia*, which have concentrated on the language and, more specifically, the type of plurilingualism used by the writer in the novel. See, e.g., Clelia Martignoni, Cinzia Lucchelli and Elisabetta Cammarata (eds), *La scrittura infinita di Alberto Arbasino. Studi su 'Fratelli d'Italia'*, Biblioteca di Autografo, 4 (Novara: Interlinea, 1999); and Chantal Randoing, 'Il plurilinguismo del romanzo-conversazione in *Fratelli d'Italia* di Alberto Arbasino', *Collection de l'ÉCRIT*, 11 (2007), 359–75.

Very few studies have addressed fictional spaces, urban descriptions or the writers' relationship with nature and the landscape.[29] A significant exception is the research which Marco Paoli has conducted on the representation of urban space in Scerbanenco's crime novels: a study to which Chapter 2 of this book is certainly indebted.[30] One of the main arguments in existing studies dedicated to the writers examined here is the idea that they have allegedly not received adequate attention from critics and are generally more talked about than read.[31] With the exception of Arbasino and Ginzburg, two major names in post-war Italian culture, and, one could argue, of Fruttero & Lucentini, a highly successful writing pair and prominent editors at the prestigious Einaudi publishing house, these writers are, for different reasons, considered to be marginal, discordant voices within the Italian literary tradition. This is particularly true in the case of Bianciardi, Volponi, Scerbanenco and Ortese, who have been labelled irregular and rebellious, also due to the difficulty of classifying their writings within the main literary trends of their time.[32]

---

29 See, e.g., Maria-Luise Caputo-Mayr, 'La funzione della natura e del paesaggio nei romanzi di Guido Piovene', *Italica*, 50 (1973), 53–65.

30 Marco Paoli, *Giorgio Scerbanenco: Urban Space, Violence and Gender Identity in Post-War Italian Crime Fiction*, Moving Texts/Testi mobili, 8 (Brussels: Lang, 2016).

31 Talking about Bianciardi, Gian Paolo Serino claims that, 'il vero dramma di Luciano Bianciardi è di essere più commentato che letto. Ancora oggi molti conoscono *La vita agra*, ma ben pochi l'hanno letto davvero' [When it comes to Luciano Bianciardi, the real tragedy is that he is more talked about than read. Even today, many know *La vita agra*, but very few have actually read it] (Gian Paolo Serino, *Luciano Bianciardi. Il precario esistenziale* (Florence: Clichy, 2015), p. 20).

32 In the case of Bianciardi, this issue is often raised together with the question of his bad-tempered, solitary personality, his prose allegedly possessing a similar, nervous quality. Pino Corrias uses the definition 'anarchico' [anarchist], while other critics have described Bianciardi as 'eretico' [heretical] and 'scrittore fuori dal coro' [a discordant, non-conformist literary voice]. See Pino Corrias, *Vita agra di un anarchico. Luciano Bianciardi a Milano* (Milan: Baldini & Castoldi, 1996); Giuseppe Muraca, *Utopisti ed eretici nella letteratura italiana contemporanea. Saggi su Silone, Bilenchi, Fortini, Pasolini, Bianciardi, Roversi e Bellocchio* (Soveria Mannelli: Rubbettino, 2000); and Giuseppe Muraca, *Luciano Bianciardi. Uno scrittore fuori dal coro* (Pistoia: Centro di Documentazione, 2012). A more recent book by Gian Paolo Serino, *Il precario esistenziale* (2015), confirms that to this day this image of Bianciardi continues to exert fascination over his readers and the wider intellectual community. Volponi has also been described as 'fuori dal coro, anti-canonico' [non-conformist, anti-canonical] and 'diverso' [different]. See Salvatore Ritrovato and Donatella Marchi, 'Nota', in *Pianeta Volponi*, ed. by Ritrovato and Marchi, pp. 7–8 (p. 7); and Alfonso Berardinelli, 'Volponi, uno scrittore "diverso"', in *Paolo Volponi. Il coraggio dell'utopia*, ed. by Massimo Raffaeli (Ancona: Transeuropa, 1997), pp. 11–18.

It is true that these authors show a non-normative approach to writing. They engage with 'marginal' literary genres (notably, crime fiction and travel writing) and with the popular press, as in the case of Bianciardi, while Volponi inaugurates the minor literary trend of *allegorismo* in the Italian literature of those years.[33] By employing formats such as the detective story and reportage, these writers have contributed to shifting the boundaries of the Italian literary canon in the post-war years. The authors' non-identification with the canon therefore needs to be read less in terms of opposition to the literary establishment, for they are still part of a certain high, or at least official, culture, and more in terms of the inability to associate them with the dominant literary trends and aesthetics of the time. Arbasino, a leading exponent of the Italian *Neoavanguardia* [Neo-Avantgarde], may be seen as an exception, even though that movement, later formalized in the textbooks, sought precisely to break with canonical definitions of what constitutes literature. Chapters 3 and 4 focus on female authors, Ginzburg and Ortese, to counterbalance the exclusively male viewpoint of the previous two chapters. As a case study exploring the small-town environment of the northern provinces, Ginzburg's *Le voci della sera* serves to problematize further the image of the North, which is often identified with major urban conglomerations (chiefly Milan) and treated in a rather monolithic way as the rich and more advanced half of the country.

Other Italian authors have engaged with the new realities of urbanization and industrialization. Amongst them one may mention Giovanni Testori, Ottiero Ottieri and Goffredo Parise, the latter two specifically concerned with the Italian corporate environment in the boom years. Testori's cycle *I segreti di Milano* [*The Secrets of Milan*] depicts the Milan of the suburbs, the prostitutes and proletarians who work in auto-repair shops and small workshops; and it does so with a style that still relies considerably on realism.[34] The most visible absence here is perhaps that of Italo Calvino. Among his books, those

---

33   As Monica Jansen points out, many critics regard *Le mosche del capitale* as 'la prima scrittura allegorica che attacca direttamente la società capitalistica moderna' [the first allegorical piece of writing that directly attacks modern capitalist society] (Monica Jansen, *Il dibattito sul postmoderno in Italia. In bilico tra dialettica e ambiguità* (Florence: Franco Cesati, 2002), p. 275).

34   See Marco Forti, 'Temi industriali della narrativa italiana', *Il Menabò*, 4 (1961), 213–39. *I segreti di Milano* includes *Il ponte della Ghisolfa* [*The Ghisolfa Bridge*] (1958), followed by the short story *La Gilda del Mac Mahon* [*Mac Mahon's Gilda*] (1959), the comedies *La Maria Brasca* [*Maria Brasca*] (1960) and *L'Arialda* [*Arialda*] (1960) and the novel *Il fabbricone* [*The Factory*] (1961).

that are more concerned with the transformations of post-war Italy are *Marcovaldo ovvero Le stagioni in città* [*Marcovaldo: Or, The Seasons in the City*] (1963), which narrates the difficulties that the main character Marcovaldo experiences in adjusting to big-city life after leaving the countryside; *La speculazione edilizia* [*A Plunge into Real Estate*] (1963), which addresses building speculation in the Ligurian Riviera; and *La nuvola di smog* [*Smog*] (1958), which tackles the issue of pollution, a rising concern in Italian society in those years. Calvino's work has received a great deal of critical attention, to the point where his views have come almost to define – within Italy and outside – the literary response to that period. For this reason, this book seeks to foreground other authors and texts which have not been as extensively read or discussed.

Between Modernity and Postmodernity

The analysis of how literary texts capture Italy's post-war socio-spatial transformations is supported by theories of space, which employ some of the formulations and arguments which have propelled the so-called 'spatial turn' in postmodern theory. The rejection of historical grand narratives centred on the idea of the universal and linear progression of history in favour of spatial categories for the study of reality has been identified by Fredric Jameson, Edward Soja, David Harvey and Umberto Eco, amongst other scholars, as one of the key features of the transition from the modern to the postmodern paradigm. Postmodern theories sought to offer a framework through which to make sense of the increasingly globalized and interconnected world that developed after the end of the Second World War with the unprecedented dissemination of information and communication technologies. Among the intellectuals whose work has led to the 'rediscovery' of space, one may certainly include Michel Foucault and Henri Lefebvre, whose writing provides an important point of reference for the analysis in Chapters 1 and 2. The relevance which Lefebvre's analysis of social space has gained in Anglo-American scholarship, especially after *La production de l'espace* was translated into English in 1991, has led a scholar such as Michael Dear to claim that Lefebvre was primarily responsible for re-orientating social theory away from analyses of time towards analyses of space.[35]

---

35 Michael J. Dear, *The Postmodern Urban Condition* (Oxford: Blackwell, 2000), p. 47.

Romano Luperini has pointed out that 'la condizione postmoderna comincia a essere avvertita, in Italia, già durante il cosiddetto "miracolo economico", ma si afferma in modo chiaro solo a partire dagli anni Settanta' [the postmodern condition already begins to make itself felt in Italy during the so-called 'economic miracle', but it is only from the 1970s onwards that it clearly and distinctly asserts itself].[36] The time frame of this book coincides with the slow gestation of postmodern ideas that began to infiltrate Italian intellectual debate and literary production from the second half of the 1950s and witnessed a more systematic consolidation in the 1980s. The economic and socio-cultural changes of the late 1950s began to undermine the hierarchical opposition, traditionally championed by the Italian intellectual establishment, between highbrow and lowbrow culture. The expansion of a wealthier, cultivated middle class meant that access to money and culture was granted to larger swathes of the Italian population and had the effect of reconfiguring the cultural landscape and traditional ways of producing and apprehending culture. Literature was directly affected by these social changes and writers and publishers responded in various ways to calls to redefine the distinctions between niche and popular culture.[37] Scholars of contemporary Italian culture and society stress the predominantly negative connotations traditionally held by mass culture in Italy.[38] David Forgacs and Stephen Gundle, for instance, have shown that since Fascism, and subsequently with the post-war Christian Democrat (Democrazia Cristiana; DC) governments – so in those years in which Italian civil society was under the sway of the two opposing institutions of the Catholic Church and the Italian Communist Party (Partito Comunista Italiano; PCI) – mass culture was denigrated as the product of passive indoctrination.[39] As Forgacs

---

36 Romano Luperini, *Controtempo. Critica e letteratura fra moderno e postmoderno: proposte, polemiche e bilanci di fine secolo* (Naples: Liguori, 1999), p. 170.

37 Caesar and Caesar, *Modern Italian Literature*, p. 9.

38 Popular culture has instead been treated as the equivalent of folklore, i.e., a spontaneous, grassroots form of cultural expression that cannot be controlled or imposed from above. Hence while mass culture evokes 'falsehood' and refers mostly to cultural products embodying the American hegemonic model, popular culture retains an 'aura of authenticity' (Zygmunt G. Barański and Robert Lumley, 'Turbulent Transitions: An Introduction', in *Culture and Conflict in Postwar Italy: Essays on Mass and Popular Culture*, ed. by Zygmunt G. Barański and Robert Lumley, University of Reading European and International Studies (London: Macmillan, 1990), pp. 1–17 (pp. 10–12)).

39 David Forgacs and Stephen Gundle, *Mass Culture and Italian Society from Fascism to the Cold War* (Bloomington, IN: Indiana University Press, 2007), pp. 1–2.

and Gundle argue, however, one should not underestimate the role of mass-media communication in increasing participation in the broader cultural debate, in raising socio-political awareness and in challenging conservative views on gender, sexuality and race.[40] They also stress that, in Italy, the mass media have contributed to fostering a sense of community and belonging.[41] As much as there were attempts by post-war governments to control social and cultural life, it would therefore be as mistaken to think of Italian culture monolithically as it would be to consider the people on the receiving end as merely passive agents.[42]

Umberto Eco was certainly one of the most acute observers of the post-war socio-cultural transformations, as well as a protagonist in the modernization of Italian culture through a prolific production of novels and critical essays. Already in *Opera aperta* [*The Open Work*] (1962), and subsequently in *Apocalittici e integrati* [*Apocalyptic and Integrated Intellectuals*] (1964),[43] Eco tackles trends such as the hybridization of forms of culture and explores the extent to which the opposition between popular culture, as genuine and autonomous, and mass culture, as merely the expression of (American) capitalist ideology, was called into question from the 1950s onwards. Eco's questioning of traditional cultural categories and deep-rooted assumptions about what constitutes good literature – especially his idea that mass culture can be an object of critical and literary analysis alongside subject matter traditionally seen as worthier of intellectual speculation – sparked heated debate amongst Italian intellectuals.[44] While postmodern thought was, therefore, met with resistance, if not open hostility, by an intellectual establishment that was still advocating an idea of elitist and classical culture as legitimate, the assimilation of postmodern

40   Forgacs and Gundle, *Mass Culture and Italian Society*, p. 2.

41   Forgacs and Gundle, *Mass Culture and Italian Society*, p. 17.

42   Against Pier Paolo Pasolini's idea of an 'anthropological revolution' that allegedly occurred in post-war Italian society, John Foot maintains that the cultural consumer negotiates models and notions of truth, occasionally producing forms of opposition and resistance (Foot, *Milan since the Miracle*, pp. 21–23).

43   *Apocalittici e integrati* introduced the now-famous distinction between the intellectuals who rejected stylistic and conceptual innovations altogether (apocalyptic) and the opposing group of intellectuals who, on the contrary, saluted the efforts at renewal enthusiastically, often showing a lack of critical judgement (integrated).

44   See Eco's reconstruction of the reception of *Opera aperta* and *Apocalittici e integrati* in later editions of these works, specifically, *Opera aperta*, 3rd edn (Milan: Bompiani, 1976 [1962]); and *Apocalittici e integrati*, 7th edn (Milan: Bompiani, 1988 [1964]).

ideas in Italy began at an early stage. Monica Jansen shows how the formulations of postmodern thinkers such as Jameson, Deleuze, Habermas and Lyotard found fertile ground within Italy's philosophical debate. Gianni Vattimo's weak-thought philosophy, in particular, was an attempt to re-orient Italian contemporary philosophy towards the relativism of postmodern theory and in opposition to dominant ideologies.[45] Italian architecture also incorporated postmodern ideas from an early stage, mostly through the Post-Modern movement of Charles Jencks.[46] Interdisciplinarity, another peculiarity of Italian postmodernism according to Jansen, could be witnessed in the cross-fertilization between different disciplines.[47] Literary journals such as *Alfabeta* and *Il Verri* testify, for instance, to the interaction between contemporary philosophy and literary criticism in those years.[48] The literary movements of the *Neoavanguardia* and the *Gruppo 93* in poetry (the latter created in 1989) developed within this context as a peculiar re-articulation of postmodern poetics and stylistics.

While periodization inevitably has a degree of arbitrariness, some critics treat 1956 as the beginning of a new phase in Italian literature by highlighting the continuities between the 1930s and 1940s and the fact that Neo-Realism, developed in the latter decade, re-semanticized some of the traits of the Realism of the 1930s.[49] The Hungarian Uprising of 1956 had deep repercussions for the Italian political and cultural climate, prompting a new intellectual openness that pre-dated by just two years the economic boom of 1958. Fittingly in the context of this book, in 1956 Piovene concluded his documentary journey through the Italian Peninsula before publishing *Viaggio in Italia* the following year. The end of the 1970s, when this study concludes, marked a further turning point in Italian literary production and intellectual debate, for the following decade witnessed the consolidation of postmodern ideas in all aspects of Italian cultural life. Significantly, the first Biennale of International Architecture, held in Venice in 1980 and organized by Italian architect Paolo Portoghesi, was largely inspired by Jencks's Post-Modern movement.[50] In 1979 Lyotard's *La*

---

45   Jansen, *Il dibattitto sul postmoderno in Italia*, p. 14.

46   Jansen, *Il dibattitto sul postmoderno in Italia*, p. 29.

47   Jansen, *Il dibattitto sul postmoderno in Italia*, p. 16.

48   Jansen, *Il dibattitto sul postmoderno in Italia*, p. 20.

49   Caesar and Caesar, *Modern Italian Literature*, p. 188. See also Anna Maria Torriglia, *Broken Time, Fragmented Space: A Cultural Map for Postwar Italy*, Toronto Italian Studies (Toronto: University of Toronto Press, 2002), pp. xii–xiii.

50   Jansen, *Il dibattitto sul postmoderno in Italia*, p. 42.

condition postmoderne [*The Postmodern Condition*] appeared in France, while in Italy Italo Calvino published his *Se una notte d'inverno un viaggiatore* [*If on a Winter's Night a Traveller*], which is widely regarded as one of the foremost examples of meta-literary fiction in the Italian contemporary tradition.[51] As confirmation of the new trend, Umberto Eco's *Il nome della rosa* [*The Name of the Rose*] came out the following year, in 1980. *Le mosche del capitale*, published in 1989, and *La lente scura*, published in 1991, may appear to be exceptions to the time period embraced by this book. However, *La lente scura* is a collection of travel pieces which had previously appeared in various newspapers and magazines. As for *Le mosche del capitale*, its publication was merely post-dated: Volponi had started to work on the book in 1975 and the story is set in 1970s Turin.[52]

Whilst a coherent framework of postmodern theories was yet to be consolidated in Italy in the years surveyed in this book, the privileged status of highbrow culture had been shaken, paving the way for the far-reaching cultural turn. The texts examined here bear witness to this cultural transition and must have absorbed, if only osmotically and without full-blown critical awareness (at least initially), impulses and reflections that were organized more systematically during the following decades. One may argue that the texts are at the intersection of two epochs; and while they retain some of the central themes of modernity, such as anxiety and alienation, they also anticipate the contours of postmodern literature. Their attention to space, in particular, is a way of challenging dominant categories and hierarchies that have shaped the built environment and its use. Hence the emphasis on the appropriation of urban spaces, as well as on the unfathomable elements of the urban environment, may be read as a rejection of the functional and 'clean' space of architectural Modernism, which embodies the Western value of rationality. The physical fabric of urban and provincial territory is apprehended in the selected writings as the stage on which the tensions between

---

51 Jennifer Burns, *Fragments of Impegno: Interpretations of Commitment in Contemporary Italian Narrative, 1980–2000* (Leeds: Northern Universities Press, 2001), pp. 8–9.

52 Interestingly enough, 1989 (year of publication of *Le mosche del capitale*) is another crucial date in both the consolidation of postmodern culture (marking the fall of the Berlin Wall and the radical evolution of the international geo-political situation) and, more specifically, in the development of the postmodern debate in Italy. Indeed, it was in 1989 that Remo Ceserani published his translation of Fredric Jameson's highly influential essay *Postmodernism, or, the Cultural Logic of Late Capitalism*, Post-Contemporary Interventions (London: Verso, 1991).

tradition and change are tangibly played out, in terms, for instance, of the changing use of spaces, the construction and destruction of the built environment, the evolving infrastructure and new architectural styles. Space itself is, therefore, a key protagonist (and antagonist).

The examined texts are also innovative in their modernization of narrative styles and structures which, in the 1950s, had been defined by realism as the dominant aesthetic; and in the emergence of perspectives which increasingly called into question all-encompassing narratives and the illusion of the mastery of the writer-observer. The work of Ortese and Arbasino, for example, questions the socially constructed ideas of gender and sexuality with which space is imbued. *Fratelli d'Italia* plays with linguistic experimentalism and references to the past (one of the distinguishing features of Italian postmodern literature), re-articulating and re-inventing the tradition of the Grand Tour. This double nature, marked by the co-existence of elements of tradition and innovation, has been seen as specific to post-war Italian culture[53] and brings us back to the interpretation of the Italian boom years as a problematic transition in which conservative tendencies co-exist with new trends.[54] Whilst the presence of some features of postmodern culture is discussed with regard to selected writings, postmodernism is a highly diversified and somewhat controversial notion, which has, more often than not, been overused. In addition, and as already pointed out, the reception of postmodernism in Italy has been particularly problematic: unsurprisingly, in a context still largely dominated by an elitist idea of high culture, postmodern ideas encountered significant resistance. Nevertheless, this study is interested in exploring the unfolding, among the writers analysed in this book, of a tension towards a different understanding of modernity, an understanding which may be broadly associated with the framework of postmodern theories slowly infiltrating the Italian cultural debate during those years and, with more evidence, also at the cusp of the 1980s, the point at which this book ends.

One may argue that the progression of the chapters in this book follows the movement towards postmodern arguments in Italian culture, as the focus of the analysis shifts outwards from the centre of the important industrial cities of the North to the secondary,

---

53   Caesar and Caesar, *Modern Italian Literature*, p. 191.

54   The co-existence of innovation and tradition may also be read in relation to Jameson's notion of cultural dominance as a predominant aesthetics or cultural paradigm that emerges within a given historical context and always incorporates pre-existing, residual forms of culture (Jameson, *Postmodernism*, pp. 3–4).

marginalized environments of a small Piedmontese town and Southern Italy in order to call into question dominant perspectives on the Italian Peninsula.

Structure and Approach

The chapters of this book explore how the selected writings conceptualize Italians' changing experiences of space from the second half of the 1950s to the end of the 1970s. The post-war modernization process was experienced as a rupture at the level of everyday individual existence, for it had profound consequences on how Italians lived and thought. This book is concerned with how the built environment responded to and sought to accommodate these changes, as well as with its users' apprehension of the changing space. The first three chapters deal with the big-city and small-town environments. The focus of the last chapter broadens to the level of the national space. Throughout this study space is regarded as the locus where anxieties about changing social structures, values, gender roles and relations play out. Anxiety may be a response to rapid transformations and changing urban conditions. It is also an epistemic category which is often evoked to make sense of urban experience. Hilde Heynen claims, for instance, that anxiety is 'inherent' in the modern city.[55] Anthony Vidler has explored the ways in which modern urban experience is conducive to the uncanny. In Freud's first theorization of this concept, the built environment fosters the emergence of a feeling of uncanniness, since he recounts the uncomfortable experience of losing his way in the unknown Italian city of Genoa.[56] Georg Simmel and Walter Benjamin have also argued that modern urban life induces new forms of neurosis.[57] At the same time, the rejection of urban lifestyles and values may be ideologically biased: a reaction to modernization that often manifests itself as nostalgia for cities of the past, which were believed to facilitate social relationships. The model of the harmonious built environment *par excellence*, the Renaissance city, resonates especially in Italian culture. In the novels analysed in Chapters 1 and 2, one perceives the absence

---

55 Hilde Heynen, *Architecture and Modernity: A Critique* (Cambridge, MA: MIT Press, 1999), p. 72.

56 Sigmund Freud, 'The Uncanny', in *The Uncanny*, trans. by David McLintock (London: Penguin, 2003), pp. 121–62; first published as 'Das Unheimliche', *Imago*, 5 (1919), 297–324.

57 Richard J. Williams, *The Anxious City: English Urbanism in the Late Twentieth Century* (London: Routledge, 2004), p. 8.

of a more architecturally pleasant city and a more harmonious relationship between people and their urban environment, which are set against the perceived 'lack of legibility' and outright ugliness of post-Second World War cities.[58]

The case study of Italy's socio-spatial transformations over the course of roughly two decades is explored here though several different literary genres which present their own distinctive interpretations of reality. Chapter 1 examines how Bianciardi's and Volponi's novels engage with contemporary social issues by choosing the cities of Milan and Turin as the focus of their criticism of post-war, capitalist-driven urbanization. In their novels Milan and Turin are centres of power and wealth where political and economic elites have aligned to exploit the working classes and maintain the status quo. The urban layout reproduces these relations of power and fosters continuous productivity. Thus, it poses problems for social control. The writers perceive an authoritarian threat in a built environment that encourages uniformity and atomization. If, for instance, the act of walking is a way for urban dwellers to appropriate their environment, a type of spatial layout that limits the walkability of the city arguably prevents them from relating to urban space more meaningfully and creatively and from gathering to create a community. The chapter explores how Bianciardi and Volponi conceptualize the interrelation between the space of industry and the city, their representation of the architecture of capitalism and its disenfranchising effect, as well as the link they establish between disciplinary power, its spatial concretization and industrial productivity.

A focal point in the chapter is the work of Foucault and Lefebvre, which has been pivotal in deconstructing the idea of space as a neutral milieu and emphasizing instead its active role in upholding and perpetuating relations of power.[59] In *Discipline and Punish* Foucault traces the evolution of mechanisms of power, that is, of the techniques implemented by power in order to maintain the dominant social

---

58 Nan Ellin, *Postmodern Urbanism* (New York: Princeton Architectural Press, 1999 [1996]), p. 4.

59 Other scholars have also explored issues of power and space. David Harvey, Michael Dear, Manuel Castells and Sharon Zukin have positioned the economic question at the heart of their geographical explorations. A similar observation applies to scholars who have taken Foucault's work forward, e.g., Miles Ogborn, who has drawn on Foucault's theories to investigate the regulation of urban behaviour, mostly focusing on the beginning of the modern era (Miles Ogborn, *Spaces of Modernity: London's Geographies, 1680–1780* (New York: Guilford, 1998)). It is also interesting to mention that more recent studies have raised the

order, from the Middle Ages to contemporary society. He argues that these techniques of power have always existed, but in mostly isolated, fragmented form until the seventeenth and eighteenth centuries, when they were organized into a comprehensive disciplinary system aimed at controlling the population as a whole.[60] At that point in history, a shift can be registered to new forms of disciplinary power involved with the control of individuals and their conduct or behaviour. For Foucault, power has a fundamental spatial element. Jeremy Crampton and Stuart Elden fittingly point out that spatial issues permeate Foucault's analyses of power and knowledge, providing the backbone for his research, even when this makes no explicit mention of geography.[61] Indeed, as will be shown in more detail in Chapter 1, Foucault maintains that spatial organization is crucial for power over the social body to be exercised continuously and consistently through a rational distribution and partitioning of individuals in space. Foucault has also examined the role of architecture, most famously the model of the Panopticon, in regulating the conduct of individuals. The Milan described by Bianciardi, the factory environment of *Memoriale* and Bovino, the industrial city portrayed by Volponi in *Le mosche del capitale*, are all disciplinary environments which are organized in ways that maximize efficiency and instil quiescence in a social body that has been rendered malleable and docile.

The notion of space developed by Lefebvre is less theoretical and more implicated in everyday social and economic activities. He rejects the union of space and reason in the Western epistemologico-philosophical tradition, which, in his view, accounts for the idea of space as a 'mental thing', that is, an abstract category disconnected from lived experience.[62] Lefebvre argues that this view has generated

---

question of the panopticon city, based on the idea that modern technologies of surveillance, such as the CCTV cameras widespread in our modern cities, have turned the city itself into a panopticon.

60   Michel Foucault, 'The Incorporation of the Hospital into Modern Technology', trans. by Edgar Knowlton Jr., William J. King and Stuart Elden, in *Space, Knowledge and Power: Foucault and Geography*, ed. by Jeremy W. Crampton and Stuart Elden (Aldershot: Ashgate, 2007), pp. 141–51 (p. 146). This is the translation of a lecture, 'L'incorporation de l'hôpital dans la technologie moderne', given by Foucault in 1974 and subsequently published in *Hermès* (1988), 2, 30–40.

61   Jeremy W. Crampton and Stuart Elden, 'Introduction', in *Space, Knowledge and Power*, ed. by Crampton and Elden, pp. 1–16 (pp. 8–9).

62   Henri Lefebvre, *Production of Space*, trans. by Donald Nicholson-Smith (Oxford: Blackwell, 1991), p. 3; first published as *La production de l'espace*, Société et urbanisme, 9 (Paris: Anthropos, 1974).

the 'illusion of transparency', namely, the idea that space can be fully comprehended and controlled by the power of reason by illuminating and conquering it.[63] Particularly relevant here is Lefebvre's idea that, as much as power seeks to master space for its purposes, often having recourse to violent means, the latter is never fully controllable. Power therefore engenders forms of resistance. In a Freudian-like paradox, those elements which are repressed into the margins fuel the urban unconscious and come back to haunt us.[64]

The Production of Space is concerned with the political and economic implications of space that reflect and consolidate relations of production.[65] Lefebvre applies Marxist tools to the analysis of how, throughout history, people have manipulated and shaped the natural environment for religious, social and economic purposes. His history of spatial modes of production culminates with the abstract space of modern capitalist societies. Chapter 1 of this book draws on some key notions in Lefebvre's analysis of capitalist abstract space: the colonization of social space by capitalism, namely, how capitalist social relations are internalized and inscribe themselves into all aspects of everyday life;[66] and the logic of visualization based on the predominance of the eye as a means to apprehend, measure and simplify reality, an approach which began with the discovery of linear perspective in the Renaissance.[67] A geometrical and measurable space is useful to a mercantile, profit-oriented society and, indeed, its rise coincided with the development of commercial capital in the Italian city-states.[68] The centrality of this objectifying gaze contributes to the increasing process of abstraction or de-materialization of space in neo-capitalist societies.

---

63   Lefebvre, *Production of Space*, pp. 27–29.

64   As Roger Luckhurst puts it, the more urban redesign tries to jettison certain aspects, the more likely it is that these return to haunt city dwellers in the form of the repressed (Roger Luckhurst, 'The Contemporary London Gothic and the Limits of the Spectral Turn', *Textual Practice*, 16 (2002), 527–46 (p. 532)).

65   Chris Butler argues that 'Lefebvre sees production extending beyond the economic confines of the labour process. It encompasses products in a strict sense alongside creative work (such as artistic forms and the built environment) and the social relations of production. Hence Lefebvre re-crafts and expands Marx's model of commodity production to explain how space is produced and contributes to the reproduction of the social relations of capitalism' (Chris Butler, *Henri Lefebvre: Spatial Politics, Everyday Life and the Right to the City*, Nomikoi: Critical Legal Thinkers (Abingdon: Routledge, 2012), p. 43).

66   Butler, *Henri Lefebvre*, p. 51.

67   Derek Gregory, *Geographical Imaginations* (Oxford: Blackwell, 1994), p. 389.

68   Gregory, *Geographical Imaginations*, p. 390.

By examining urban descriptions that evoke feelings of estrangement and uneasiness in the crime novels of Scerbanenco and Fruttero & Lucentini, Chapter 2 further explores the sense of disorientation induced by unprecedented transformations. The chapter explores the interrelations between crime and urbanization with a special focus on the periphery, an area often deemed dangerous, dark and gloomy. Scerbanenco and Fruttero & Lucentini mark a turning point in the tradition of Italian crime literature thanks to the vast popularity enjoyed by their novels. Up until the 1960s crime fiction in Italy consisted primarily of translations of foreign, mostly Anglo-American, authors.[69] The censorial attitude of the Fascist regime towards detective stories set in Italy, which could potentially convey an unpalatable image of the country, meant that foreign and fictional settings provided a safer choice for Italian writers.[70] The fact that Scerbanenco and Fruttero & Lucentini chose to set their crime stories in the concrete setting of the Milan and Turin of the 1960s and 1970s therefore introduced an important element of novelty. Following their example, Italian crime writers increasingly produced stories with a strong geographical connotation that gave rise to several local traditions.[71]

The chapter draws on the renewed interest in the unconscious and irrational in critical theory, as shown, for instance, by the reappraisal of the Freudian notion of the uncanny. Since Freud's theorization in his seminal essay in 1919, the idea of uncanniness has denoted the feelings of unease and estrangement that arise when something familiar suddenly appears in a different light and turns unfamiliar

---

69 Giuliana Pieri, 'Introduction', in *Italian Crime Fiction*, ed. by Pieri, pp. 1–5 (p. 1).

70 Luca Crovi, *Tutti i colori del giallo. Il giallo italiano da De Marchi a Scerbanenco a Camilleri* (Venice: Marsilio, 2002), p. 52.

71 Many studies have concentrated on the topographical connotations that Italian crime fiction develops from at least the late 1960s onwards. Massimo Carloni, for instance, maintains that, especially in the period from 1966 to 1978, 'gli autori che esordiscono o ritornano alla narrativa d'indagine trovano nella connessione tra vicenda poliziesca e ambientazione metropolitana e provinciale un nucleo irrinunciabile e caratterizzante attorno al quale costruire i loro romanzi' [authors who try their hand at or return to crime fiction find in the link between the detective story and the metropolitan and provincial setting a characteristic and indispensable core around which to build their novels] (Massimo Carloni, *L'Italia in giallo. Geografia e storia del giallo italiano contemporaneo* (Reggio Emilia: Diabasis, 2006 [1994]), p. 12). The first part of Carloni's *L'Italia in giallo* is organized into chapters dedicated to specific places: 'Milano', 'Provincia', 'Roma', 'Torino' and 'Bologna e Napoli'.

and menacing. The uncanny is a key notion in the discussion in Chapter 2, especially through Vidler's interpretation of it as the return of the repressed that becomes visible in the built environment and Mark Fisher's treatment of the related but distinct notions of the weird and the eerie. Vidler argues that as the 'quintessential bourgeois kind of fear',[72] the uncanny has been at the heart of architectural representations since the end of the eighteenth century: while the haunted house is a recurring theme in Romantic literature, with the rise of the modern metropolis at the end of the following century the uncanny moves from the home interior to the interior of the mind and acquires further connotations, coming to coincide with 'metropolitan illness'.[73] The enlarged spaces and crowds of the big city marked a shift in sensorial and aesthetic perception. Something similar happened with the rapid transformation of Italian society in the post-war period and the rise, during that time, of a functional type of space that embodied the values of industrial productivity. Whilst the category of the uncanny pertains to urban experience *tout court*, Chapter 2 aims to contextualize it historically as the anxiety that marked the post-war transition in Italy, the rapid spatial and social changes and the uneasy relationship with the past. The texts hint at a gap in our understanding and representation of space, at the impossibility fully to grasp and master it.

Once again, the equation between space and rationality engrained in Western thought is called into question.[74] A product of the Enlightenment, the modern city was supposed to stand as the bulwark of society: the rational organization of people and functions of public life as opposed to the state of nature.[75] If it is true that mastering space is an illusion, the unpredictable which urbanists and social theorists of the eighteenth century sought to suppress continued to be part of urban life, challenging its rational principles.[76]

72 Anthony Vidler, *The Architectural Uncanny: Essays in the Modern Unhomely* (London: The MIT Press, 1992), p. 4.

73 Vidler, *The Architectural Uncanny*, p. 6.

74 Gregory argues that 'in the course of the nineteenth century dominant conceptions of space installed within the political imaginary of the West a presumptive identity between "rationality" and "space"; that the one was inscribed within the other' (Gregory, *Geographical Imaginations*, p. 137).

75 Richard Lehan, *The City in Literature: An Intellectual and Cultural History* (Berkeley, CA: University of California Press, 1998), p. 3.

76 Lehan claims: 'What the city casts off became another force that challenged it from within' (Lehan, *The City in Literature*, p. 8).

Richard Lehan explores the forms taken by this archetypical struggle between urban order and disorder in the course of history: from the figure of Dionysus in Greek mythology to carnivalesque rituals; and from the mob of the modern metropolis, perceived as a threat, to the Freudian notion of the uncanny as the return of the repressed.[77] The city ultimately contains both principles, rational and irrational, and urban life is inevitably involved with a degree of uncertainty and unpredictability.[78]

The city, crime literature and the uncanny are closely connected. Detective stories were born out of the big-city environment and the density of people and things that led to a rise in crime and the creation of an institutionalized police force.[79] The aesthetics of fear and estrangement at the heart of the uncanny is also at home in mystery and detective stories. The greater anonymity and sense of impunity that the individual experiences in the big city are, according to Benjamin, 'at the origin of the detective story'.[80] The crowd permeates the urban fiction of the nineteenth and twentieth centuries. The writings of Baudelaire, Poe and Dickens document the appearance of this somewhat disturbing and menacing entity in the context of rising Paris and London.[81] In this regard, Lehan points out that the idea of the

---

77   Lehan, *The City in Literature*, p. 6.

78   Lehan identifies two spheres that shape modern urban life: on the one hand, the official, rational space of state power and, on the other, the underground, often repressed, life of the city. As he puts it, 'there are always two cities at work: one visible, the other invisible; one of the surface, the other underground or hidden; one a realm of mastery and control, the other of mystery and turmoil' (Lehan, *The City in Literature*, p. 273).

79   Barbara Pezzotti, *The Importance of Place in Italian Contemporary Crime Fiction: A Bloody Journey*, The Farleigh Dickinson University Press Series in Italian Studies (Madison, WI: Farleigh Dickinson University Press, 2012), p. 7.

80   Walter Benjamin, *The Writer of Modern Life: Essays on Charles Baudelaire*, ed. by Michael W. Jennings, trans. by Howard Eiland and others (Cambridge, MA: Belknap Press, 2006), p. 72. As Benjamin points out, 'the original social content of the detective story focused on the obliteration of the individual's traces in the big-city crowd' (Benjamin, *The Writer of Modern Life*, p. 74). This work is a translation of selections from Walter Benjamin, *Gesammelte Schriften*, ed. by Rolf Tiedemann and Hermann Schweppenhäuser (Frankfurt a.M.: Suhrkamp, 1972).

81   Benjamin writes that 'Poe's famous tale "The Man of the Crowd" is something like an X-ray of a detective story. It does away with all the drapery that a crime represents. Only the armature remains: the pursuer, the crowd, and an unknown man who manages to walk through London in such a way that he always remains in the middle of the crowd' (Benjamin, *The Writer of Modern Life*, p. 79).

man of the crowd as threat also needs to be read in conjunction with the advance of totalitarianism at the turn of the twentieth century.[82] The crowd, however, is not only menacing: it also can offer protection. For instance, the literary type of the *flâneur* – which enjoyed a great vogue in nineteenth-century Paris in conjunction with the rise of department stores, grand boulevards and the first gas street-lighting – finds in city crowds a source of vitality and inspiration.[83] For the *flâneur* the colourful bustle of the city streets has the same exhilarating effect as the *panoramas,* a stereoscopic form of entertainment and the forerunner of modern cinema, which developed in Paris in the same years.[84] The *flâneur* seeks the strange and unfamiliar as an antidote to the *spleen* of bourgeois life. The uncanny can, therefore, also become an inspiration for artistic experimentation and has, indeed, been a source of creativity, especially for avant-garde movements:

> Expressionist artists and writers from Kubìn to Kafka explored the less nostalgic conditions of the modern uncanny, pressing the themes of the double, the automat, and derealization into service as symptoms of posthistorical existence. Symbolists, futurists, dadaists, and of course surrealists and metaphysical artists found in the uncanny a state between dream and awakening particularly susceptible to exploitation. In this way, the uncanny was renewed as an aesthetic category, but now reconceived as the very sign of modermism's propensity for shock and disturbance.[85]

Chapters 3 and 4 move away from the industrial cities, the heart of economic activity, to foreground more marginal and tangential perspectives. In Chapter 3 the analysis of Ginzburg's *Le voci della sera* enables the problematization of common representations of the provinces, and specifically of the provincial city, beyond the opposition to the big city as supposedly the only one conducive to a 'real' urban experience. Chapter 4 addresses mobility as one of the defining aspects of the post-war years: not only the modern exaltation of movement, but also the mass internal migration of Italians from the impoverished areas of the country and the documentary reportage

---

82 Lehan, *The City in Literature,* p. xv.

83 David Frisby, *Cityscapes of Modernity: Critical Explorations* (Cambridge: Polity, 2001), p. 31.

84 Benjamin, *The Writer of Modern Life,* pp. 33–34. As Benjamin puts it, the flâneur 'seeks refuge in the crowd. [...] The crowd is the veil through which the familiar city beckons to the flâneur as phantasmagoria – now a landscape, now a room' (Benjamin, *The Writer of Modern Life,* p. 40).

85 Vidler, *The Architectural Uncanny,* p. 8.

by writers and intellectuals who sought to make sense of phenomena of modernization across the Peninsula. This latter type of mobility, which was not constrained by social status or modelled on some pre-packaged idea of journey around Italy but was, rather, motivated by critical investigation and reflexive self-exploration, resulted in new ways of narrating the Italian national space and identity. Through the perspective of two female writers, Ginzburg and Ortese, in contrast to the selected male authors in the previous two chapters, Chapters 3 and 4 also tackle the issue of women's agency in a built environment and social space which primarily accommodate the needs of men.

Ginzburg's *Le voci della sera* allows us to particularize the image of the Italian North by moving out of the major urban centres to look at a small town in the Piedmont region. The specifically gendered connotation of the novel enables a discussion around space which takes into account the point of view of marginalized subjects, like women, whose agency has traditionally been limited and regulated. The analysis in Chapter 3, therefore, relies on ideas about gender as it looks at how certain stereotypes and social conventions, as well as human relationships, are influenced and shaped by the provincial setting of *Le voci della sera*. Ginzburg's gender-specific perspective enables us to reflect more effectively on the alleged peripherality of the small town portrayed in the novel.

The chapter challenges the over-fixed opposition between big and provincial, or smaller, cities by showing how in *Le voci della sera* such a distinction is more nuanced and often played out around a dynamic of (more or less) imaginative escape from, and longing for, the provincial hometown. The relationship of Elsa and Tommasino creates continuity between city and province as it unfolds in both these environments. More subtle degrees of differentiation may prevent the risk of employing a monolithic notion of the provinces as an entity with fixed characteristics which is totally separate from, and subordinated to, the big city. This dichotomy fails to recognize, for instance, that smaller cities have often played an important part in propelling modernization in their national contexts and that, historically, capital cities have, therefore, not been the only places where innovations have originated and subsequently spread to the rest of the country.[86] In the case of some smaller towns, their

---

86 Ceserani mentions the examples of Germany and Great Britain, where smaller cities have traditionally been important, wealthy, commercial centres that have produced an educated, forward-thinking middle class (Remo Ceserani, 'Dalla piccola città alla cosmopoli: Premessa: Scene di provincia', *L'Asino d'oro*, 1 (1990), 3–7 (p. 6)).

development actually went hand in hand with that of major urban centres.[87] The qualities ascribed to the provincial town vary not only according to the specific national and regional context, but also historically across the modern era. One should also differentiate between the small town and the countryside, which a particular modern sensibility has perhaps too hastily constituted as a more salubrious, uncorrupted alternative to the metropolitan environment, which is often perceived as overstimulating and threatening. Hence it is noteworthy that existing critical studies on literary geographies tend to reproduce the supposed polarization between the country and city (overwhelmingly intended as the big metropolis) with little interest, at least in the Italian context, devoted to the intermediate space which is the provincial town.[88] Many studies tend to focus on the notion of margin, which is applicable to different domains (the city has its own margins), again testifying to how the province has found little room in Italian literary studies.

Differences between smaller cities should also be emphasized. One can think, for example, of those smaller centres that, especially in the second half of the twentieth century, have *de facto* been incorporated into wider metropolitan regions and now mainly serve as commuter villages and towns for those working in the city. Arguably they present a different situation from provincial cities which are not immediately connected to metropolitan areas and which may rely more on their unique characteristics and features to build a sense of their own identity. This is just one example of the almost kaleidoscopic distinctions and peculiarities which ought to be considered on a case-by-case basis. The predominant tendency is instead to classify cities either in terms of their size or of quantifiable parameters such as their population or GDP; and to do so both worldwide, with the so-called 'alpha' cities (New York, London, Paris, Tokyo) at the top, and in

---

87   Marcello Flores, for instance, points out that in the Italian city of Udine electric lighting was introduced almost at the same time as in Milan and Paris (Marcello Flores, 'La provincia come categoria storiografica', *L'Asino d'oro*, 1 (1990), 8–20 (p. 16)).

88   One example is Raymond Williams, *The Country and the City* (London: Chatto and Windus, 1973). An exception is provided by the work of Jason Finch, Lieven Ameel and Markku Salmela referred to in Chapter 3. Finch, Ameel and Salmela address phenomena of urban peripherality that have generally been overlooked in literary urban studies, which have traditionally privileged the study of the world's so-called 'first' cities. See in particular Jason Finch, Lieven Ameel and Markku Salmela (eds), *Literary Second Cities* (Basingstoke: Palgrave Macmillan, 2017).

national contexts, where smaller centres are usually subordinated to the capital city.[89] Finch, Ameel and Salmela suggest that the way around the hierarchical scheme according to which cities are perceived and classified as 'primary' and 'secondary' is to focus on a different set of parameters, such as the specific functions of a town or city, the types of experience it enables and the urban networks to which it may belong.[90] The implications are important. In the first place, it means that there is no such thing as a canonical urban experience, or at least that this is not, as widely believed, the prerogative of people who live in big cities, for smaller and mid-sized cities evoke their unique kind of urban experience. A further implication is that cities may simultaneously be secondary, for instance in relation to the capital city of their country, and primary, in terms of their unique functions and peculiarities.

In questioning common views of the *provincia* [provinces], Chapter 3 also points to the fact that the boom was not an exclusively metropolitan phenomenon. Smaller cities that were mostly concentrated in the Centre-North regions of the country created diffused industrialization through a constellation of small- and medium-scale companies specializing in a particular trade and focusing on product quality. From the end of the 1950s onwards these often family-run businesses could rely on the increasing purchasing power of the Italian population as well as on the growing appeal and reputation on the international market of the label 'Made in Italy'. While some towns and regions grew wealthier, territorial imbalances persisted and were actually exacerbated by uneven development. This was not only the case for the South, despite some awkward attempts by Italian governments at fostering socio-economic development there, but also for traditionally impoverished areas in the North, to the extent that some argue that the two halves of the country actually had more in common than is generally believed.[91]

The idea of the margin returns in Chapter 4. Chiefly referring here to the Italian South, it reminds us that the other side of the rapidly burgeoning urban centres of the North is the emptying of the

89   Jason Finch, Lieven Ameel and Markku Salmela, 'The Second City in Literary Urban Studies: Methods, Approaches, Key Thematics', in *Literary Second Cities*, ed. by. Finch, Ameel and Salmela, pp. 3–30 (pp. 3–4).

90   Finch, Ameel and Salmela, 'The Second City', p. 5.

91   See, e.g., Clarissa Clò, 'Visions of Italy Beyond the North/South Divide: Regional Documentaries and Global Identities', in *Negotiating Italian Identities*, ed. by Norma Bouchard (= *Annali d'Italianistica*, 24 (2006)), pp. 41–60.

countryside through poverty and emigration. It also reflects patterns of dominance, exclusion and subordination within the nation territory. The intermingled feelings of hope and disorientation which characterized the Italian post-war transition were a major factor in inducing Italian writers to take to the roads of Italy in the 1950s and 1960s with the aim of getting to know their country better. As Anna Maria Torriglia points out, the journey is increasingly conceptualized in post-war Italian literature and cinema as a figure of discovery and self-discovery for intellectuals and ordinary Italians alike.[92] Many Italians, intellectuals amongst them, had in various ways supported the Fascist regime and were now eager to find new sources of identification and inspiration. Travel took multiple forms in the 1950s and 1960s. It did not involve only the journeys of exploration by writers and intellectuals discussed in Chapter 4, but also the mass internal migration of poorer Italians, mostly along the South-to-North trajectory. Paul Ginsborg reports that between 1955 and 1971 some 9,140,000 Italians moved to a place in the Peninsula outside their region of origin, with Milan, Turin and other cities in the North registering the largest number of arrivals.[93] In those years there also emerged a culture of *villeggiatura*, the annual escape from the city that for the first time was within virtually everyone's means. Thanks to the expansion of the road network and railway system, travelling became easier and faster.

The chapter explores the (re-)discovery of the Italian territory in the aftermath of the Second World War through Ortese's *La lente scura*, Piovene's *Viaggio in Italia* and Arbasino's *Fratelli d'Italia*. These three samples of Italian domestic travel writing provide different, yet complementary views on Italy's changing geography and enable a discussion of the correlation between identity, gender, sexuality and space in travel writing. By looking at arguments developed in eco-feminist theory, such as the similarities between the subordination of women and nature, this section examines how Ortese's gender-specific take on the Italian journey calls into question dominant ways of portraying Italy at the convergence between a contemplative kind of foreign gaze and nationalist rhetoric. Ortese's point of view is less systematic and authoritative, but precisely for this reason more effective at subverting stereotypes than Piovene's *Viaggio in Italia*, which in this chapter represents the dominant tradition of male travel writing with its supposedly objective perspective. *Viaggio in Italia* is

92 Torriglia, *Broken Time*, pp. 118–19.
93 Ginsborg, *A History of Contemporary Italy*, p. 219.

an extensive documentary account of what Piovene observed and methodically noted down as he travelled from North to South, one region after the other, from 1953 to 1956. Arbasino's *Fratelli d'Italia* is the account of four intellectual friends, showcasers of sophisticated tastes and a cosmopolitan lifestyle, who embark on yet another kind of journey. Continuing the exploration of the positioning of the author in travel writing and its implications in terms of gender and sexuality, the chapter examines the queer perspective on the Italian journey and the postmodern re-articulation of the tradition of the Grand Tour found in *Fratelli d'Italia*.

The travel writings of Ortese, Piovene and Arbasino are presented as examples of the critical investigation of the post-war modernization process and the problematization of dominant ways of looking at Italy, which have largely been codified by the Grand Tour. The latter is crucial to the understanding of the evolution of travel writing in Italy, for Grand Tour travellers have largely shaped the subsequent tradition of Italian travelogues and the very image (and geography) of Italy in the European imagination. Whilst it is true that attitudes towards Italy in travel literature remain for the most part foreign and contemplative, one can challenge the assumption that travel accounts of Italy are the exclusive domain of non-Italian authors. Italian domestic travel accounts developed at almost the same time as foreign ones but have attracted less critical attention. Luca Clerici provides the first comprehensive study of travel accounts written by Italian authors travelling through Italy from the early eighteenth century to the late twentieth century.[94] Italian travel writers have had to come to terms with the inherited tropes of the Grand Tour in order to surpass them. Arbasino's *Fratelli d'Italia* is especially emblematic in this regard as an example of the meta-appropriation of tradition.

Chapter 4 also hints at how travel writing provides an opportunity to reflect on Italy's diversification and problematic sense of national identity. The nation-building process was still not fully accomplished in the post-war years and was, indeed, again at stake at later stages in Italian history: during the bloody sequence of domestic terrorist attacks which beset Italy from the end of the 1960s to the early 1980s, known as *anni di piombo* [Years of Lead]; and with the fall of the so-called First Republic following the Tangentopoli scandal and

---

94   See in particular Luca Clerici (ed.), *Il viaggiatore meravigliato. Italiani in Italia 1714–1996* (Milan: Il Saggiatore, 1999); and Luca Clerici, *Viaggiatori italiani in Italia, 1700–1998. Per una bibliografia* (Milan: Bonnard, 1999).

constitutional crisis of the 1990s.[95] At the root of the country's historical fragmentation lie strong territorial differences but also ideological divisions exacerbated by the inability of post-war governments both to promote a strong vision of national identity based on a critical public reckoning with the past and to tackle long-standing social issues.[96] This unresolved definition of Italianness and the willingness to explore the country in order to come to grips with its diversification characterize Italian travel writing of the post-Unification and post-war periods alike. Travel accounts of these two epochs share the sense of discovery and appropriation of the national territory, as well as an educational intent. In the post-war years mass media played a pedagogical role through the many travel documentaries produced for the radio and newly born television, a tendency of which *Viaggio in Italia*, written for Radio RAI, is clearly an example.

95 Jennifer Burns writes that 'Italy in the 1990s is therefore a country whose national identity has been tested perhaps more acutely than at any time since the *Risorgimento*' (Burns, *Fragments of Impegno*, p. 4). *Tangentopoli* [Bribe City] was the name given to a huge corruption scandal that brought down the old political establishment.

96 As Minghelli puts it, 'the persistently absent cultural elaboration of the past leading to a confused sense of any collective project' (Minghelli, 'Icons of Remorse', p. 400).

1. Authoritarian City: Milan and Turin for Luciano Bianciardi and Paolo Volponi

Taking the Leap: Two Writers Moving North

In 1954 Luciano Bianciardi left his hometown of Grosseto in Tuscany to join Giangiacomo Feltrinelli's newly founded publishing house in Milan (currently one of the most important publishers in Italy). In Tuscany he had been working as a school teacher and librarian and had acquired a certain notoriety as a political militant and contributor to major national newspapers. Depictions of Grosseto may be found across Bianciardi's oeuvre. They sketch a tableau of provincial life, with its human types and routine social interaction taking place in the streets and squares of the old centre; and resurface as memories of youth and an alternative to hectic metropolitan life in the works of the Milanese years, *L'integrazione* and *La vita agra*. Both novels are heavily autobiographical. They retrace Bianciardi's relocation to Milan and provide an account of life in the big city as hyper-competitive, isolating and alienating. In *L'integrazione* Luciano, the main character and author's namesake (as will be the case again in *La vita agra*), moves to Milan with his brother Marcello. The two siblings reflect different attitudes in the way they adjust to life in the big city (Marcello being more pragmatic and disillusioned from the start; Luciano soon wanting to go back to a more tranquil life in Tuscany) and eventually come to embody two opposite tales of urban self-realization: Luciano becomes the 'integrated' one to whom the book title alludes, fully compliant with the lifestyle of an ambitious Milanese. Marcello struggles to make ends meet with precarious forms of employment, writing anything from romance novels to articles for newspapers and magazines, encyclopaedia entries and translations (something which reflects much more closely Bianciardi's actual experience in Milan). *L'integrazione* establishes a clear dichotomy between Grosseto's village-like atmosphere, allegedly more in tune with nature and its cycles, and the alienating bustle of the big city. Memories of small-town life indulge somewhat in nostalgia and in the celebration of a romanticized past, especially when emphasizing the sense of community and human solidarity that seems impossible to retrieve in Milan.

La vita agra narrates Bianciardi's experience in Milan as he gradually lets go of his plans and ideals. Themes touched upon in the previous novel reach fuller artistic maturity here. *La vita agra* is a more iconic portrayal of big-city life and its pitfalls than *L'integrazione*, in which Bianciardi focuses mainly on his work days at Feltrinelli. Bianciardi had somehow reached a professional and personal standstill as he started questioning his Socialist ideals and commitment as an intellectual after the incident in the Southern Tuscan mine of Ribolla in which forty-three miners lost their lives in 1954. He knew some of them personally and at the time of the incident was researching their working and living conditions for a reportage series that he co-authored with Carlo Cassola.[1] The tragedy had a profound effect on him and influenced his decision to accept Feltrinelli's invitation to move to Milan and join his publishing house.[2] One can therefore imagine that he set out for Milan harbouring hopes that the big city would bring renewed inspiration and professional recognition. In *La vita agra* Luciano arrives in the Northern capital with the main purpose of vindicating the miners by blowing up the head office of the Montecatini industrial group, which owned the Ribolla mine and is headquartered in Milan. As the novel proceeds, however, Luciano's subversive plans gradually wane while he finds himself more and more settled in a life of routine with precarious employment as translator. The excerpt below, from an article which Bianciardi wrote for *Il Contemporaneo*, sums up the trajectory of the main character in the novel: a rebel against the

---

1 The articles have been merged into Luciano Bianciardi and Carlo Cassola, *I minatori della Maremma* (Bari: Laterza, 1956).

2 Corrias claims that, following the funeral of the forty-three miners, 'Luciano torna a Grosseto sfinito e frastornato dall'enormità della tragedia. È qui che si chiude la sua prima vita, anche se ancora non lo sa' [Luciano returns to Grosseto exhausted and bewildered by the enormity of the tragedy. It is here that the first part of his life comes to a close, even if as yet he does not know it] (Corrias, *Vita agra di un anarchico*, p. 76).

status quo in the early days of his arrival in Milan who loses sight of his ideals and eventually gives in to the logic of the capitalist city:

> Persino quel che mi pareva chiaro, la posizione del nemico nei palazzoni di dieci piani, fra via Turati e via della Moscova a Milano non mi è parso più tanto chiaro. Perché qui le acque si mischiano e si confondono. L'intellettuale diventa un pezzo dell'apparato burocratico commerciale, diventa un ragioniere.[3]

> [Even what had seemed clear to me, the position of the enemy in the ten-storey blocks of flats between via Turati and via della Moscova in Milan, no longer seemed so clear to me. Because here the waters mix and merge. The intellectual becomes a piece of the commercial bureaucratic apparatus, he becomes an accountant.]

The Luciano who sets foot in Milan for the first time can clearly locate his 'enemy' in the high-rise office buildings of the areas around the via Turati and via della Moscova. He plans to blow them up but, as we shall see, because he needs to work long hours to keep up with the cost of living in the big city, he becomes just another pawn in the 'commercial bureaucratic apparatus' that he had once intended to overthrow.

Scholars and biographers of Bianciardi have iterated the importance of Milan in the existential and professional trajectory of the writer and his antagonism towards the culture of profit embodied by the Northern capital. In this regard, some studies have also explored the idea that for Bianciardi the disillusionment of the Milanese years prompted a seemingly unresolvable fracture.[4] Bianciardi's controversial relationship with Milan and the implications of the boom in terms of emerging consumerist culture and lifestyles have been at the heart of many studies, which have also highlighted the writer's opposition to neo-capitalism and the contradictions of his stance in the context of the counterculture movement of the 1960s.[5] The fact remains

---

3   Luciano Bianciardi, 'Lettera da Milano', *Il Contemporaneo*, 5 February 1955 (in Crainz, *Storia del miracolo italiano*, p. 110).

4   Maria Clotilde Angelini, for example, analyses how *Il lavoro culturale* (Milan: Feltrinelli, 1957) and *L'integrazione* reveal Bianciardi's gradual disillusionment with metropolitan life and his looking back with nostalgia to the life and ideals he had repudiated by leaving Grosseto (Maria Clotilde Angelini, *Luciano Bianciardi* (Florence: La nuova Italia, 1980)). The idea of fracture is clearly present also in Mario Terrosi and Alberto Gessani, *L'intellettuale disintegrato. Luciano Bianciardi*, Bibliotheca Ianua, 9 (Rome: Ianua, 1985).

5   See, e.g., Velio Abati and others (eds), *Luciano Bianciardi tra neocapitalismo e contestazione* (Rome: Editori riuniti, 1992). It is significant that the editors

that Bianciardi's success as a writer is quite controversially tied to Milan as *La vita agra* is by far his most read and cited book. After the publication of *La vita agra* Bianciardi gradually withdrew from public life, perhaps seeing in his own success the self-fulfilling prophecy of the commodification of intellectual work. A downward spiral into depression and alcoholism eventually led to his death in 1971.

Paolo Volponi left another Central Italian town, Urbino in the region of Le Marche, driven by a similar restlessness and a desire to see the more advanced North beyond the narrow confines of his provincial world. He moved first to Milan, where, crucially, he met the industrialist Adriano Olivetti, head of the famous typewriter manufacturers, who entrusted Volponi with a job assignment in Rome. In 1956 Volponi moved to the Olivetti headquarters in Ivrea, in the metropolitan area of Turin, where he was appointed head of the social services division. The Ivrea experience was a crucial one: Volponi stayed there from 1956 to 1966, even after Olivetti's death in 1960. The landscapes, colours and sounds of rural Marche and of the Appennines which had imbued his early poetic production gave way to novels inspired by the industrial world.[6] Volponi, like several other intellectuals of the time, was drawn to Olivetti's ambition and charisma, in particular the entrepreneur's aspiration to restructure Italian industry, starting with his own company, so that the rights and wellbeing of the workers would form the core of its ethos. Olivetti wished to ensure better working conditions, welfare services such as nurseries, a good work–life balance and the pursuit of intellectual interests (the Ivrea factory had a library and rooms for film screenings).[7] A recurring theme in the literary criticism on Volponi is utopia, to be understood precisely as the possibility of creating a

---

chose this particular title for the volume of an important conference held in Grosseto, Bianciardi's birthplace, to commemorate the twentieth anniversary of the author's death, with contributions which address various aspects of his life and writing career. Another example is provided by the research of John Mastrogianakos, who examines how the style (embedded text) of *La vita agra* represents a narrative of subversion against the consumerist society that the book portrays in its frame narrative (John Mastrogianakos, 'Embedded Narratives of Subversion in Luciano Bianciardi's *La vita agra*', *Forum Italicum*, 37 (2003), 121–46).

6   Gian Carlo Ferretti, *Paolo Volponi* (Florence: La Nuova Italia, 1972), p. 8.

7   Claire Provost and Simone Lai, 'Story of Cities #21: Olivetti tries to build the ideal "human city" for its workers', *The Guardian*, 13 April 2016 <https://www. theguardian.com/cities/2016/apr/13/story-cities-21-adriano-olivetti-ivrea-italy-typewriter-factory-human-city> [accessed 8 March 2022].

more humane industry in which technical know-how is infused by Humanist knowledge and sensitivity, as Olivetti envisaged.[8]

Nevertheless, Volponi's books seem to tell an altogether different story. They provide a pessimistic account of the industrial environment, emphasizing in particular its alienating effects. This is clearly the case in *Memoriale*, which tells the life story of Albino Saluggia, the first-person narrator and author of the biographical memoir alluded to in the title. Albino is a Second World War veteran who returns from a German prison camp to his place of origin in the countryside near Candia, in Piedmont, and goes on to find employment in a big company just outside the city of Turin, which is clearly inspired by the Ivrea-based Olivetti. The narrated facts take place between 1948 and 1956, thus during the transition period that leads to the economic boom proper. Albino is an outcast, somebody who does not fit in and whose neurosis belongs more broadly to a social class and economic system. If Volponi depicts a hostile, alienating factory environment, it is, however, because he measured it against a possible alternative. He was critical towards certain aspects of industry, not towards industry *per se*. Quite the contrary, he believed that, if managed wisely, industry might produce the conditions that would free individuals from the need to work unsocial hours to support themselves and their families.[9] Even after Olivetti's death, Volponi strove to take forward the entrepreneur's ideals of a democratization of the industrial system, a robust assistance-plan for the workers and a more harmonious integration between the factory and the urban fabric.[10]

---

8   Examples include Ferdinando Virdia, 'Il tema è sempre l'utopia', *La fiera letteraria*, 12 (1974), 18–19; Daniele Fioretti, *Utopia and Dystopia in Postwar Italian Literature: Pasolini, Calvino, Sanguineti, Volponi*, Italian and Italian American Studies (Basingstoke: Palgrave Macmillan, 2017); and Raffaeli (ed.), *Paolo Volponi*.

9   Volponi claims that 'l'industria non è ancora in grado di garantire a tutti la possibilità di esprimere la propria intelligenza e di farla fruttificare nel vantaggio comune. Questa è la vera forma di sfruttamento che ancora esiste. Ma tutto ciò verrà corretto proprio attraverso l'industria stessa […]. In sostanza, io credo nell'industria perché, se controllata, potrà produrre gli strumenti per la liberazione dell'uomo dal bisogno, dal lavoro, dalla fatica' [industry is not yet able to guarantee everyone the opportunity to express his intelligence and make it bear fruit for the common good. This is the real form of exploitation that still exists. However, all this will be corrected through industry itself […]. Basically, I believe in industry because, if controlled, it will be able to produce the tools for the liberation of man from need, from work, from exhaustion] (Ferretti, *Paolo Volponi*, p. 6).

10   See Adriano Olivetti, *Città dell'uomo* (Milan: Edizioni di Comunità, 1960).

Volponi left Olivetti for Fiat in 1971, having gradually grown apart from management, who in his view had proved unable or unwilling to carry forward the projects of the late Adriano Olivetti. *Le mosche del capitale* was written after the conclusion of his two-year controversial experience at the Italian flagship car-manufacturer, where he served as an adviser to the leadership on issues concerning the integration of the factory into its urban environment. At Fiat, Volponi was confronted by a very different, more conservative corporate environment. He eventually resigned as he felt that his proposals had gone largely unheard.[11] In *Le mosche del capitale* Bruno Saraccini (in whom one may recognize the author himself) quits the MFM company (Olivetti) after he is denied promotion to Managing Director. He then takes up a new job at Megagruppo (Fiat), bringing with him his progressive views on working conditions and legislation. He is soon confronted by the reality of everyday work at Megagruppo, where the workers demanding more rights and a more humane work environment are discriminated against and risk being fired. He resigns and goes back to MFM in a lesser capacity. The novel gives an unapologetic portrayal of industrial power as always opposed to the collective good in its relentless pursuit of profit. Autobiographical and allegorical elements intertwine in the dehumanizing corporate environment, where characters have no real depth or dimension outside their role in the workplace and objects become animated and can speak. Alienation is no longer a condition restricted to the work environment, as in *Memoriale*: it has spread to colour everything in the novel with its dull, despairing quality. As a theme, alienation also speaks of the crisis undergone in those years by the working class as a self-conscious and traditionally identifiable entity.[12]

Bianciardi and Volponi therefore provide a particularly insightful commentary on the Northern urban industrial society of the 1960s and 1970s from a perspective informed by direct knowledge of its industrial system. While Volponi worked as an industrial manager at both Olivetti and Fiat, Bianciardi was part of the group of intellectuals who contributed to establishing the Feltrinelli Publishing House in its very early stages, an experience he narrates in *L'integrazione*. At the same time the two writers originally came from the small-town environment of Central Italy and were, in this sense, outsiders who arguably perceived the social and urban changes underway all the more acutely.

---

11   Walter Pedullà, 'Vita e opere di Paolo Volponi', in *Paolo Volponi* (= *L'Illuminista*, 24 (2008)), pp. 25–36 (p. 33).

12   Pedullà, 'Vita e opere di Paolo Volponi', p. 33.

La vita agra and *Memoriale* are rooted in the complex transition of the Italian boom years, during which radical innovations in the lifestyles and values of the Italian people overlapped with the persistence of more traditional, conservative attitudes. In 1960 the issue of Fascist legacies in the Republic once again came under the spotlight when the transitional government, led by Fernando Tambroni, looked to form a tactical alliance with the neo-Fascist Italian Social Movement (Movimento Sociale Italiano; MSI) founded in 1946 by former members of the Italian Social Republic. This sparked protests and demonstrations.[13] Despite achieving only modest results at the national elections, the Far Right could count on the support of powerful sectors of Italian society, specifically amongst the Civil Service, landowners, police and army, and was therefore able to influence the agenda of the Christian Democrat governments.[14] The climate of the Cold War made an overtly authoritarian shift in Italy seem like a realistic possibility. All this explains the widespread feeling, particularly on the Left, that the struggle against Fascism did not conclude with the Resistance and the transition to the post-war Republic.[15]

In the novels examined in this chapter, the ghost of authoritarianism lingers as an insidious threat, lying just beneath the level of consciousness. Allusions to the past are made through characters who have only pretended to disavow their Fascist views and now feel legitimized to embrace them again, as well as through the recurring war imagery. Bianciardi and Volponi detect the threat of an authoritarian revival in the industrial architecture that is the expression of political authority and the kind of urban layout that fosters individualism and productivity. In 1929 George Bataille was already pointing out the connection of architecture to power and how the 'architecture of the majority' disenfranchises the less powerful.[16] This chapter refers to Lefebvre's analysis of social space in capitalist societies to make sense of the writers' apprehension of the modern

---

13 Paolo Pombeni, 'Christian Democracy in Power, 1946–63', in *Oxford Handbook of Italian Politics*, ed. by Erik Jones and Gianfranco Pasquino, Oxford Handbooks (Oxford: Oxford University Press, 2015), pp. 255–67 (p. 263).

14 Duggan, 'Italy in the Cold War Years', p. 9.

15 Duggan, 'Italy in the Cold War Years', p. 6.

16 Jill Stoner, *Toward a Minor Architecture* (Cambridge, MA: MIT Press, 2012), p. 5. George Bataille's reflections have been collected in Denis Hollier (ed.), *Against Architecture: The Writings of Georges Bataille*, trans. by Betsy Wing (Cambridge, MA: MIT Press, 1992 [1989]).

big city and the descriptions of besieged public spaces that, in the novels, prompt the feeling of a corporate takeover of everyday life. It also draws on Foucault's notion of disciplinary power and its spatial organization, particularly in the concluding section of the chapter, which explores textual descriptions of forms of social control which aim at increasing efficiency and productivity.

Colonization of Space: Industry and Urban Space

When Bianciardi moved to Milan, the city was being radically transformed by industrialization and a dramatic wave of immigration from the poorer areas of the country. For those coming from the impoverished regions of rural Italy, the psychological and cultural process of adjustment to the urban-industrial society of Northern Italy was anything but straightforward. As Ginsborg points out:

> For the immigrants from the rural South the first impressions of the northern cities were bewildering and often frightening. What struck them most were the wide streets full of traffic, the neon lights and advertisement boards, the way the northerners dressed. [...] these were cities which seemed not just of another country, but of another planet.[17]

This experience is replicated by Marcello and Luciano in *L'integrazione*. As they arrive for the first time in Milan, the absolute dominance of automobiles, which form a seemingly incessant stream down the city's streets, and the marginal space which is allocated to pedestrians make a deep impression on them:

> Non c'è dunque motivo di meraviglia se di quest'altra città, nuova, grande, importante, a noi che ci arrivammo con un balzo solo di cinquecento chilometri, prima e più di ogni altra cosa sembrassero differenti le strade. Ci sorprese anzitutto la scarsa parte che di ogni strada toccava a noi pedoni. (*I*, pp. 10–11)

> [There is therefore no reason to be surprised if in this other city – new, large and important – more than anything else the roads seemed different, at least to those of us who reached it with a journey of only five hundred kilometres. Above all, we were surprised by how small a part of each street fell to us pedestrians.]

L'integrazione, Bianciardi's first Milanese book, opens with praise of the act of walking for leisure, an activity that has traditionally cemented community life in Grosseto, where people find one another,

17 Ginsborg, *A History of Contemporary Italy*, p. 222.

socialize and seemingly inhabit their urban environment more fully through this *passeggio* [walking at a leisurely pace]: a custom that even today may still be observed in the old centres of any small city or village in Italy. In the first few pages of the book, the emphasis on the slow pace of life in Grosseto is linked to the idea that people in the Tuscan town still live in a harmonious relationship with nature and the cycle of the seasons (*I*, pp. 14–15). The dichotomy between Grosseto and Milan is established here once and for all. As life in the Northern capital takes its course, Grosseto becomes for Bianciardi a distant reverie and the image of an old Italy that seems about to be swept away by economic progress.

At the beginning of *La vita agra* Luciano lives in the Brera quarter, which in the book is called Braida (also Braida Guercia and Braida del Guercio), an allusion to the Braidense National Library, located in the Palazzo di Brera. In this chapter the toponyms Brera and Braida will be used interchangeably. The area of Braida has a bohemian spirit and is chiefly frequented by young, and mostly penniless, would-be intellectuals, 'pittori capelluti, ragazze dai piedi sporchi, fotografi affamati' [hairy painters, girls with dirty feet, penniless photographers] (*VA*, p. 94; *HL*, p. 91). In the novel Braida plays an important role in protecting a sense of identity that is under threat in the wider city, for it provides Luciano with familiar co-ordinates that makes him feel safer, if not completely at home. Bianciardi describes Brera as an 'island' and 'citadel' to which to retreat from urban threats which, in the novel, are often symbolized by the rise in road traffic:

> Era una strada tranquilla e tutta *nostra*; il traffico quasi non ci si azzardava, ma anche in via della Braida, che pure è centrale e frequentata, le auto sembravano riconoscere che questa era zona *nostra* e rallentavano più del dovuto, e i piloti non s'arrabbiavano né facevano le corna se un pedone uscito dal caffè delle Antille traversava senza guardare, obbligandoli a una secca frenata. Per tacito consenso insomma quella era *la nostra isola, la nostra cittadella*. (*VA*, p. 14)[18]

> [It was a quiet street, and entirely *our own*; traffic hardly ventured into it, but even in the Via della Braida, which is a busy, central street, drivers seemed to recognise that this was *our* part of the world and slowed down more than was absolutely necessary, and did not get angry or make rude gestures if a pedestrian coming out of the Antilles crossed the road without looking and forced them to jam on their brakes. In short, by tacit general consent, this was *our little island, our citadel*.] (*HL*, p. 14)

18 My emphasis.

Luciano claims ownership over this part of Milan, seemingly still untouched by urban progress, through the repetition of the possessive pronoun *nostra* [our/ours]. Car drivers seem to recognize that this is not their territory and show respect: on the rare occasions on which they venture into the Via della Braida, where traffic is normally very light, they slow down to give way to those who come and go from the many bars and cafés in the area, refraining from honking, making angry gestures and from all the repertoire of their usually aggressive behaviour. Luciano reacts to the complexity and perceived dangerousness of city life by seeking refuge in a well-defined area of Milan, the artistic and bohemian Brera. His preference for spaces within Milan which he perceives as safe and protective expresses a rejection of the capitalist way of life that is rampant in the Northern capital. Later in the novel he moves out of Brera into an apartment on the periphery, where he feels confused and threatened by the hostile environment and hectic pace of urban transformations unfolding all around him.

Luciano is aware that Brera, with its bohemian, artsy spirit, reflects a false image of the city of Milan.[19] As he puts it, 'non si capisce Parigi standosene barbicato a Montmartre, né Londra abitando a Chelsea' [you don't know Paris if you never set foot outside Montmartre, or London from living in Chelsea] (*VA*, p. 94; *HL*, p. 91). He is able to grasp the real essence of Milan for the first time only when he moves into a flat further out of the centre with his girlfriend Anna. Life in the periphery unveils to Luciano the real city beyond the elitist, somewhat artificial Brera. It is at this point in the novel that his metamorphosis into one of the city's 'grigi abitatori' [grey inhabitants] (*VA*, p. 94; *HL*, p. 91) really begins. In the novel the peripheries, which in those years accommodated an increasing number of people from the lower-middle class and petty clerks working in industry in the city, are a bleak, melancholic place. In the following extract, for example, the description of a disused freight yard close to the apartment that Luciano and Anna share with a married couple from the Alto Adige is reminiscent of some pages from Giorgio Scerbanenco's Milanese crime novels (examined in the next chapter), with their *noir* atmosphere and the presence of destitute humanity and lowlife. Bianciardi effects explicit dehumanization since the human element is degraded

---

19   He says: 'Finché fossimo rimasti nell'isola attorno alla Braida del Guercio, della città noi avremmo visto soltanto una fettina esigua, atipica, anzi falsa' [As long as we remained in the island round the Braida del Guercio, all we saw of it was a narrow, untypical, actually false and unreal sector] (*VA*, p. 94; *HL*, p. 91).

to shadows and larvae: 'Di notte si riempiva di larve indistinte in quella scarsa luce frammezzo alla nebbia che si abbioccolava sugli sterpi. A sostare nella strada vicina, le vedevi, contro i lumi opposti e lontani, muoversi, sparire, incontrarsi, dividersi ancora, scomparire' [In the dim, foggy light that hung over the whole area at night it was haunted by shadowy ghosts. If you stopped in the neighbouring street you caught glimpses of them against the distant lights opposite as they moved, vanished, met, separated again, and again vanished] (*VA*, p. 100; *HL*, p. 97).

Opening up to the city beyond the confines of Brera confirms Luciano's inability to adapt to metropolitan life and towards the end of the novel prompts his elaboration of an alternative idea of society, one based on the rejection of modern urban lifestyles and the false needs created by consumerist culture.[20] Halfway between serious and facetious, this ideal model of society is a fusion of the anti-urban philosophical and artistic traditions with the hippie counterculture of the 1960s; it envisages the return to a pre-urban condition through self-organized forms of collective that abandon private property and live as close to a state of nature as possible. The 'intellectual resentment'[21] towards the city in Western culture finds one of its first and most famous advocates in Jean-Jacques Rousseau, with his celebration of the noble savage and rural values.[22] Anti-urban sentiments reverberate through the Romantic literary tradition, which rejects modern urban life by praising the mystic and instinctive qualities of nature that have allegedly been sacrificed to the materialist parameters of modern city life.[23] The imagery of the city as a site of corruption and alienation imbues many Modernist texts. This critical view of the modern city – which arose at an earlier

---

20   He asserts: 'Occorre che la gente impari a non muoversi, a non collaborare, a non produrre, a non farsi nascere bisogni nuovi, e anzi a rinunziare a quelli che ha' [People must learn not to hurry, not to co-operate, not to produce, not to acquire new needs, but instead to give up their existing needs] (*VA*, p. 160; *HL*, p. 155).

21   Lehan, *The City in Literature*, p. xv.

22   See, e.g., Rousseau's *Discours sur l'origine et les fondements de l'inégalité parmi les hommes* (1755) and his *Du contrat social* (1762).

23   Lehan claims: 'The Enlightenment depicted the city as a powerful grid superimposed upon the natural, and the romantics questioned what that grid repressed: the naturalists, who shared the romantics' doubt, depicted the city as an energy system and an alienating mechanism that inculcated a degenerative process by creating a diseased center outside of nature' (Lehan, *The City in Literature*, p. 70).

stage elsewhere in Europe, especially in England and France, due to the prior development in these countries of industrial capitalism and commercialism and therefore of the modern metropolis – is embodied most notably by the work of Ezra Pound, T. S. Eliot and James Joyce. Although they are reworked and adapted to the peculiar context of 1960s Milan, Bianciardi employs some of the traditional motifs that have been applied to the description of the metropolis in literary and artistic traditions and in the sociological analysis of the effects of rapid urbanization. These include, in particular, individualism and the feelings of detachment and alienation which result from the overstimulation of metropolitan life and its distancing from nature.

Let us now go back to the depiction of central Milan in *La vita agra*. Just outside Brera, heavy traffic means that one needs to pay close attention to avoid being run over. For this reason, one may overlook the tower blocks of the city's business district, which Bianciardi describes as 'un blocco militaresco, coi suoi ponti levatoi, le sue muraglie imprendibili, i suoi camminamenti coperti, le sue aree bertesche' [a fortress complete with drawbridges, impregnable walls, covered passageways, and aerial corridors] (*VA*, p. 32; *HL*, p. 31). *La vita agra* was written in the same years that witnessed the creation in Milan of the Velasca and Pirelli Towers (1960 and 1961 respectively), which sparked debate about the diverse interpretations of Modernism in architecture.[24] The 'Pirellone', as the Pirelli tower is colloquially known, is certainly one of the iconographic symbols of the boom. It also features in the initial sequence of Michelangelo Antonioni's film *La notte* [*The Night*] (1961), with the surrounding skyscrapers and highways reflected by its glass surfaces, all indicators of Milan's rapid industrial growth.[25] The war rhetoric of besieged public spaces in Bianciardi's description of these buildings suggests that capital has increasingly colonized everyday life, thanks to the mobility and ubiquity of information and financial flows that sustain the global economy, of which these skyscrapers are a tangible concretization.[26]

---

24   See Halldóra Arnardóttir, 'Architecture and Modernity in Post-war Milan', in *Italian Cityscapes: Culture and Urban Change in Contemporary Italy*, ed. by Robert Lumley and John Foot (Exeter: University of Exeter Press, 2004), pp. 90–99.

25   John David Rhodes, 'Antonioni and the Development of Style', in *Antonioni: Centenary Essays*, ed. by Laura Rascaroli and John David Rhodes (London: Palgrave Macmillan, 2011), pp. 276–300 (p. 286).

26   Lefebvre argues that the abstract space of neo-capitalist societies 'is founded on the vast network of banks, business centres and major productive entities, as also on motorways, airports and information lattices' (Lefebvre, *Production of Space*, p. 53).

Capitalism, as Lefebvre puts it, 'has subordinated everything to its own operations by extending itself to space as a whole'.[27]

Through the spectacular action of blowing up the Montecatini Building, which is Luciano's intent at the beginning of *La vita agra*, he aims to erase from Milan's cityscape a symbol of capitalist wealth and exploitation: the skyscraper with its density of offices. Albino, the first-person narrator of *Memoriale*, somehow echoes Luciano's self-appointed mission when he says that he intends to unmask the deception and injustices of the industrial system from within. Albino's position, however, is more complicated, since, as will be discussed later, his point of view as narrator is overtly not entirely reliable. Luciano's declaration of war on the new Milan is reaffirmed through the military metaphors scattered through *La vita agra* to suggest that modern metropolitan life is replete with risks and dangers. In the following extract, for instance, the act of sharing a cigarette with the friend and room-mate Carlone is the pretext for Luciano to remember the war and a particular night under the Allied bombing of Foggia, in Southern Italy, while serving in the Italian Army during the Second World War:

> Carlone e io, vecchi compagni contubernali del numero otto terzo piano, amici come soltanto sono amici due uomini quando intorno c'è il pericolo. Come una notte di settembre, vicino a Lecce, quando scendevano rossi i bengala, grappoli dell'ira, uva della collera, insomma the grapes of wrath perché erano bombe inglesi, e fu Dodi a destarmi e mi vide le mani tremare e mi ci mise una sigaretta e la fumammo vicini accosto al muretto del vigneto, mentre di lassù scaricavano tonnellate di tritolo addosso ai tedeschi della Goering in fuga verso nord. Così ora con Carlone la sigaretta scambiata è un pegno di amicizia a difesa contro quest'altra collera grigia della città che si stringe attorno a noi e minaccia quest'isola nostra. (*VA*, pp. 24–25)

> [Carlone and I, old friends who shared a third-floor room at No. 8, united by friendship of the kind that exists only when danger threatens – as on that September night near Lecce when the red flares came down, followed by the grapes of wrath – they were in fact British bombs – and Dodi woke me, and then noticed that my hands were trembling and put a cigarette in my mouth, and we smoked it together sitting up against the vineyard wall while they unloaded tons of the stuff on Georing's [*sic*] Germans fleeing north. Similarly

---

27 Henri Lefebvre, *The Survival of Capitalism: Reproduction of the Relations of Production*, trans. by Frank Bryant (London: Allison and Busby, 1976), pp. 37–38; originally published as *La survie du capitalism. La reproduction des rapports de production* (Paris: Anthropos, 1973).

now, exchanging cigarettes with Carlone was a pledge of friendship
and an act of defence against the grey wrath of the city that oppressed
us on all sides and threatened our little island.] (*HL*, p. 24)

The bombing raid is compared to the bourgeoning city that, in
its seemingly relentless expansion, threatens to incorporate areas
which still conserve an intimate, almost village-like atmosphere,
such as Brera, which Luciano calls 'our island'. Once again the Brera
microcosm embodies for Luciano a counter-space of resistance to
the official city. A cigarette smoked in good company is a way to
pluck up courage, in the present as well as during the war. In a
similar way, Luciano's sentimental bond with his girlfriend Anna
is so strong and exclusive because the two lovers grab onto it as
a defence against the solitude and precariousness of big city life.
The urgency of love is justified by the existential uncertainty of
the current 'tempi di guerra e di rivoluzioni' [times of war and
revolution] (*VA*, p. 62; *HL*, p. 61).

Bianciardi's descriptions of the roadworks that proliferated
across Milan in those years are a further example of the perceived
takeover of public space in the novel. Alongside new buildings
and housing estates, the post-war era witnessed the construction of
the underground, the first line of which was inaugurated in 1964.
Ermanno Olmi's film *Il posto* [*The Job*] (1961) immortalizes the works
for the *metropolitana* in the Piazza San Babila and emphasizes the rise
in car traffic and noise, for instance in the sequence that features the
two young protagonists struggling to cross a congested thoroughfare.
The periphery south of the city centre, where Luciano and Anna go
to live, is a constantly changing landscape of roadworks as groups of
workers arrive every day to dig new holes:

> Intanto sono arrivati gli operai coi picconi e scavano la fossa. [...]
> Aperta la buca, se ne vanno. Il giorno dopo altri operai provvedono
> a rimettere a posto la terra scavata, che risulta sempre troppa e
> fa montarozzo, sicché bisogna far venire il rullo compressore a
> schiacciarla, e poi un'altra macchina a stendere altro asfalto, bitume
> e ghiaino. Gli scavatori intanto si sono spostati un poco più in là,
> sempre sul marciapiede, e scavano una fossa nuova, che sarà riempita
> puntualmente il giorno dopo. (*VA*, p. 168)

> [Meanwhile a gang of workmen has turned up with picks and begun
> digging a trench. [...] When they have dug their trench they go away.
> Next day another gang turns up and puts back in the trench the earth
> dug up by the first gang. But there's always too much of it, and it won't
> all go in, so they send for a steam-roller to force it in, and then another

mechanical monster comes along and spreads asphalt, bitumen and gravel on top. Meanwhile the trench-diggers have moved along and are digging another trench, again on the pavement, which will be duly filled in next day too.] (*HL*, p. 163)

Luciano is bewildered at the apparent senselessness of the excavations, which are repeatedly done and undone. He argues that no one really understands what these works are for and even tries an experiment to validate his theory: pretending to be a roadworker, he digs a hole in the street at night. Nobody seems to notice or pay any attention to him and the following day other workers are already undoing his work and filling the hole again, just as they normally do.[28] Luciano's frustration at the frenzy of construction which has turned Milan into a *città-cantiere* [a city of building sites], with deep holes in the pavement and the constant noise of pneumatic drills, clashes with the blasé attitude that is generally exhibited by the Milanese population. They pay no attention to this 'dissennato scavare' [senseless excavation] (*VA*, p. 169; *HL*, p. 164), interpreting it as a positive sign of progress.[29]

Excessive roadworks produce a feeling of oppression and limit the ability to move around the urban environment, giving the impression of a city that is almost under siege. The construction site outside Marcello's place, at the end of *L'integrazione*, resembles the 'complicato tracciato delle trincee e dei camminamenti' [a complicated layout of trenches and passageways] (*I*, p 107). In Fruttero & Lucentini's

---

28   Luciano recounts the incident as follows: 'Per motivi di ricerca sociologica ho provato anch'io, una volta, a mettermi panni dimessi, camicia senza colletto, calzoni turchini sporchi di calce, la barba lunga e i capelli scarruffati. Ho provato, in questa tenuta, e munito di piccone, paline bianche e rosse a strisce e lanternino cieco per la notte [...] ho provato a scavare uno spicchio di strada, e poi a lasciarci la buca. Nessuno me lo ha vietato, e anzi il giorno dopo c'erano operai a disfare il mio lavoro, a riempire la mia buca, guidati da un geometra in camicia bianca ma senza cravatta, serio' [I once tried a sociological experiment. I put on my oldest clothes, a collarless shirt, a pair of paint-stained blue trousers, didn't shave or brush my hair, and, armed with a pick, some stakes painted with red and white stripes, and a storm lantern for the night [...] dug a hole in the road, and left it overnight. Nobody interfered and, when I went back next day, sure enough a gang of workmen were busy undoing my work and filling the hole again, under the supervision of a very serious, white shirted but tieless surveyor] (*VA*, p. 169; *HL*, p. 164).

29   'Per i rumori lavorativi c'è rispetto sommo, invece, e in quel dissennato scavare tutti vedono il segno del progresso' [Noise made by men working, however, are treated with supreme respect, and all this senseless excavation is regarded as a sign of progress] (*VA*, p. 169; *HL*, p. 164).

La donna della domenica the diggers are compared to the claws of a monster that destroys the built environment for the sake of destruction alone (*DD*, pp. 226–27). David Harvey's theory of a 'spatial fix' may help us to make sense of the relentless demolition and reconstruction of the built environment described by Bianciardi. Harvey explains the interventions of capitalism in the built environment as a way of resolving the recurring economic crises caused by a cyclical surplus of capital by allowing new forms of capital flow. These solutions, however, are always temporary, for ultimately capitalism relies on these recurrent economic crises for survival – one of the contradictions inherent in the capitalist economy.[30] When Lefebvre writes that state power 'endures only by virtue of violence directed towards a space',[31] he points to the kind of imperialistic control over space that ensures continuous economic growth along the lines of Harvey.

In Volponi's *Memoriale* and *Le mosche del capitale* industry has conquered urban space. The latter has turned into a sort of appendix to the industrial system whose interests it serves. In *Memoriale* urban descriptions are marginal since few depict Albino's reprise from work at the factory and therefore his outings in the city. The urban setting assumes more relevance in *Le mosche del capitale*, even though it is still squeezed by the dominant space of industry. In *Le mosche del capitale* Salisborgo C. and Bovino, where the industrial plants of the fictional companies MFM and Megagruppo are respectively located, are clearly Ivrea and Turin, seats of Olivetti and Fiat. It may be argued that *Le mosche del capitale* adheres to the image of Turin as a *città-azienda* [a one-industry town] in the shadow of the giant car manufacturer, an image that will be put aside by Fruttero & Lucentini in favour of a more composite representation of Turin.[32]

Albino lives in the countryside and commutes to the city to work at the factory. He therefore has little time left for a leisurely exploration of the urban space. Initially, he expresses indifference to, and even rejection of, city life and its values due to his preference for the simplified lifestyle of the country, with its rhythms dictated by the seasons and the times of day. In the mid-1950s, at the time when *Memoriale* was written, Italy was still largely an agrarian country

---

30 David Harvey, 'Globalization and the Spatial Fix', *Geographische Revue*, 2 (2001), 23–30; and David Harvey, *The Limits to Capital* (London: Verso, 2006 [1982]), pp. 373–412. See also Gregory, *Geographical Imaginations*, p. 380.

31 Lefebvre, *Production of Space*, p. 280.

32 Carloni, *L'Italia in giallo*, p. 83.

with a considerable number of people, like Albino's family in the novel, still employed in agriculture:

> Io non potrei vivere in città, pensavo, dove mi sento solo e dove vedo benissimo che la gente è cattiva, troppo furba e interessata. […] Trovare una strada è una fatica e così sapere dove andare. Io amo la campagna che dice prima, con strade e viottoli, che cosa si deve fare e che si fa vedere tutta, onestamente. (*M*, pp. 13–14)

> [I couldn't live in the city, I thought, not in the city where I feel alone and where I can see that people are mean and tricky, interested only in what they can get out of you. […] It is hard work to find a street in the city and to know where to go. I love the country with its roads and lanes that tell you what you should do, the country that reveals itself at a glance, openly and honestly.] (*MM*, pp. 7–8)

To Albino the countryside discloses itself without deception, shows itself for what it is. The city, by contrast, with its intricate networks of roads may confuse and mislead. Clearly, here Albino chooses the safety of what is known and familiar. One should bear in mind that, over the years of Adriano Olivetti's leadership, Ivrea expanded considerably to accommodate the factory workers and their families. The population of Ivrea approximately doubled in those years from fifteen thousand to thirty thousand.[33] Gradually, however, Albino's resistance gives way to a more open disposition. As his factory life proceeds, the stimuli and opportunities that the urban environment has to offer become a welcome distraction from the repetitiveness of work:

> La sera uscivo lentamente dalla fabbrica perché non avevo voglia di correre ancora a prendere il treno, a ricacciarmi in questa altra fabbrica […] andavo adagio verso il centro della città; passavo un momento in biblioteca, sceglievo a lungo ma senza riuscire a trovare un libro che mi piacesse e camminavo fermandomi davanti a tutti i negozi. […] Dopo andavo al cinema. (*M*, pp. 163–64)

> [In the evening I would walk slowly out of the factory because I didn't want to run to catch the train and plunge myself into this other factory […] I would walk slowly toward the center of the city. I would go into the library for a minute and browse slowly among the books without ever finding one I liked. Then I would continue my walk, stopping at all the shop windows. […] Afterwards I would go to the movies.] (*MM*, p. 120)

The commuter train is a continuation of the factory experience: an oppressive environment that one may imagine packed with workers

---

33   Provost and Lai, 'Story of Cities'.

who have just finished their shift and are heading home, weary, before starting all over again the next day. Instead of getting on the train, Albino takes his time and wanders through the city. The colourful variety of the streets, the different shops and the cultural offerings, the public library and the cinema provide a respite from the repetitiveness of his job. Albino's walking unhurriedly and without a clear direction also expresses a distancing from the relentless rhythms and efficiency-mindedness of the factory.

Volponi's work has frequently been placed by critics within the context of the Italian *romanzo industriale* [industrial novel] that developed in the 1950s and 1960s. Many of the works that belong to this genre and, most notably perhaps, those of Ottiero Ottieri and Volponi have focused on the theme of the alienation and mental illness which derive from the distancing from nature, repetitiveness and apparent lack of meaning of industrial work.[34] Bianciardi's 'anger trilogy' addresses similar themes, expressing frustration at the commodification of intellectual work in the consumerist society of the 1960s.[35] The Italian *romanzo industriale* became established as a genre within a relatively short period of time.[36] This can be roughly circumscribed by the publication in 1957 of Ottieri's *Tempi stretti* [*Tight Times*] and Bianciardi's *Il lavoro culturale* [*Cultural Work*] and then by that of Goffredo Parise's *Il padrone* [*The Boss*] in 1965.[37] Industrial

---

34 Industry as 'second nature' is a central theme in Michelangelo Antonioni's film *Il deserto rosso* [*Red Desert*] (1964). On this topic, see issue 4 of the literary magazine *Il Menabò*, published in 1961, and Giorgio Barberi Squarotti, 'La letteratura e la "nuova natura" creata dell'industria', in *Letteratura e industria. Atti del XV Congresso A.I.S.L.L.I., Torino, 15–19 maggio 1994*, ed. by Giorgio Bàrberi Squarotti and Carlo Ossola, Biblioteca dell'Archivum Romanicum, 276, 2 vols (Florence: Olschki, 1997), i, *Dal Medioevo al primo Novecento*, pp. 25–42.

35 The 'anger trilogy' comprises *Il lavoro culturale*, *L'integrazione* and *La vita agra*.

36 Carlo Varotti, 'Fabbrica', in *Luoghi della letteratura italiana*, ed. by Gian Mario Anselmi and Gino Ruozzi (Milan: Mondadori, 2003), pp. 180–90 (p. 180).

37 Rocco Capozzi, 'Dalla "Letteratura e industria" all'industria del postmoderno', *Annali d'Italianistica*, 9 (1991), 144–57 (p. 144). Other authors who have participated in this particular trend are Giovanni Arpino (*Gli anni del giudizio* [*The Judgment Years*] (1958); *Una nuvola d'ira* [*A Cloud of Anger*] (1962)); Lucio Mastronardi, with his trilogy that bears witness to the transformations in the productive environment in Vigevano, from workshops to small industries; Vasco Pratolini (*Costanza della ragione* [*The Constancy of Reason*] (1962)); and Alberto Bevilacqua (*La Califfa* [*Califfa*] (1964)). Calvino was another protagonist of this season, both with books that address post-war modernization and industrial development and by participating directly in the debate on the renewal of Italian literature through new languages and ways of representation, with articles published in journals and magazines. Many of these industrial

literature somehow exhausted its *raison d'être* in the 1980s, when class divisions were redefined and the (white Italian) working class joined the ranks of the lower-middle classes in conjunction with further transformations in the job market, the development of other sectors of the economy and the delocalization of industrial production.[38] The *romanzo industriale* needs to be seen not only as a type of novel that addresses factory life as its main topic, but also as one that undertakes a revision of language and style in order to explore more effectively the socio-economic changes of those years and their repercussions on the working class.[39] The debate on literature and industry reached a mature conceptualization with *Il Menabò*, a literary magazine founded by Elio Vittorini and Italo Calvino, and specifically with its 1961 issue, which was entirely dedicated to the question of how literature can most effectively document the new reality of industrialization.[40]

One of the peculiarities of the tradition of Italian industrial literature is that many of the writers who wrote about the industrial environment were themselves involved at different levels within Italian industry.[41] In this regard Volponi is certainly an emblematic figure. The co-operation between writers and industry was made possible thanks to a group of innovative industrialists like Vittorio Valletta, Oscar Sinigaglia, Enrico Mattei and Adriano Olivetti, who entrusted many writers, including Leonardo Sinisgalli, Franco Fortini, Giovanni Giudici, Ottieri and Volponi himself, with important roles

---

novels are collected in Giorgio Bigatti and Giuseppe Lupo (eds), *Fabbrica di carta. I libri che raccontano l'Italia industriale*, Percorsi Laterza (Rome: Laterza, 2013).

38   Varotti, 'Fabbrica', pp. 180–81.

39   Piergiorgio Mori, *Scrittori nel boom. Il romanzo industriale negli anni del miracolo italiano* (Rome: EdiLet-Edilazio, 2011), p. 8. In this regard Mori notices that 'il romanzo industriale fotografa quella parte d'Italia scontenta e delusa dal benessere decantato dalle cifre e amplificato dalla televisione e dai mezzi di informazione' [the industrial novel captures that part of Italy unhappy and disappointed by the image of well-being projected by the statistics and amplified by television and the media] (Mori, *Scrittori nel boom*, p. 306).

40   Giorgio Barberi Squarotti, *Storia della civiltà letteraria italiana*, 6 vols (Turin: UTET, 1996), v, *Il secondo Ottocento e il Novecento*, p. 1666. The editorial director Vittorini and other contributors felt that this was a particularly relevant issue in Italy and called for renewed literary modes of expression and representation. The fact that the issue of *Il Menabò* for 1961 sparked lively debate can be seen as symptomatic of the centrality that these themes had assumed in the Italian culture of those years. See Mori, *Scrittori nel boom*, p. 33.

41   Mori, *Scrittori nel boom*, p. 11.

in their companies.[42] Volponi's oeuvre critcizes a model of industry that is founded on the exploitation of the working class at the hands of the capitalist elite; it is not against industrial progress *per se*.[43] Volponi believed that industry should incorporate not only technical knowhow but also a more human-centred approach. In this sense his disillusion, perhaps most evident in *Le mosche del capitale*, reveals more broadly the failure of the project to reform Italian industry championed by Olivetti. After the entrepreneur's death, his company experienced financial problems due to poor strategic choices and the newly unfavourable situation of the Italian economy, whilst his Socialist projects and initiatives gradually lost momentum.[44]

The theme of *spaesamento* [uprootedness] is central in *Memoriale* and Albino's illness, as it is more generally in Volponi's work. Fabrizio Scrivano focuses on the movement of the characters' leaving behind familiar places and stresses the non-compatibility of spaces in *Memoriale*, particularly in terms of the dichotomy between the countryside and urban-industrial environment.[45] Owing to the hypertrophic growth of industry, a further incompatibility and lack of balance emerge between the space of production and the space of leisure. The imposing size of the factory building suggests that, even though architectonically separate from the city, seemingly not an integral part of it and almost a foreign body, the factory dominates the mindsets of the city dwellers:

> La fabbrica in quel posto è costruita e in quello stesso posto resterà; non entrerà mai nel paese, non avrà mai un mercato davanti, una fiera, dei crocchi di persone, i fiori le fontane, un porticato. Davanti non si fermerà nessuno, solo chi starà male o chi lavorerà o non avrà un lavoro. (*M*, p. 262)

---

42   Bàrberi Squarotti describes the Olivetti Company as 'quel centro di fervide discussioni sul mondo della fabbrica, sulla condizione operaia, sull'organizzazione della vita e del tempo libero [...] con il movimento di Comunità fondato da Adriano Olivetti con programma di fare della fabbrica un luogo di umano incontro oltre che di lavoro' [that centre of fervent discussions on the world of the factory, on the condition of the workers, on the organization of life and leisure [...] with the Community Movement founded by Adriano Olivetti with a programme of making the factory a place of human encounter as well as work] (Bàrberi Squarotti, *Il secondo Ottocento e il Novecento*, p. 1666).

43   Capozzi, 'Dalla "Letteratura e industria"', p. 146.

44   Franco Amatori and Andrea Colli, *Impresa e industria in Italia dall'Unità a oggi* (Venice: Marsilio, 1999), pp. 269–70.

45   Fabrizio Scrivano, 'Individuo, società e territorio nei romanzi di Paolo Volponi. Le soluzioni narrative di *Memoriale* e *La strada per Roma*', *Esperienze letterarie*, 25 (2000), 88–104.

[The factory is built in one place, and it will always remain in the same place. The factory will never come into town. It will never have a market or a fair in front of its doors. It will never be surrounded by people, or flowers, or fountains, or arcades. No one will stand in front of it – only those who are not well, those who work in the factory, or those who want to work there.] (*MM*, pp. 194–95)

In the space of economic production one does not find recognizable urban features such as local markets, fairs, green spaces, fountains and the kind of user-friendly architecture which ensures that people are able to orientate themselves and fosters social interaction. Everything here has a function and there is no place for the leisure activities that normally take place in a town or city. There is no room for idleness. Volponi goes further to suggest that the factory has replaced the traditional urban environment and is organized like a town in its own right:

Pensavo anche a quello che l'ultima volta mi aveva detto l'impiegato dell'Ufficio Personale: 'Deve far conto che la fabbrica sia un paese, del quale un uomo deve accettare le leggi' […]. Come potevo considerare la fabbrica un paese? A Candia avrei potuto vivere in tanti modi ma in fabbrica nell'unico modo comandato. (*M*, pp. 238–39)

[I also thought about something the clerk in the Personnel Department had told me the last time: 'You must pretend that the factory is a town, and a man must accept its laws' […]. But how could I pretend that the factory was a town? In Candia I could live in many different ways, but in the factory there was only one way to live: under orders.] (*MM*, p. 177)

The workers live in the factory and for the factory. They must embrace its ideology and comply with its regulations. For Albino, this means leaving behind the freedom he enjoys in the outside world to live according to his own nature.

During the course of the novel Albino develops tuberculosis, whilst his mental condition deteriorates. He experiences several episodes of sickness that keep him off work, at home or in medical rehabilitation centres to recover. In his vulnerable mental and emotional state he becomes the victim of fraud at the hands of Palmarucci, with whom he engages in conversation on a train journey back home. Having learnt about his health issues, Palmarucci introduces Albino to the fake healer Dr Fioravanti, who pretends to cure his tuberculosis with injections of an allegedly miraculous serum. Palmarucci has moved to the North from his hometown of Gubbio in Umbria. As he begins to spend more time with Albino, establishing with him a bond of trust, the two men share their impressions of the urban environment where they now live and work. In the half-drunk monologue quoted below, with only Albino as his audience, Palmarucci launches into praise of small-town and village life:

> Stanno tutti dentro la fabbrica, che non si vede nemmeno. È messa fuori, come da noi i carceri o i cimiteri. A passarle davanti mette paura. In giro ci sono sole donne, vecchi e malati. La domenica poi, non c'è più nessuno. Non ho nemmeno capito da che parte siano le chiese. Meglio un paese; un paese qualunque delle mie parti. (*M*, p. 219)

> [Everyone is in the factory, and it is not even in the city. It is outside the city where we put our jails and our cemeteries. When you walk by it frightens you. The only people you see around are women, old men, and invalids. On Sunday there isn't a soul to be found. I don't even know where the churches are. A small town in my part of the country, any small town, is better than this.] (*MM*, p. 161)

Palmarucci looks back with regret at his hometown, which, like many other people in those years, he had left behind to move to the richer North. He recalls with nostalgia the occasions for socializing and the livelier town atmosphere. Now, as he looks around, the streets are empty with everyone at work at this time of day, as if the factory had sucked the life out of the city. The factory is compared by Palmarucci to a prison, a space of containment and re-education. According to Foucault, as the scale of production increases factories become highly hierarchized, disciplinary places that ensure 'an intense, continuous supervision'.[46] Prisons, buildings which are normally located outside city centres, as removed as possible from our everyday experience and immediate consciousness, by virtue of this very displacement acquire an amplified and almost transcendental power to orientate individuals' behaviour and attitudes. It is not their visibility, but the certainty of punishment which lies behind their walls that transforms the conscience of individuals and, in the minds of those who developed the idea of this kind of administrative apparatus, provides a hold on the conduct of potential criminals.[47] Palmarucci

46 Michel Foucault, *Discipline and Punish: The Birth of the Prison,* trans. by Alan Sheridan (London: Penguin, 1995), p. 174; originally published as *Surveiller et punir: Naissance de la prison* (Paris: Gallimard, 1975).
47 With the rise of disciplinary power, writes Foucault, punishment 'will tend to become the most hidden part of the penal process. This has several consequences: it leaves the domain of more or less everyday perception and enters that of abstract consciousness; its effectiveness is seen as resulting from its inevitability, not from its visible intensity; it is the certainty of being punished

also compares the factory to a cemetery, a site that elicits feelings related to illness and death and, at least since modern times, has also been pushed out to the edges of the city. Here one has another example of the absolute dominance of the factory over the lives of urban dwellers, despite its peripheral location and its presence not being visible to Palmarucci and Albino on this particular occasion.

In *Le mosche del capitale* Turin's fictional counterpart Bovino is described as 'la città sottomessa' [the subjugated city] (*MC*, p. 125); by now we know that it is subjugated to the logic of capital. The adjective *bovino* [bovine] itself evokes dullness and unconditional obedience. The identity of Turin is bound to the presence of Fiat, Italy's giant automotive manufacturer, which dominated car production in the post-war years. In the novel we are mostly given glimpses of Bovino from the windows of the company headquarters that dominate the city from their vantage point, a view from on high that reverses Bianciardi's street-level gaze in *La vita agra*. The principle, however, remains the same: as Lefebvre argues, the verticality of buildings refers symbolically to an implicitly authoritarian power:

> The arrogant verticality of skyscrapers, and especially of public and state buildings, introduces a phallic or more precisely a phallocratic element into the visual realm; the purpose of this display, of this need to impress, is to convey an impression of authority to each spectator. Verticality and great height have ever been the spatial expression of potentially violent power.[48]

In the novel the economy grows and fosters urban expansion at the price of the increasing exploitation and marginalization of the lower classes. Urban geography and housing distribution reproduce these relations of power. The working classes live in tower blocks and cheap houses in less-sought-after areas of the city, in a kind of proletarian trend towards suburbanization that Turin shared with Milan and other Italian cities in those years.[49] A number of housing

---

and not the horrifying spectacle of public punishment that must discourage crime' (Foucault, *Discipline and Punish*, p. 9). Again in Foucault's words, prison walls embody the 'monotonous figure, at once material and symbolic, of the power to punish' (Foucault, *Discipline and Punish*, p. 116).

48   Lefebvre, *Production of Space*, p. 98.

49   In this regard, see, e.g., the description of Milan's *coree* in John Foot, 'Revisiting the *Coree*. Self-construction, Memory and Immigration on the Milanese Periphery, 1950–2000', in *Italian Cityscapes*, ed. by Lumley and Foot, pp. 46–60; and Rome's *borgate* in John David Rhodes, *Stupendous, Miserable City: Pasolini's Rome* (Minneapolis, MN: University of Minnesota Press, 2007), p. 2.

estates sprang up in the two Northern cities to accommodate immigrant and unskilled workers and became, often infamously, known as places of crime and social isolation. This is discussed in more detail in Chapter 2, which analyses common ideas associated with the periphery. In the boom years one may observe the general trend of the displacement of working-class people from the central areas of the main cities in order to make them available 'for luxury housing and administrative offices'.[50] One should bear in mind, however, that several factors, including gender, sexuality and ethnic background, concur to shape the social geography of the city and, therefore, parameters based strictly on wealth and socio-economic factors prove insufficient to account for the complexity of urban space. That said, there is no doubt that city centres concentrate wealth (as the realm of the privileged classes), power (through the presence of institutional buildings) and tradition (monuments as signifiers which convey meaning related to the collective identity and national history of a particular social group).

We have seen examples of how the space of industrial production, the space of capital, moulds the environment in which the characters of Bianciardi and Volponi live. Bianciardi's use of vocabulary relating to military sieges points to the imperialist-like expansion of capital into everyday life through its network of architectural and communication infrastructures. Rampant car traffic and the pervasiveness of road works, which constantly re-shape the urban landscape, limit freedom of movement and force people to the same itineraries and places within the city. In Volponi's novels one finds the same kind of tension as the urban environment recedes to the background and is devoid of features which are not relevant to economic growth. There emerge a non-compatibility and imbalance between the space of work and leisure, since the former dominates the urban environment and the lives of its inhabitants. Albino's

---

50   Gianfranco Petrillo, 'The Two Waves: Milan as a City of Immigration, 1955–1995', in *Italian Cityscapes*, ed. by Lumley and Foot, pp. 31–45 (p. 39). Mario Sechi observes that, in Volponi's oeuvre, the contradictions of industrial development are reflected in 'una specie di malattia degenerativa della crescita urbanistica' [a kind of degenerative disease of urban growth]. As Sechi puts it, 'l'organismo urbano sembra impotente a ricucire e a suturare le lacerazioni che la crescita puramente quantitativa degli spazi edificati, e l'ammassamento di nuove ondate migratorie, hanno prodotto' [the urban organism seems powerless to mend and suture the lacerations that the purely quantitative growth of built-up spaces and the accumulation of new migratory waves have produced] (Mario Sechi, 'Centri e periferie di città in Pier Paolo Pasolini e Paolo Volponi', *Urbanistica*, 125 (2004), 90–96 (pp. 94–95)).

internal conflicts leave way, in *Le mosche del capitale*, to characters who have been flattened out by their becoming just a cog in the capitalist machine.

Industrial Architecture

The high-rise buildings which sprang up in Milan following the extraordinary development of tertiary industry and are immortalized by Bianciardi in *La vita agra* have become a trademark of the city as financial capital. Bianciardi's futuristic, dystopian descriptions convey the idea that these megastructures are the spatial concretization of industrial capitalism and political bureaucracy, with their inherent degree of violence and social inequality. Once again, these buildings, projecting upwards, are a reminder of the power of economic and political elites:

> Raro perciò che ci si avveda del torracchione irto in cima di parafulmini, antenne, radar. Solo a tratti, quando fa specchio il sole su quel lucido, ti accade di levare gli occhi verso il torracchione di vetro e d'alluminio, di vedere una strada privata ingombra di auto in sosta, stranamente tacita in quel quartiere centrale, di girare attorno all'isolato, scoprendo un'intera cittadella – tre o quattro torracchioni simili, di vetro, di alluminio, di pietra lustrata. (*VA*, p. 31)

> [That's why you rarely notice the big tower with all those lightning conductors and antennae and radar apparatus on top. Only rarely, when the shiny mass happens to catch and reflect the sun, do you raise your eyes towards the huge glass and aluminium structure and notice a private street crowded with parked cars, strangely quiet in that central area; and if you walk round the isolated block you discover a whole citadel – three or four similar towers built of glass and aluminium and shiny stone.] (*HL*, p. 31)

The *torracchione* which Luciano intends to blow up – and which arguably embodies the fusion of the Pirelli Building and the Montecatini head office in the Via della Moscova, the latter designed by Giò Ponti and completed in 1938 – is a hostile and uncanny entity. Its smooth, impenetrable surfaces almost belie its human manufacture. With the lighting conductor on the top, it is reminiscent of another grotesque, sinister building, the Villa Pirobutirro in Gadda's *La cognizione del dolore* [*The Experience of Pain*] (1963).

Heavy car traffic diverts attention so that, quite remarkably, one may not immediately notice these skyscrapers looming threateningly, forming what in the familiar siege language Bianciardi describes as a citadel. The office blocks and skyscrapers are the main target of

Luciano's personal war on the new Milan, for they concentrate wealth and power and concretize capitalist relations of power. Luciano envisages 'i cervelli, lo stato maggiore' [the brains, the general staff] (*VA*, p. 32; *HL*, p. 31), that is, the oligarchy of industrialists and technocrats with full decision-making power in their hands who work behind the translucent windows of these multinational corporations. Their course of action has deep repercussions not only for the population in Milan but also for the rest of the country, as shown by the Ribolla mining incident. Ignoring health and safety concerns, guided only by the goal of profit, just a few days before the accident the head office had been insisting that not a man, not a ton of lignite, not a working day be wasted (*VA*, p. 38; *HL*, p. 37). A trait of the capitalist city is, for Lefebvre, its being the centre of decision-making.[51] This 'domination of and by centrality' may refer to both the dominance of the so-called Alpha cities,[52] major urban centres that are essential nodes in the global economy, and to the perceived greater importance for financial or institutional reasons of certain urban areas over others. In the case of Italy, this is especially true for Milan, which has been a major industrial centre since Italy's first industrial revolution at the beginning of the nineteenth century and which, with the post-war economic boom, consolidated the role of financial capital of the country that it has maintained up to the present day.

The emphasis on the changing scale of the built environment and on modern building materials (glass, metal) hints at feelings of alienation and inhumanity, at the idea that urban space is no longer the domain of the human and humanity has somehow been surpassed. Changing urban proportions affect the way in which city dwellers perceive the built environment and may undermine their ability to relate empathetically to it.[53] Feelings of anxiety may, therefore, be projected onto buildings, which are assigned their

---

51   As Lefebvre puts it, '[t]his centre, gathering together training and information, capacities of organization and institutional decision-making, appears as a project in the making of a new centrality, that of *power*' (Henri Lefebvre, 'Industrialization and Urbanization', in *Writings on Cities*, ed. and trans. by Eleonore Kofman and Elizabeth Lebas (Cambridge, MA: Blackwell, 1996), pp. 65–85 (p. 73)).

52   Henri Lefebvre, 'Perspective or Prospective?', in *Writings on Cities*, pp. 160–74 (p. 161).

53   Will Self, 'Will Self on the Meaning of Skyscrapers: From the Tower of Babel to the Shard', *The Guardian*, 27 March 2015 <http://www.theguardian.com/books/2015/mar/27/will-self-on-the-meaning-of-skyscrapers> [accessed 20 May 2015].

own strange and unsettling qualities.[54] Milan's Stazione Centrale provides an interesting example. As the main gateway through which masses of people and material goods entered and left Milan in the boom years, the Stazione Centrale became 'a monument to the industrial city'.[55] In *Silenzio a Milano* [*Silence in Milan*] (1958) Anna Maria Ortese lingers on the exact measurements of the height and surface area of the Stazione Centrale and on the description of the construction materials. The impressive height of the arrival hall and the steel canopies make it resemble a cathedral or a mountain to those who arrive here for the first time and are struck by this kind of grand, almost awe-inspiring architecture.[56] The opening scene of Visconti's film *Rocco e i suoi Fratelli* [*Rocco and His Brothers*] (1960) features a Southern family arriving in Milan Stazione Centrale. Like Ortese, Visconti also lingers on the stone and marble entrance hall of the station, emphasizing the contrast between architecture which conveys the values of economic progress and power and the family's humble condition. In his crime story 'Stazione centrale ammazzare subito' [Central Station Kill Immediately] (1969) Giorgio Scerbanenco describes the Stazione Centrale as 'un pianeta a sé' [a planet unto itself] and 'una riserva di pellerossa nel mezzo della città' [an Indian reservation in the middle of the city].[57] The exoticizing and pejorative term *pellerossa*, literally 'red skin', further cuts the station out of the space and time of the rest of the city, conveying the idea of a place that was increasingly regarded as ambiguous and even disreputable. In the 1960s the station became a focal point for travellers and commuters, a place of socialization for the groups of immigrants and workers who gathered in the cafés of the adjacent square,[58] but also a transit site that provided a suitable environment for crime and illegality. In *La vita agra* the station is the arrival point of the 'treni del sonno' [sleepy trains] which every day, in the early morning, carry crowds of workers from the hinterland into the city. By means of another military metaphor, Bianciardi describes them

---

54 Vidler argues that 'the "uncanny" is not a property of the space itself nor can it be provoked by any particular spatial conformation; it is, in its aesthetic dimension, a representation of a mental state of projection' (Vidler, *The Architectural Uncanny*, p. 11).

55 Foot, *Milan since the Miracle*, p. 7.

56 Anna Maria Ortese, *Silenzio a Milano* (Bari: Laterza, 1958), pp. 7–9.

57 Giorgio Scerbanenco, 'Stazione centrale ammazzare subito', in *Milano calibro 9* (Milan: Garzanti, 1993 [1969]), pp. 93–110 (p. 93).

58 Foot, *Milan since the Miracle*, pp. 7–8.

as 'battaglioni di gente grigia, con gli occhi gonfi, in marcia spalla a spalla' [battalions of grey, swollen-eyed people, who march shoulder to shoulder] (*VA*, pp. 53–54; *HL*, p. 52).

The *fabbrica* of *Memoriale* possess a similar estranging quality. Some descriptions, like the one quoted below, emphasize, for example, the analogy with the human body. Here the *fabbrica* is a gigantic organism with grotesque anthropomorphic traits and fragmented body parts: 'Aspettavo soprattutto di entrare nel corpo della fabbrica, di arrivare di fronte alle macchine, alla bocca del rumore' [I looked forward above all to entering the interior [*corpo*] of the factory and coming face to face with those machines, with the source [*bocca*] of all that noise].[59] Other, more frequent, descriptions borrow elements from the natural world so as to suggest that the *fabbrica* exists in an immutable reality to whose eternal laws the city and its inhabitants are subjugated. *Memoriale* is dominated by this presence: the factory is 'grande più della stessa città' [bigger than the city it has conquered] (*M*, p. 7; *MM*, p. 3). The novel repeatedly stresses the imposing and threatening size of the factory, which looms over the pavement and obstructs the view of the surrounding countryside:

> La fabbrica, grandissima e bassa, ronzava indifferente, ferma come il lago di Candia in certe sere in cui è il solo, in mezzo a tutto il paesaggio, ad avere luce. Nemmeno in Germania avevo visto una fabbrica così grande; così tutta grande subito sulla strada. (*M*, p. 19)

> [The huge low building hummed indifferently. It was still, like the lake in Candia when it alone in all the countryside reflects the light. Not even in Germany had I seen such a large factory. Huge, sitting squarely on the street.] (*MM*, p. 12)

Like the calm water of the lake in Candia, indifferent to Albino's ruminations when in his many sleepless nights he observes the reflections of moonlight playing on its surface, the *fabbrica* remains deaf to his protests and anguish. It shares with nature the indifference to human suffering.

Further analogies are made to institutions of Italian public life. In continuation of the previous extract, the *fabbrica* is compared to a church and a courthouse; its governing body to judiciary power and ecclesiastical authorities. The factory is immovable and imperturbable, like these powers, which may see themselves as representatives of an objective and absolute law, but may indeed be unfair or corrupt. One may read here distrust towards the judiciary system and its collusion

---

59   This part is missing from *The Memorandum*.

with political power, as well as a rejection of the ideology of the Catholic Church, which was still exerting a dominant influence over the Italian society of those years. The passage also contains another element of uncanny anthropomorphizing, the incessant noise of industrial machinery resembling someone with shortness of breath after running a lap:

> La fabbrica era invece immobile come una chiesa o un tribunale, e si sentiva da fuori che dentro, proprio come in una chiesa, in un dentro alto e vuoto, si svolgevano le funzioni di centinaia di lavori. Dopo un momento il lavoro sembrava tutto uguale; la fabbrica era tutta uguale e da qualsiasi parte mandava lo stesso rumore, più che un rumore, un affanno, un ansimare forte. (*M*, p. 19)

> [But the factory was immovable, solid, and silent, like a church or a courthouse, and from the outside you knew that the interior was just like a church; you knew that in a high and empty space a thousand different kinds of jobs were getting done. After a second the work seemed all the same. The factory was the same in all parts, and it emitted the same humming noise from every side. It was more than just a hum. It was like a panting sound or a loud gasp.] (*MM*, p. 12)

The opening scene of *Le mosche del capitale* has echoes of these descriptions. It captures the city dwellers asleep and unaware while the capitalist machine, here embodied by a gigantic calculator, is relentlessly at work, fuelling economic expansion and urban growth. Bovino has taken on its own life or, more appropriately, the life of capital. The feeling is that of a lurking threat coming from the ubiquity of capital:

> La grande città industriale riempie la notte di febbraio senza luna, tre ore prima dell'alba. Dormono tutti o quasi, e anche coloro che sono svegli giacciono smemorati e persi. [...] Il sonno si spande senza alcuna innocenza, e non per fisico gravame, ma come ulteriore dato e calcolo delle compatibilità favorevoli al capitale. Tutta la città gli è sottoposta; così ciascun dormiente, ciascuno nel suo posto e letto, nel proprio sonno come in quello più grande e generale che si svuota di vapori. Il calcolatore guida e controlla, concede rincorre codifica assume imprime. (*MC*, pp. 5–6)

> [The large industrial city fills the moonless February night, three hours before dawn. Almost all of them are asleep, and even those who are awake lie there oblivious and lost. [...] Sleep spreads without any innocence, and not as a physical burden, but as a further piece of data and calculation of the combinations favourable to capital. The whole city is subject to it; so each sleeper, each in that bed where

they belong, in their own sleep as in the larger and more general one
that exhales an enormous breath. The computer guides and controls,
enables, searches, encodes, accepts and imprints.]

This is a numb sleep, without memory or dreams, not innocent
but culpable, as if the whole urban population were to be held
accountable for letting capital perpetrate its injustices in the name
of modernization and profit. Even those who are awake are almost
in a stupor. Capital does not need critical and engaged people. The
characters in the novel are devoid of any personality traits that do
not revolve around the spheres of industrial work and productivity.
The urban setting is perhaps more relevant to the narration than in
Memoriale; it is, however, a city that is almost abstract and rarefied,
where traditional urban features have become scarce and fainter. It is
Turin and yet it could also be any place or no place at all.

The perceived lack of legibility of the urban landscape, which
signals a loss of control over it, brings about a crisis of representation.
Through the character of Astolfo (head of Megagruppo with Donna
Fulgenzia, respectively inspired by Umberto and Gianni Agnelli), in *Le
mosche del capitale* Volponi voices the idea that literature is inadequate
to portray the transformations of the city in the advanced phase of
capitalist development: 'Astolfo dolente e ispirato gli mostra la città
dalla vetrata centrale del suo ufficio all'undicesimo piano. Recita che
è brutta e che abbrutisce anche l'industria. È così brutta e sfatta che
non è più raccontabile' [Sorrowful and inspired, Astolfo shows him
the city from the central window of his office on the eleventh floor. He
says that it is ugly and that it also makes the industry look ugly. It's
so ugly and untidy that it beggars description] (*MC*, p. 122). Astolfo,
looking down from his office on the eleventh floor of the corporate
building, reaffirms the dominant, objectifying kind of gaze that in the
novel is cast on the city below from on high and from the perspective
of the ruling classes. He claims that the city is ugly and shabby and
that cannot be narrated, or rather that it is not worth narrating. He
seems to think that it is redundant and dispensable. One may find, in
Astolfo's monologue, echoes of the idea that the metaphor of the city
as a legible text has been surpassed in advanced industrial societies.
It would, therefore, take a new artistic form, one able to break with
traditional modes of representation, to convey the new urban reality.

Milan's skyscrapers in *La vita agra* and the corporate buildings
in *Memoriale* and *Le mosche del capitale* signify and concretize deeply
unequal relations of power at the heart of Italian society in the
1960s and 1970s. The imposing verticality of these buildings and the
perception of them as being out of scale convey the impossible fight of

Luciano, Albino and other characters against political and economic power. These coercive architectures (and the dominant organization of space, as we shall see below) have the effect of disenfranchising the characters of Bianciardi and Volponi as well as the many users of space that are reduced, as Lefebvre puts it, to 'passivity and silence'.[60]

Discipline and Productivity

Hinting at Foucault in their introduction to Bianciardi's collected oeuvre, Massimo Coppola and Alberto Piccinini maintain that the emergence of advertising-driven consumerism in post-war Italian society betrays a new form of bio-political control: 'Nella sua opera Bianciardi si misura con i nuovi dispositivi di controllo biopolitico, che coincide con l'affermarsi, proprio in quel tempo, della società dei consumi' [In his work Bianciardi comes to terms with the new biopolitical mechanisms of control, which coincide with the emergence, at that time, of consumer society].[61] Foucault argues that at the turn of the eighteenth and nineteenth centuries an evolution in the Western penal system can be registered which coincides with the rise of disciplinary power: in other words, of rationally organized and hierarchical methods of surveillance that develop in conjunction with 'an extension and refinement of punitive practices'.[62] Discipline exercised on a societal scale entails ever more sophisticated forms of bio-political control of the human body and of people's behaviour and conduct.[63] In *La vita agra* control and economic productivity,

---

60   Lefebvre, *Production of Space*, p. 56.

61   Massimo Coppola and Alberto Piccinini, 'Luciano Bianciardi, l'io opaco', in Luciano Bianciardi, *L'antimeridiano. Tutte le opere*, ed. by Luciana Bianciardi, Massimo Coppola and Alberto Piccinini, 2 vols (Milan: Mondadori, 2005–08), I (2005), *Saggi e romanzi, racconti, diari giovanili*, pp. v–xxxv (p. xxxiv).

62   Foucault, *Discipline and Punish*, p. 77. This shift takes place in conjunction with complex historical transformations, such as the demographic growth of the eighteenth century, the increase in production and rise in school population and, therefore, the presence of larger groups of individuals to be supervised (Foucault, *Discipline and Punish*, p. 218).

63   Foucault writes that towards the end of the eighteenth century 'a whole corpus of individualizing knowledge was being organized that took as its field of reference not so much the crime committed [...] but the potentiality of danger that lies hidden in an individual and which is manifested in his observed everyday conduct' (Foucault, *Discipline and Punish*, p. 126). Similarly, he writes that 'this punitive intervention must rest on a studied manipulation of the individual' (Foucault, *Discipline and Punish*, p. 126).

core values in Milanese society, form an indissoluble pair: continued productivity to preserve the status quo requires new forms of social control and the orientation of what people do, buy and consume. Bianciardi explicitly links increased industrial productivity and new levels of consumption when he writes that 'faranno insorgere bisogni mai sentiti prima. [...] Purché tutti lavorino, purché siano pronti a scarpinare, a fare polvere, a pestare i piedi, a tafanarsi l'un l'altro dalla mattina alla sera' [needs previously unheard of will arise. [...] Provided, that is to say, everyone works hard and is always ready to lift his feet, wear out shoe leather, kick up the dust, and pester his fellows from morning till night] (*VA*, p. 158; *HL*, p. 153). The new *benessere* relies on a growth in productivity. It fosters competition and forms of labour exploitation which are intrinsic to capitalism. People in Milan are expected to contribute to economic growth and the prestige of Milan as a great international city through their work and by paying taxes, which disproportionately hit the poorer.

In his analysis of disciplinary power, Foucault shows that this has an essential spatial component, for it relies on the rational principle of the segmentation and distribution of space and of individuals within it in order to enable supervision.[64] The disciplinary discourse reverberates in *La vita agra* through an urban layout which fosters a rational, purpose-oriented way of moving across the city, where automobiles – fast-moving vehicles that can transport one quickly from one point to another – have an uncontested central role.[65] Bearing in mind Foucault's idea of apparatus, or *dispositif*, as any set of practices and strategies that aim to train, control and therefore 'normalize' the behaviour of individuals,[66] it can be argued that the

---

64   As Foucault puts it, 'discipline proceeds from the distribution of individuals in space' (Foucault, *Discipline and Punish*, p. 141). This can either be realised in enclosed and supervised places – not only prisons but boarding schools, military barracks, workshops and factories, places of confinement of vagabonds – or through the partitioning of individuals in space, where each of them occupies a precise place to avoid concentration and gatherings and to make it possible to supervise them more effectively. Foucault goes on to explain this latter point more in detail, claiming that disciplinary power does not assign individuals to a fixed position but, rather, places them within a network of power relations (Foucault, *Discipline and Punish*, pp. 145–46).

65   See, e.g., Nicholas R. Fyfe, 'Introduction: Reading the Street', in *Images of the Street: Planning, Identity and Control in Public Space*, ed. by Nicholas R. Fyfe (London: Routledge, 1998), pp. 1–10 (pp. 2–3).

66   Foucault does not provide a proper definition of apparatus. He claims, for instance, that the model of surveillance embodied by Jeremy Bentham's

way in which movement is organized and regulated in *La vita agra* links modern Milan to the functioning of the apparatus. On the one hand, Bianciardi argues that modern transport only guarantees a false freedom of movement, for it funnels people to specific areas and itineraries within the city, chiefly the journey from home to work and vice versa. This limited freedom comes at a price that not everyone can bear, for not everyone can afford a car or the cost of commuting by public transport. On the other hand, the dominance of car traffic marginalizes specific categories of city users such as cyclists and pedestrians, relegating the latter to 'una fettuccia di marciapiede' [narrow pavement] (*VA*, p. 31; *HL*, p. 30) with cars zooming past on all sides. Mobility in Milan is production-oriented and elitist. Modern street planning, influenced by theories on the rational distribution of space developed primarily by Le Corbusier, privileges efficient, fast mobility while limiting the walkability of the city.[67] As Michel De Certeau argues, the act of walking becomes a way of subverting established and imposed itineraries, for instance by creating shortcuts or opting for alternative routes.[68] By re-working official and accepted routes, one may reclaim urban spaces and enable a different experience of the city. Similarly, in *La vita agra*, walking is a way truly to appropriate urban space, which as such is viewed with suspicion and actively discouraged by authorities in the city.

In the novel street planning follows a principle of spatial rationality and regulation that influences the behaviour of car drivers and passers-by. The latter, portrayed as perpetually walking at a hectic pace, oblivious to the world around them, assume the contours of the blasé metropolitan crowd that has populated early sociological studies and the literary imagination with its fluctuating physiognomy, at least from Baudelaire onwards. Among the Milanese crowd one may pick

---

Panopticon represents an 'architectural apparatus', for it concretizes the need of power to rationalize space in order to exert more efficiently and consistently its control on the social body (Foucault, *Discipline and Punish*, p. 201). Giorgio Agamben writes: 'I shall call an apparatus literally anything that has in some way the capacity to capture, orient, determine, intercept, model, control, or secure the gestures, behaviors, opinions, or discourses of living beings' (Giorgio Agamben, 'What Is an Apparatus?', in *What Is an Apparatus? and Other Essays*, trans. by David Kishik and Stefan Pedatella, Meridian: Crossing Aesthetics (Stanford, CA: Stanford University Press, 2009), pp. 1–24 (p. 14)).

67   Fyfe, 'Introduction', pp. 2–3.

68   Michel de Certeau, *The Practice of Everyday Life*, trans. by Steven F. Rendall (Berkeley, CA: University of California Press, 1984), pp. 97–105; originally published as *L'Invention du Quotidien* (Paris: Union générale d'éditions, 1980).

out the secretaries, a new professional figure in the post-war era, from their nervous, steady walk, their heels tapping rhythmically on the pavement.[69] Once again, one can assume that they are on their way to work or, conversely, that they have just left the office and are heading home. Behind the wheel, car drivers undergo a sort of animalistic mutation. Their cars, described as 'lupi' [wolves], become a sort of grotesque prosthetic extension of their body (*VA*, p. 165; *HL*, p. 159). Bianciardi assigns to cars monstruous animalistic traits, for example when he compares a few vehicles that have been parked with their wheels on the sidewalk to 'grosse bestie ferme lì per orinare' [big beasts stopping there to urinate] (*I*, p. 17). In *La vita agra* Luciano even observes that it is possible to determine the day of the week by the particular way in which car drivers unleash their anger and vent at other drivers or pedestrians: 'rabbiosi sempre, il lunedì la loro ira è alacre e scattante, stanca e inviperita il sabato' [always angry traffic, but on Monday its anger is lively and explosive, and on Saturday it's tired and morose] (*VA*, p. 164; *HL*, p. 159). As seen above, Luciano's emotional connection with Brera also relies on the relative lack of road traffic in the area, which contributes to its aura of safety and comfort.

The Milanese do not walk: they march at a round pace. Luciano's incompatibility with metropolitan life is betrayed by his own way of walking, which, on the contrary, is slow and meditative, hence unconventional.[70] This kind of wandering is apparently inefficient and, as such, cannot be accommodated in a disciplinary spatial regime that requires productivity. In other words, Luciano's unproductive way of walking is a direct challenge to the urban-industrial society where he lives, a society that is reluctant 'to consider the uneconomical or unjustified'.[71] Unlike the stream of

---

69   Cf. Bianciardi's description: 'Picchiettano dalla mattina alla sera, coi tacchi a spillo, sugli impiantiti lucidati a cera, e poi su un pezzetto di marciapiede, fino alla fermata del tram' [They trip about all day long on their stiletto heels on the shining, polished office floors, and then along the strip of pavement as far as the tram stop] (*VA*, p. 106; *HL*, pp. 102–03).

70   Luciano says: 'Io non cammino, non marcio: strascico i piedi, io, mi fermo per strada, addirittura torno indietro, guardo di qua e guardo di là, anche quando non c'è da traversare' [I don't walk, or march; I drag my feet, keep stopping and looking back, or gazing all round even when I am not about to cross the road] (*VA*, p. 107; *HL*, p. 104).

71   Kristin Thompson, 'The Concept of Cinematic Excess', in *Narrative, Apparatus, Ideology: A Film Theory Reader*, ed. by Philip Rosen (New York: Columbia University Press, 1986), pp. 130–42 (p. 136). A parallel may be drawn with Michelangelo Antonioni's cinema and its aesthetic of waste and excess. Karl

seemingly robotic passers-by hurrying to work, Luciano pauses, goes back and observes his surroundings. This 'odd' demeanour makes him resemble something of a maverick and ends up attracting the attention of the vice squad: 'Sorpreso in atteggiamento sospetto, diceva appunto al telefono quel maresciallo del buon costume, dopo che mi ebbe fermato, caricato sul furgone nero e portato in questura' [Caught acting in a suspicious manner was what the vice-squad inspector said about me on the telephone after he had stopped me, put me in a black maria and taken me to the police station] (*VA*, p. 107; *HL*, p. 104). Walking for leisure is penalized in an urban system that encourages conformity by prioritizing work and productivity over other, perhaps more creative and unconventional pursuits.[72] Merlin Coverley also argues that cities have become 'increasingly hostile to the pedestrian' and that 'walking is seen as contrary to the spirit of the modern city with its promotion of swift circulation'.[73] Luciano observes that after living in Milan for some time people turn into automatons or ghosts as they move about the city deprived of vitality. He once again likens labour productivity and this kind of fast, efficient road mobility when he claims that the fact that he 'cannot walk' has led not only to his arrest but also to the termination of his job at the company where he works at the beginning of the novel (inspired by the experience at the Feltrinelli Publishing House): 'una volta mi arrestarono per strada, soltanto perché non so camminare. E poi mi licenziarono, per lo stesso motivo' [I don't know how to walk even, and once I was arrested in the street for just that reason. In the end I lost my job for the same reason] (*VA*, p. 107; *HL*, p. 104).

Disciplinary power activates a mechanism of self-regulation and instils passivity, relying on the fact that its technologies of power operate constantly, as in the archetypical model of Jeremy Bentham's Panopticon discussed by Foucault. This is a circular building with a guard tower in the centre and prisoners placed in cells around the perimeter: from their position the invigilators can virtually see the

---

Schoonover has pointed out that Antonioni fills the frame with uneconomical objects that appear to have no narrative or semantic utility in order to challenge the spectator's eye, which is trained to find a coherent meaning (Karl Schoonover, 'Antonioni's Waste Management', in *Antonioni*, ed. by. Rascaroli and Rhodes, pp. 235–53 (pp. 235–39)).

72   Foucault writes that 'specific to disciplinary penality is non-observance, that which does not measure up to the rule, that departs from it. The whole indefinite domain of the non-conforming is punishable' (Foucault, *Discipline and Punish*, pp. 178–79).

73   Merlin Coverley, *Psychogeography* (Harpenden: Pocket Essentials, 2010 [2006]), p. 12.

inmates at all times, whilst the latter cannot see what lies outside their cells. As Foucault puts it, the principle of the constant visibility of the inmate by the invigilator 'assures the automatic functioning of power' without direct action but through mind conditioning,[74] for the inmates are aware that they could potentially be watched at all times.[75] Foucault's panopticism as a model of permanent control draws on this interdependency of spatial order and the visibility of the subjects to be supervised. As such, the Panopticon is 'an architectural apparatus'[76] that can be implemented in different contexts (not only prisons but hospitals, workshops and schools)[77] and potentially in any situation in which individuals need to be trained and supervised. As a generalizable model, the Panopticon responds to the need of power to rationalize space in order to exert more easily and consistently its control and ultimately become 'coextensive with society'.[78] Panopticism inaugurates 'generalized surveillance':[79] the focus moves from enclosed institutions to disciplinary mechanisms spread throughout the social body, giving rise to a disciplinary society. The corporate tower that Luciano intends to blow up at the beginning of *La vita agra* is yet another version of the Panopticon. It is equipped with surveillance cameras that are able to acquire information about everyone entering the building. Luciano is aware that he is being 'observed' while inspecting the building and the surrounding area, trying to figure out how to effect entry. The security guards at the entrance – described as 'ex-carabinieri e secondini di Portolongone allontanati dal corpo per eccesso di rigore, bluastri in faccia e con gli occhi cattivi' [former *carabinieri* from Portolungone who had been dismissed for excessive

---

74 Foucault, *Discipline and Punish*, p. 201. Foucault writes that 'he who is subjected to a field of visibility, and who knows it, [...] inscribes in himself the power relations in which he simultaneously plays both roles; he becomes the principle of his own subjection' (Foucault, *Discipline and Punish*, pp. 202–03). He further argues that disciplinary power 'imposes on those whom it subjects a principle of compulsory visibility. [...] Their visibility assures the hold of the power that is exercised over them. It is the fact of being constantly seen, of being able always to be seen, that maintains the disciplined invidivual in his subjection' (Foucault, *Discipline and Punish*, p. 187).

75 See also David Murakami Wood, 'Beyond the Panopticon? Foucault and Surveillance Studies', in *Space, Knowledge and Power*, ed. by Crampton and Elden, pp. 245–63 (p. 248).

76 Foucault, *Discipline and Punish*, p. 201.

77 Foucault, *Discipline and Punish*, p. 205.

78 Foucault, *Discipline and Punish*, p. 82.

79 Foucault, *Discipline and Punish*, p. 209.

severity, and they all had bluish faces and evil eyes] (*VA*, p. 32; *HL*, p. 32) – recall a Fascist squad threatening to confront any intruder.

Similarly, the factory in *Memoriale* is a panoptical institution that exerts a disciplinary power over its workers. An analogy with Bianciardi's hasty passers-by may be found in the workers that leave the *fabbrica* after work. Tired and numb at the end of their shift, they part hurriedly, oblivious to what is going on around them: 'Improvvisamente la gente cominciò a uscire [...]. Molti si buttavano sulle biciclette e sui motorscooter; altri andavano a piedi di qua e di là sui marciapiedi, sicurissimi per una direzione che sembravano aver preso a caso' [Suddenly a mass of people started streaming out of the building [...]. Many of the men rode off on their bicycles or on their motor scooters while others, very sure of themselves, sauntered off in directions that seemed to have been chosen at random] (*M*, p. 23; *MM*, p. 15). Discipline is an essential value in the factory's work environment. It maintains workers in a passive state and ensures that they continue to carry out their tasks on the assembly line without questioning the orders they receive from their superiors. Indeed, Foucault asserts that:

> discipline produces subjected and practised bodies, 'docile' bodies. Discipline increases the forces of the body (in economic terms of utility) and diminishes these same forces (in political terms of obedience). In short, it dissociates power from the body; on the one hand, it turns it into an 'aptitude', a 'capacity', which it seeks to increase; on the other hand, it reverses the course of the energy, the power that might result from it, and turns it into a relation of strict subjection.[80]

On several occasions factory life is presented as a continuation of the experience of war and particularly of Albino's period of internment in the German labour camp.[81] The analogy between war and industry

---

80 Foucault, *Discipline and Punish*, p. 138.

81 Examples include: 'Il treno partiva verso sera ed era un treno operaio che fermava a tutte le stazioni. Era affollato come una tradotta militare, soprattutto da operai che lasciavano le fabbriche di Torino' [The train left in the early evening. It was a train used by all factory workers, and it stopped at every station along the way. It was crowded as a military train, filled with workers returning home after leaving the factories in Turin] (*M*, p. 12; *MM*, pp. 6–7); 'Io avevo paura di questo inizio, soprattutto paura che la fabbrica potesse assomigliare all'esercito' [I feared those first moments, and most of all I feared that the factory might resemble the army] (*M*, p. 53; *MM*, p. 37); 'Vestivano tutti allo stesso modo, o così mi sembrava per l'uniformità dell'ambiente, delle macchine e del lavoro che poteva annullare le piccole differenze' [All the men were dressed alike, and I thought that the sameness of the place, the machines, and the work would succeed in voiding any small differences] (*M*, p. 55; *MM*, p. 38).

is, indeed, a major thread in the novel. Albino observes, for example, that 'mai come durante il lavoro io ho pensato alla prigionia' [while I worked I thought about the prison camp] (*M*, p. 22; *MM*, p. 14). In the introductory meeting between Albino and the hiring manager on the first day of work, the latter once again likens the factory and military experience: '[T]u hai fatto il soldato per molti anni e conosci il valore della disciplina e dell'ubbidienza. Queste due virtù sono basilari anche nella fabbrica' [You've been a soldier for many years so you must know the values of discipline and obedience. These are also two basic principles of the factory] (*M*, p. 30; *MM*, p. 20). The manager points out that discipline and obedience are essential qualities in a soldier as well as in a factory worker and that, as a former soldier, Albino will find it easier to adjust to the rhythms and requirements of industrial work. For Albino, the factory environment becomes a new battlefield on which to prove his real value once and for all. By throwing himself wholeheartedly into his new job, he intends to demonstrate that he is better and more efficient than his colleagues. This over-commitment, however, soon leads him to physical and mental exhaustion and to numerous admissions to hospital on the advice of the company doctors. Albino lives in a state of acute internal conflict: he alternately praises and fiercely opposes, and even loathes, industry and its mechanisms. This conflict almost reaches madness, since 'la fabbrica mi sembrava un edificio senza senso e sentivo che una parte del mio cervello stava facendo violenza su di me per trattenermi in quel luogo ostile e innaturale' [the factory seemed like a meaningless building, but I still felt as if a part of my brain was forcing me to stay in that hostile, unnatural place] (*M*, p. 23; *MM*, p. 15).

Albino suffers from paranoid neurosis and may therefore be seen as a typical example of an unreliable narrator who is bound to cast doubt on the truth of the narrated facts. While this is certainly true to an extent (for instance, Albino's belief that the company doctors diagnose him with fake illnesses and prescribe periods of leave deliberately to penalize him and keep him away from work is clearly delusional), there are more complex issues at stake with the point of view he brings as narrator of the story. Albino embodies an urban-industrial malaise that is rooted in neo-capitalist societies.[82]

---

82 Volponi explains the choice of Albino Saluggia as the main character in *Memoriale* as follows: 'Perché ho scelto un nevrotico a protagonista del mio romanzo? Un nevrotico ha una capacità di interpretazione della realtà più dolente, ma più acuta [...] ma anche perché un nevrotico è *un ribelle*. In un uomo sano avrei trovato uno che ha già ceduto qualcosa alla fabbrica' [Why did

His experience is generalizable. A disclaimer at the beginning of the novel informs us that the narrated facts are not relatable only to a single and specific city, but are instead generalizable because 'la città industriale non ha identità' [the industrial complex has not been identified]. In other words, *Memoriale* could be set in any city in the era of global capitalism, in which differences are flattened out between places which are more interconnected than ever before. Later in his memoir, Albino iterates this point:

> Il problema è quello dell'industria in generale, tutta, dalle sue città e quartieri ai treni e ai pullman che la servono, alle sue fotografie sui giornali, ai suoi operai, tanti come un esercito, come il mio lago, che batte la testa sempre sulla stessa sponda. (*M*, pp. 176–77)

> [This is the problem of all industry in general, from the cities where it grows to the trains and buses that serve it, from its image in the newspapers to its workers, vast as an army, an army like my lake, always beating its head against the same shore.] (*MM*, p. 129)

Albino shows awareness of industrial capitalism as a transnational phenomenon and of the system that sustains it: technologies, cities across the globe and the means of transport and communication through which material goods and transactions reach different places, the publicity and mass media and the countless low-wage workers who keep this system running. It is interesting to note the presence of another military metaphor when Albino refers to factory workers as an army in disarray with no clear direction, like the waves of Lake Candia that keep breaking monotonously on the same shore.

The end of *Memoriale* appears to confirm the idea that Albino's malaise is more generally rooted in society. After all the issues he has created with his neurotic behaviour and the efforts the factory doctors have made to facilitate his recovery, despite the fact that he has even denounced their supposedly persecutory behaviour to the head of the company, Albino is fired for prompting the kitchen staff to join the other workers on strike. We readers are left with the doubt that Albino was right after all: if there is no real conspiracy against him, it is nonetheless true that industry does not work for the good and in the interest of its workers. Quite the contrary: Albino's illness and obsession feed on the environment of the factory and blur into the kind of alienation that

---

I choose a neurotic to be the protagonist of my novel? A neurotic, because of his suffering, has a more acute ability to interpret reality [...] but also because a neurotic is a rebel. In a healthy man I would have found someone who had already ceded something of himself to the factory] (Ferretti, *Paolo Volponi*, p. 29).

is typical of such repetitive, isolating work. The relentless background noise of industrial machinery in particular embodies the spellbinding power of the *fabbrica*. The workers move in unison with the constant hum of the machines, as if hypnotized:

> Il rumore mi rapiva; il sentire andare tutta la fabbrica con un solo motore mi trascinava e mi obbligava a tenere con il mio lavoro il ritmo che tutta la fabbrica aveva. Non potevo trattenermi, come una foglia di un grande albero scosso in tutti i suoi rami dal vento. (*M*, p. 62)

> [The noise fascinated me. All parts of the factory throbbed in unison and, driven by this beat, I was compelled to adapt the rhythm of my work to that gigantic pulse. I couldn't stop myself; I was like a leaf of a great tree whose every branch shook in the wind.] (*MM*, p. 43)

Albino's awareness of the alienating quality of his factory work grows as the story proceeds. Hence it does not come as a complete surprise that at the end of the novel he takes a clear stance against it, since he finds himself in agreement with the demands for improvement of the factory's working conditions outlined in the flyer distributed by members of the FIOM union during the workers' industrial action. Albino is frustrated in his hopes of finding in the factory a means towards a better life and compensation for his existential sense of non-belonging. His disillusion mirrors Volponi's own frustrated aspirations for improvements in Italian industry, especially after Olivetti's death and the failure of his reform project. As seen above, Volponi believed that industry should provide not only economic stability for workers and their families and the fulfilment of their basic needs, but should also address their cultural and intellectual development in order to lead to a real improvement in their lives.[83]

Social malaise reaches a climax in *Le mosche del capitale*. Here people live confined to either their home or the workplace. The action takes place almost exclusively in indoor spaces; and even as the characters, primarily the industrial managers, move through the urban space, they do so by car in order to reach their destination quickly and efficiently. One may argue that Bovino is reminiscent of Foucault's plague-stricken town as 'a compact model of the disciplinary mechanism'.[84] Foucault argues that the plague regulations and containment measures implemented in sixteenth

---

83 Emanuele Zinato, 'Paolo Volponi: letteratura e industria', *Doppiozero*, 27 August 2012 <http://www.doppiozero.com/materiali/made-in/paolo-volponi-letteratura-e-industria> [accessed 20 February 2018].

84 Foucault, *Discipline and Punish*, p. 197.

and seventeenth-century towns when an epidemic broke out betray more broadly an ancestral fear of contagion, understood as any potential element of chaos and challenge to the status quo.[85] A similar utopia/dystopia of the 'perfectly governed', 'immobilized'[86] city is realized in *Le mosche del capitale*. Any potential threat to the dominant order has been neutralized and the city of Bovino has turned into a disciplined, aseptic space with docile, passive citizens. The beginning of the novel is particularly emblematic in this regard since, as seen above, it captures the inhabitants of Bovino in a dreamless sleep which resembles lethargy.

Fascist Legacies

Le mosche del capitale contains several references to the question of Fascist legacies in post-war Italian society. The issue is raised, for instance, through the character of Radames, a security guard at MFM. In a speech replete with Fascist and imperialist tropes, Radames calls for the necessary infiltration of authoritarian elements into the Italian public administration, police and judicial and school systems in order to exert control over democratic institutions:

> Dobbiamo cioè tendere a moltiplicarci, a fare entrare le nostre credenze e le nostre volontà in tutte le branche vitali dell'organizzazione nazionale, soprattutto in quelle dei pubblici poteri e della pubblica amministrazione ... di tutti i bracci secolari dello stato, dalla magistratura all'esercito, dai carabinieri alla finanza ... Magari fino alle scuole ai collegi ai centri alle organizzazioni sportive. [...] potremo con grande forza e nuove capacità, davvero uniti, andare a conquistare e mettere ordine in altre regioni e in altri territori. (*MC*, p. 92)

> [We must, therefore, tend to multiply, to make our beliefs and wills enter all the vital branches of the national organization, especially those of the public authorities and the public administration ... of all the secular arms of the state, from the judiciary to the army, from the *carabinieri* to finance .... Maybe including schools, colleges, centres and sports organizations. [...] We shall be able, with great strength and new abilities, truly united, to conquer and bring order to other regions and other territories.]

85 He claims: 'Behind the disciplinary mechanisms can be read the haunting memory of "contagions", of the plague, of rebellions, crimes, vagabondage, desertions, people who appear and disappear, live and die in disorder' (Foucault, *Discipline and Punish*, p. 198).

86 Foucault, *Discipline and Punish*, p. 198.

Through Radames's speech, which indicates the hard-line approach which the industrial leadership should take in order to erase 'ogni principio di opposizione e di intralcio all'industria' [any principle of opposition or hindrance to the industry] (*MC*, p. 91) and 'tutti i nemici, di cui è pieno il mondo, anche le nostre case, le nostre città, soprattutto le nostre fabbriche' [all the enemies of which the world is full, even in our homes, our cities and especially in our factories] (*MC*, p. 90), Volponi denounces the abuses perpetrated by the Italian political and industrial elites in those years. Industrial management at Fiat and other companies aligned with the repressive measures taken by the Christian Democrat governments: for example, the creation of anti-strike rewards and practices of discrimination against members of the Italian General Confederation of Labour (Confederazione Generale Italiana del Lavoro; CGIL), Italy's largest union. In this regard Crainz asserts:

> L'iniziativa delle direzioni aziendali – alla Fiat e altrove – si coniugava al quadro politico dei primi anni cinquanta che abbiamo già delineato: nelle fabbriche più che altrove si coglie il clima generale 'degli anni della libertà congelata', gli anni in cui sull'eguaglianza prevale 'la regola della discriminazione'.[87]

> [The initiatives of the company management – at Fiat and elsewhere – combine with the political framework of the early 1950s that we have already outlined: in factories, more than elsewhere, the general climate 'of the years of suspended freedom' manifests itself, the years in which 'the rule of discrimination' prevails over equality.]

In *Memoriale*, too, one may find examples of characters who are supposedly converted former Fascists but actually still harbour feelings of nostalgia for Italy's totalitarian past. Albino's line manager Grosset claims, for instance, that their colleague, the engineer Pignotti, only pretended to repudiate his pro-Fascist ideals until it was sufficiently safe to embrace them again. According to Grosset, Pignotti aspires to rule the factory and would be willing to use violence on the least pretext to maintain discipline:

> Pignotti ci farebbe lavorare con le bastonate se appena potesse. A che punto siamo ricaduti in pochi anni. Il caro ingegner Pignotti subito dopo la liberazione sembrava il più mansueto degli agnelli [...]. Si vede che tutte le vecchie ambizioni lo hanno ripreso. Vuol comandare, vuol comandare a tutti i costi. (*M*, p. 171)

---

87 Crainz, *Storia del miracolo italiano*, p. 37.

[Pignotti would beat us to make us work if he could. What have we come to in such a few years? After the liberation, our dear Pignotti was as meek as a little lamb […]. I guess all his ambitions have come back. He wants to be boss, he wants to be boss at any cost.] (*MM*, p. 125)

As pointed out in the Introduction, some of the discriminatory practices that had been widespread under the Fascist regime persisted in the post-war Republic, particularly aimed at left-wing political dissidents. The thesis of the survival of a 'Fascist mentality' in the Republic, to use Dondi's definition,[88] is based on the evidence that a real process of de-fascistization, that is, a political purge of Fascist individuals, was never accomplished, since 'after 1960, neo-fascists, whether members of the MSI or its friends, found positions in the heart of the state, in the secret services, in the military hierarchy, in a fashion that would condition Italian life for decades to come, blocking even the most timid move to the Left'.[89] Indeed, on the one hand it proved difficult to achieve a consensus on how the cleansing process was to be carried out, due to the presence in the Italian territory in the aftermath of the war of a mosaic of military and political forces with their differing views and aims.[90] On the other, the initial willingness of the political parties, and particularly the Christian Democrats, the Italian majority party throughout the 1950s, to carry out the purge grew more cautious as it became clear that a substantial portion of Italian society, including key officials, had in various degrees been involved with the regime.[91] The failure of the cleansing process, i.e., the removal from institutional positions of individuals who had in various ways collaborated with the Fascist regime, was accompanied in the post-war years by the substantial inability or unwillingness on the part of the leading sectors of Italian society to instigate critical reflection on the past in order to come to terms with Fascism and the collective responsibility of Italians in its rise and consolidation. The general tendency, which suited the needs of the reconstruction and recovery of Italy's war-battered economy, was instead to try and forget: a removal process that Ruth Ben-Ghiat

88   Dondi, 'The Fascist Mentality', pp. 141–60.

89   Dondi, 'The Fascist Mentality', p. 155.

90   Ruth Ben-Ghiat, 'Liberation: Italian Cinema and the Fascist Past, 1945–50', in *Italian Fascism*, ed. by Bosworth and Dogliani, pp. 83–101 (pp. 89–90).

91   Dondi has observed that 'at least two-thirds of the staff of the Ministry of the Interior would have to be suspended, resulting in a general paralysis of public administration' (Dondi, 'The Fascist Mentality', p. 143).

labels 'collective amnesia'.[92] A further tendency was to externalize responsibility through a narrative of victimization that saw Fascism as a foreign body and a temporary hiatus in the path of the liberal progress of the Italian nation, a thesis most notably advanced by Benedetto Croce.[93] The climate of the Cold War then meant that the Christian Democrats could be excused for the inability to 'break decisively with fascism'.[94]

In *Le mosche del capitale* there is a strong perception of the authoritarian threat that, as Dondi points out, has 'scored the path' of the Italian post-war Republic and its parliamentary parties.[95] Radames's authoritarian, imperialist views reverberate through the image of the industrial managers who march defiantly through Bovino's central streets towards the end of the novel. A historical fact, the so-called 'march of the forty thousand' took place on 14 October 1980 and was part of a strategy of intimidation carried out by industrial management at Fiat in response to a series of strikes organized by the workers. The episode led the CGIL to make concessions that were favourable to the Fiat management. In the extract below, the industrial managers march in a threatening procession like an army ready to be deployed, thereby reaffirming their power: 'I quarantamila passavano per il centro ben coperti e compatti nel grigio degli abiti e nel blu delle scarpe [...]. Quarantamila capi silenziosi e disciplinati, ben pettinati e calzati' [The forty thousand passed through the centre, well-clothed and compact in their grey suits and blue shoes [...]. Forty thousand silent and disciplined bosses, well combed and shod] (*MC*, p. 262). The episode presents an exception to the sensation that, in the novel, the characters live in indoor confinement. Here, there is appropriation of the urban space. Nevertheless, it is the kind of forcible appropriation

---

92   Ruth Ben-Ghiat, 'Fascism, Writing, and Memory: The Realist Aesthetic in Italy, 1930–1950', *The Journal of Modern History*, 67 (1995), 627–65 (p. 663). As Jonathan Dunnage observes, in post-war Italian society 'there was no far-reaching or systematic process of examination of consciences or re-education' to counterbalance the long-standing influence of the policies and propaganda of the Fascist regime on Italian civil society and the very mindset of the Italian people (Jonathan Dunnage, 'Conclusion: Facing the Past and Building for the Future in Postwar Italy', in *After the War: Violence, Justice, Continuity and Renewal in Italian Society*, ed. by Jonathan Dunnage (Market Harborough: Troubador, 1999), pp. 89–100 (p. 90)).

93   Ben-Ghiat, 'Liberation', pp. 88–89. See also Duggan, 'Italy in the Cold War Years', pp. 3–4.

94   Duggan, 'Italy in the Cold War Years', p. 16.

95   Dondi, 'The Fascist Mentality', pp. 149–50.

that is intended to intimidate and put the workers back in their place, thereby reaffirming a principle of restraint and limitation.

Bianciardi and Volponi express criticism of the transformation of Milan and Turin in the 1960s and 1970s, which are depicted as sites of social inequality, anomie and authoritative power. In shaping a certain image of post-war urban transition in Italy, they draw on traditional themes which, in the literary imagination, have been applied to the description of the modern metropolis. In this sense they describe a universal experience that pervades many literary and artistic representations of the city. Urban descriptions are also revealing of the writers' specific criticism of the bourgeois capitalism of the North and of neo-liberal, consumerist, post-war Italian society, which betrayed their aspiration for social change and for the creation of a more egalitarian society after the reconstruction period. They present the city as a symbol of capital and the paradigm of a model of civilization that has gone wrong. There emerges a portrait of the city in which impressive buildings point to the authority of state and industrial elites and the urban layout affects the behaviour of urban dwellers, enhancing their productivity and acquiescence. What the writers see as menacing and disturbing may be a reflection of the persistence of authoritarian, reactionary practices in post-war Italy aimed at those questioning the new politico-economic status quo. The writers portray urban and industrial environments where people are exploited and have their rights curtailed to accommodate the pursuit of wealth by the dominant classes. They connect political authoritarianism and economic capitalism, for the latter allies political and industrial elites and relies on the repressive intervention of state power to maintain the dominant social order.

While the work of Bianciardi and Volponi has certainly ideological implications, it does not align with a dominant left-wing political agenda.[96] The new trend towards experimental writing in Italian literature of the 1960s, which privileged form and style over content, definitely called into question a certain way of addressing political commitment.[97] The example of Bianciardi is emblematic of the growing dissent regarding the hegemonic views of the Communist Party among Italian intellectuals, particularly after the Soviet invasion of Hungary in 1956. Despite, or perhaps precisely because of, the

---

96 Assuming that such an uncritical notion of *impegno* ever existed among left-leaning Italian intellectuals, it nonetheless reveals cracks at the time at which Bianciardi and Volponi wrote (Burns, *Fragments of Impegno*, p. 1).

97 Burns, *Fragments of Impegno*, pp. 26–27.

popularity enjoyed by *La vita agra*, by far his most successful book, Bianciardi chose the path of disengagement, devoting himself to writing books on the Italian *Risorgimento* and contributions to sports magazines, thereby rejecting the label of left-wing intellectual and identification with the anti-capitalist protest movement of the 1960s and 1970s.[98] Bianciardi's gradual disillusionment with socio-political commitment is reflected in the events narrated in *La vita agra*.

The rejection of modern metropolitan life results in a subjectivist withdrawal into protective microcosms, such as Brera for Luciano and the small bedroom facing Lake Candia for Albino, perceived as spaces of resistance to the official urban–work environment. With its bohemian feel, Brera/Braida presents a direct challenge to the Milanese values of efficiency and economic profit. Escape is, however, temporary and illusory: Luciano is forced out of Brera into the 'real' city to lead a life of work and routine, with difficulties in making ends meet, whilst Albino is drawn back to the factory for which he entertains an intense love–hate relationship. The all-pervasive, unfathomable industrial city of *Le mosche del capitale* appears to seal victory for a model of capitalism that pursues profit by any means necessary at the cost of growing income inequality, the erosion of workers' rights and social isolation. Urban descriptions (and the general lack of them as characters seem to enjoy little freedom to move across the urban fabric) bear witness to Volponi's disillusionment with the current state of affairs and the persistence of a reactionary ideology.

One may argue that the anti-urban stance assumed by Bianciardi and Volponi has a conservative, elitist element to it. By retreating into Brera, for example, Bianciardi identifies with the traditional spaces of cultural value to Milan's intellectual milieu. Cities are ever-evolving and transformations in their social and physical fabric should not be dismissed too hastily as negative. One should not forget that metropolitan life is also a liberating experience since it encourages less rigid and more diluted modes of identification, which often come with a perceived greater freedom for self-expression. There is no doubt, for instance, that metropolitan life granted more freedom and wider possibilities to young people and women who left behind essentially patriarchal, traditional rural societies to move to the big city.[99] Similarly, it is the big-city environment that provides Bianciardi

---

98 Coppola and Piccinini, 'Luciano Bianciardi'; and Corrias, *Vita agra di un anarchico*.

99 Ginsborg, *A History of Contemporary Italy*, pp. 243–44.

and Volponi with the material for their successful novels. In Grosseto, Bianciardi mainly wrote preparatory works to *La vita agra*. Volponi, born in Urbino in Central Italy, moved to Ivrea to join Olivetti in his effort to reform Italian industry and drew on this experience for his industrial novels. In their novels this tension translates into a dialectic dynamic of imaginative escape and actual staying in the city which ultimately provides the source of literary imagination. The same may be said about the characters who, notwithstanding their conflictual relationship with the city, are also drawn back to it and find in it opportunities for encounters and personal and professional development, even though these are essentially negated by the nihilistic view that prevails in the end. With their contradictions, Bianciardi and Volponi embody the common existential experience of feeling 'at once aroused by the city and submerged and powerless in its vastness'.[100]

---

100 Lehan, *The City in Literature*, p. 273.

2. Uncanny City: Milan and Turin in the Crime Novels of Giorgio Scerbanenco and Fruttero & Lucentini

Introduction: Forefathers of Italian Crime Fiction

Milan and Turin have, alongside Naples, been privileged locations for mystery stories since the early stages of the genre in Italy in the late nineteenth century.[1] Nevertheless, they acquired more concrete contours only later with the work of Giorgio Scerbanenco and Fruttero & Lucentini, in which the urban setting enables the discourse on post-war transformation. Michele Righini, for example, argues that:

> ciò che viene colto dagli autori italiani è un cambiamento che investe il vivere cittadino (prima di diffondersi anche in provincia) [...]. È il boom economico degli anni sessanta che rende le nostre città – e la mentalità di chi le abita – più simili a quello che genericamente viene definito il 'modello americano', e le configura come terreno fertile per la nascita di quella stessa tradizione poliziesca che abbiamo visto fiorire oltre oceano.[2]

---

1 Giuliana Pieri has observed that 'the very beginnings of Italian crime fiction coincided with the representation of Milan, the city where, with a few exceptions, Augusto De Angelis's Commissario De Vincenzi is based' (Pieri, 'Introduction', in *Italian Crime Fiction*, ed. by Pieri, p. 133).

2 Michele Righini, 'Città degli incubi', in *Luoghi della letteratura italiana*, ed. by Anselmi and Ruozzi, pp. 142–52 (p. 145). He is supported by Luca Crovi, who writes that, with the publication of *Venere privata*, 'il giallo [...] cambia faccia e se ce lo permettete cambia persino colore, assumendo anche molte sfumature del nero. Comincia finalmente ad avere una connotazione più squisitamente nostrana e non sarà da allora più anonimo. Non è un caso che città come Milano, Roma, Napoli, Bologna, Torino, Palermo diventeranno da allora credibili scenari dei nuovi thriller italiani' [Crime literature [...] changes its aspect and, if you will allow, it even changes colour, taking on many darker hues. It finally begins to have a more decisively home-grown connotation and from now on will no

[what is captured by the Italian authors is a change that affects the life of the urban dweller (before spreading to the provinces as well) [...]. It is the economic boom of the Sixties that makes our cities – and the mentality of those who live in them – more similar to what is generically defined as the 'American model' and configures them as fertile ground for the birth of that same tradition of crime writing that we have seen flourish overseas.]

In Scerbanenco's Lamberti novels, Milan ceases to be a neutral backdrop to become, as Jennifer Burns suggests, 'the habitat which engenders, nurtures and occasionally overmasters the criminals and their crimes'.[3] Fruttero & Lucentini have paved the way for the tradition of *gialli* [detective stories] which, in their own words, look at Turin as 'la città più enigmatica, o meno nota d'Italia' [the most enigmatic, or least celebrated city in Italy] and 'uno straordinario oggetto narrativo' [an extraordinary narrative object].[4] The central role of the urban setting is just one aspect of the novelty in Scerbanenco's and Fruttero & Lucentini's crime fiction and certainly a crucial one for the present study. Fruttero & Lucentini's novels, which were met with great acclaim by readers and critics alike, contributed to the calling into question of the hierarchical distinction between high and popular literary genres particularly ingrained in the Italian tradition.[5] Scerbanenco's education, which was only up to the compulsory level, and his former employment as an ambulance assistant and columnist for a women's magazine make him a non-conventional figure within Italy's conservative literary establishment. Indeed, Burns argues: 'It is Scerbanenco's intimate and immediate understanding of "ordinary" Italian society in his *gialli* set in Italy which makes them compelling, individual, and which allows the reader to witness the emergence of a branch of crime fiction which is rooted in contemporary Italian society and its moral and social functions and malfunctions'.[6]

In order better to contextualize the innovations introduced by Scerbanenco and Fruttero & Lucentini, and the importance of the centrality they assign to the concrete urban setting, it is useful to retrace some key stages in the development of the Italian crime genre. Although Italian writers have engaged with mystery stories from as

---

longer be anonymous. It is no coincidence that cities like Milan, Rome, Naples, Bologna, Turin and Palermo will, from this point onwards, become credible settings for the new Italian thrillers] (Crovi, *Tutti i colori del giallo*, p. 21).

3   Burns, 'Founding Fathers', pp. 31–32.

4   Crovi, *Tutti i colori del giallo*, pp. 142.

5   Pezzotti, *Importance of Place*, p. 40.

6   Burns, 'Founding Fathers', p. 27.

early as the 1880s[7] and the two decades spanning the 1930s and 1940s have been seen as a 'golden age' of the genre in Italy,[8] the Italian tradition developed gradually and not without some difficulty, especially when compared to the evolution of the genre in countries such as Britain, France and the United States.[9] Maurizio Pistelli – who has carried out in-depth research on the prehistory of the Italian *giallo* and the work of proto-detective storywriters such as Emilio De Marchi, Francesco Mastriani, Jarro (pseudonym of Giulio Piccini), Federico De Roberto, Remigio Zena and Matilde Serao – points out that in the mid-nineteenth century stories began to emerge that mixed elements of mystery, suspense and murder.[10] The first proper attempt by Italian authors at detective novels can be traced back to the 1930s and the publication of a series of stories, innovative both in terms of style and narrative techniques, by the writers Alessandro Varaldo, Tito Antonio Spagnol, Augusto De Angelis and Ezio D'Errico.[11] By the end of the decade, Scerbanenco, too, had begun experimenting with crime writing, publishing a series of detective stories centred on the character of Arthur Jelling, an archivist at Boston Police Department.[12] The popular Mondadori crime series

---

7   Some argue that 1883 could be considered the official birth date of the Italian *giallo*, for it was in this year that Cletto Arrighi published his novel *La Mano Nera* [*The Black Hand*]. Nevertheless, it is perhaps more accurate to suggest 1887 as the birth date, for it witnessed the publication of *Il cappello del prete* [*The Priest's Hat*] by Emilio De Marchi, which contains many of the ingredients of the modern *giallo*. It is important to note, moreover, that there exist previous examples of texts which draw on the tradition of French feuilletons written by Victor Hugo, Alexandre Dumas and Eugène Sue and which combine elements of the *noir* and gothic literatures. One of the first and most significant examples is provided in Italy by Francesco Mastriani's feuilleton from 1852, *La cieca di Sorrento* [*The Blind Girl from Sorrento*] (Maurizio Pistelli, *Un secolo in giallo. Storia del poliziesco italiano (1860–1960)* (Rome: Donzelli, 2006), pp. 6–10, 20–25).

8   The definition of a 'golden age' is used by Pistelli, who divides his history of the Italian crime-fiction genre into its prehistory (1860–1929) and 'periodo d'oro' [golden age] (1930–40). Jane Dunnett, too, observes that 'the proliferation of crime fiction in Italy between the wars represented a publishing phenomenon of unprecedented scale' (Jane Dunnett, 'The Emergence of a New Literary Genre in Interwar Italy', in *Italian Crime Fiction*, ed. by Pieri, pp. 6–26 (p. 6)).

9   Pistelli, *Un secolo in giallo*, pp. 3–4.

10   Pistelli, *Un secolo in giallo*, p. viii.

11   Pistelli, *Un secolo in giallo*, p. viii.

12   Scerbanenco published five novels based on the character of Arthur Jelling, who works in the police archive in Boston: *Sei giorni di preavviso* [*Six Days Notice*] (1940); *La bambola cieca* [*Blind Doll*] (1941); *Nessuno è colpevole* [*Nobody is Guilty*]

Libri Gialli began publication in 1929. The series went on to exert a decisive influence on the evolution of the genre in Italy, thanks to its unprecedented success and longevity.[13] The term *giallo*, 'a short-hand term for any type of detective fiction and more widely any story that has a mystery element',[14] actually comes from the yellow cover of the Mondadori novels. As already noted, initially these mainly consisted of translations of British, French and American authors, but through the years they increasingly attracted Italian writers to the detective genre. Following the shutdown in 1941 of the Libri Gialli (together with all the other editorial initiatives in the field of crime fiction) on account of the Fascist regime, the new Giallo Mondadori series was launched after the war, in 1947, and continued to be published until 1996.[15]

The censorious attitude of the Fascist government towards crime stories certainly helps to explain the delay in the emergence of a topographical tradition within the genre of Italian crime fiction. Whilst at first the regime encouraged the publication of home-grown *gialli* in line with its politics of cultural protectionism,[16] it soon grew more intolerant due to the problematic and unpatriotic image of the country that the stories set in Italy allegedly conveyed. The regime's stance culminated in the law promulgated in 1937 by the Ministry of Popular Culture which established the rule that no crime story published in Italy should feature an Italian murderer.[17]

(1941); *L'antro dei filosofi* [*The Philosophers' Antrum*] (1942); and *Il cane che parla* [*Talking Dog*] (1942).

13   Luca Crovi itemizes the most important book series dedicated to the genre of crime fiction which were published in Italy between the 1910s and the 1930s: 'I Romanzi Polizieschi'; 'Collezione di Avventure Poliziesche'; 'Racconti d'Azione e di Mistero'; and 'Collezione Gialla' (Crovi, *Tutti i colori del giallo*, p. 37). The Mondadori series exerts an enduring influence upon the Italian crime fiction tradition and, according to Crovi, triggered 'una piccola rivoluzione all'interno del panorama letterario italiano' [a minor revolution within the Italian literary scene] (Crovi, *Tutti i colori del giallo*, p. 43).

14   Pieri, 'Introduction', p.1.

15   A ministerial decree dated 30 August 1941 provided that the publication of *gialli* be subject to authorization by the regime (Crovi, *Tutti i colori del giallo*, p. 59).

16   As from 1931 Italian publishers were required to include in their catalogue at least 15 per cent of works by Italian authors (Crovi, *Tutti i colori del giallo*, p. 44).

17   Crovi states: 'Nel 1937 il Ministero della Cultura Popolare dichiara che nei romanzi "l'assassino non deve assolutamente essere italiano e non può sfuggire in alcun modo alla giustizia"' [In 1937 the Ministry of Popular Culture declared that in the novels 'the murderer must on no account be Italian and cannot in any way be seen to escape justice'] (Crovi, *Tutti i colori del giallo*, p. 52).

This intimidating climate led Italian detective-story writers to choose exotic and stereotypical settings for their stories, locations of which the authors often had no first-hand knowledge, as in the case of Scerbanenco's Jelling novels, set in an imaginary Boston.

It is, therefore, very relevant that Scerbanenco and Fruttero & Lucentini choose the material setting of 1960s and 1970s Milan and Turin for their novels, not as a mere background, but as the functional stage for their critical discourse on contemporary Italian society. Whilst Milan had already been the setting for a number of crime stories – most notably, perhaps, Augusto De Angelis's Commissario De Vincenzi novels – Scerbanenco shaped once and for all the identity of the Northern capital as a *noir* city able to compete with Boston and Chicago, metropolitan settings of the American hard-boiled, and a role Milan has maintained in the Italian crime-fiction tradition and collective imagination.[18] On the other hand, Fruttero & Lucentini were precursors of a rich tradition of *gialli* set in Turin from the mid-1970s by authors such as Riccardo Marcato, Piero Novelli, Massimo Felisatti, Bruno Gambarotta and Margherita Oggero.[19] The tendency shown by Italian crime stories to concentrate on metropolitan areas is reaffirmed by the emergence in the 1990s of specifically local traditions, such as the Scuola dei Duri in Milan, the Gruppo 13 in Bologna and the Neonoir in Rome.[20]

Hence, it is in the time period examined in this book that the seeds for the development of a specifically Italian crime fiction tradition were sown. The 1960s marked a turning point in the debate about the specificity and legitimacy of the Italian crime genre. Until then, critics and writers of detective stories had mostly seen Italian crime stories as escapist reading or mere imitation of the British and American classics.[21] Another obstacle to the development of a proper Italian crime genre was also believed to be the absence in Italy of big cities

---

18   Burns, 'Founding Fathers', p. 32.

19   Crovi, *Tutti i colori del giallo*, pp. 143–45.

20   Elisabetta Mondello. 'Il *"noir* italiano"*. Appunti sul romanzo nero contemporaneo', in *Noir de Noir. Un'indagine pluridisciplinare*, ed. by Dieter Vermandere, Monica Jansen and Inge Lanslots, Moving Texts/Testi mobili, 2 (Brussels: Lang, 2010), pp. 23–31 (pp. 25–27).

21   Crovi identifies at least three key factors that explain why the 1960s signal a turning point in the fortunes of Italian crime fiction: the success of the popular televison series *Giallo Club*, broadcast by RAI from 1959 to 1961; the creation of *Diabolik* in 1962, which inspired similar comic-book characters and villains, including Kriminal, Satanik and Dylan Dog; and the publication of *Venere privata* by Giorgio Scerbanenco in 1966 (Crovi, *Tutti i colori del giallo*, pp. 20–21).

able to shape a convincing metropolitan tradition.[22] The development of home-grown Italian *gialli* during the period under scrutiny was fostered by urban changes, for crime fiction makes the impossibility of mastering the city into one of the main triggers of its narrative.[23] In other words, it is not fortuitous that the Italian *giallo* developed during years of unprecedented urbanization. The following analysis shows that there is clearly an interplay between Italy's post-war urban renewal and the crime stories of Giorgio Scerbanenco and Fruttero & Lucentini.

Part of the appeal of crime fiction is that it discloses a different, subterranean city behind its public façade. This chapter continues, first, to explore the feelings of disorientation and anxiety caused by rapid social change, focusing on aspects of urban life that escape comprehension in the novels of Scerbanenco and Fruttero & Lucentini. By drawing attention to these unfathomable aspects of city life it sheds light on the writers' response to rapid urban growth, the perceived break with tradition and the lack of a constructive critical elaboration of the past. The final two sections examine the link between urban growth and the development of crime with a specific focus on the periphery, a location which in the collective imagination has commonly been associated with elements of the uncanny and eerie. Throughout, the chapter draws on the idea of the uncanny as a feeling of unease that, as Freud argues, arises from the double nature of the familiar. It also refers to Fisher's analysis of the related concepts of the weird and eerie, which also denote something that exceeds the standard categories with which we apprehend the world. In addition, Vidler's work on the specific link between the built environment and the experience of the uncanny provides a central reference point. The next section of the chapter draws attention to the unfathomable aspects of city life in an attempt to shed light on the writers' response to rapid urban growth, the perceived break with tradition and the lack of a constructive critical elaboration of the past.

While it may be argued that the uncanny pertains universally to urban experience, here the aim is to contextualize it within Italy's rapid process of modernization. The official narrative of the boom period

---

22   In the 1930s De Angelis endorsed Italian crime stories, their originality and literary value, while Savinio argued that Italian culture was unable to develop a home-grown tradition of crime fiction (Crovi, *Tutti i colori del giallo*, p. 10).

23   E.g., Philip Howell argues that crime fiction portrays the city 'as a phenomenon that can be known only partially, from the vantage point of the street' (Philip Howell, 'Crime and the City Solution: Crime Fiction, Urban Knowledge, and Radical Geography', *Antipode*, 30 (1998), 357–78 (p. 367)).

exalted the achieved prosperity, the development of modern lifestyles and the diffusion of new leisure habits; and overshadowed the persistence of more traditional elements in post-war Italian society.[24] The transition of the 1950s was far more complex than the picture of widespread optimism suggests and the tension that emerged between tradition and modernity, the new that irrupts into habitual reality, did not offer neat closure. Some of the pre-existing imbalances remained or were, indeed, exacerbated, for any growth in productivity relied on inconsistencies such as the deepening economic gap between the North and South of the country and the large reservoir of cheap labour employed in the Northern industries. As seen in the previous chapter, there is a general consensus among scholars on the continuity of the state in terms of personnel and reactionary policies in the transition from pre- to post-war governments. The inability of the Italian State to implement structural reforms at this crucial point in the nation's history played a crucial part in the continued existence of unresolved social issues, widespread social dissatisfaction and the socio-political turmoil of the decades which followed.

Mysterious City

Whilst there is a tendency to think that crime literature asserts the power of reason, embodied by the detective who undertakes the enquiry, to shed light on the mysteries of the city and, in so doing, to restore order, in fact modern crime fiction is less concerned with the unitary perspective of the detective than with a distribution of meaning through a multiple-narrative viewpoint that shapes an original account of the city.[25] As Philip Howell puts it:

> Crime fiction is in truth far less interested or successful in banishing anxieties about the city than is often supposed from a reduction of the genre to the detective or 'mystery' fiction [...]. The city's mysteries are ongoing, never conclusively confronted, and victories always partial and often pyrrhic.[26]

24 Crainz discusses the example of the Vajont Dam disaster in 1963. On October 9, a landslide from nearby Monte Toc fell into the reservoir of the Vajont Dam. The impact produced an enormous wave, which destroyed several villages in the valley and killed almost two thousand people. Crainz interprets the unwillingness of Italian society to talk about the disaster at the time as due partly to the responsibilities of the Italian State in the tragedy and partly to the fact that the disaster was a powerful reminder of the persistence of a poorer Italy (Crainz, *Paese mancato*, p. 7).

25 Howell, 'Crime and the City Solution', p. 367.

26 Howell, 'Crime and the City Solution', p. 364.

The idea of mastering urban space by claiming a complete knowledge of it is ultimately unrealistic. The contemporary *noir* tends to reverberate doubt rather than to re-establish the violated order by replacing the final revelation of classic detective stories with a problematic ending which lends itself to a variety of possible interpretations and outcomes.[27]

Similarly, the Lamberti novels seem to lack a universal sense of justice.[28] Let us take the example of *Traditori di tutti*. In a break from his investigation of an international drug-smuggling network, Duca is spending an idle evening at home, solving crossword puzzles and reading magazines. One headline in particular attracts his attention:

> Su una rivista di attualità lesse il titolo *Le rivelazioni finali sul più grande traffico di droghe*, ma non lesse l'articolo perché lui non credeva alle rivelazioni finali, c'erano due buste di mescalina 6 in giro ed era stupido credere a qualsiasi rivelazione finale sulle droghe, che non finiranno mai. (*TT*, p. 186)

> [In one news magazine he read the headline: *The Great Drug-Smugglers. Full Story*. But he did not read the article, because he knew that it could not tell the full story. There were still two packets of Mescalin 6 unaccounted for and anyway the drug story was a running serial that would never end and only a fool would believe that it could.] (*DM*, p. 165)

Not only does Duca question the possibility, suggested in the captivating title, of eradicating organized crime, but he also seems aware that all case solutions are temporary and disclose further mysteries and further solutions in a potentially endless search for meaning. Duca's slightly neurotic inner thoughts, revealed to us through free indirect speech, may be read as a sign of this predicament, which questions the very possibility of any positive conclusion in Scerbanenco's novels. Vidler points out that feelings of uncanniness often arise in response to things that exceed our comprehension and provoke bewilderment.[29] The city, a reality of which we can only have partial and fragmentary knowledge, has indeed been the privileged setting for uncanny experiences in modern culture. Milan is no exception. For Duca it often elicits confusion and

---

27 Dieter Vermandere, Monica Jansen and Inge Lanslots, 'Introduzione', in *Noir de Noir*, ed. by Vermandere, Jansen and Lanslots, pp. 9–19 (pp. 9–10).

28 Burns, 'Founding Fathers', p. 34.

29 Vidler, *The Architectural Uncanny*, pp. 22–23.

incomprehension. The Lamberti novels mirror the epistemological gap in our understanding of the city in three main ways: through their open and problematic endings; by registering Milan's increasing violence; and, finally, through urban descriptions which emphasize the qualities of the built environment that elicit uncanny feelings.

The Lamberti novels leave us with an uncomfortable feeling. They convey the idea that honest people who become caught up in dangerous situations are the primary victims of widespread corruption and criminality in contemporary Milanese society. For order to be partially and momentarily restored at the end of the story, there is always someone who pays a high price. Intriguingly, this is usually a woman. In *Venere privata* Livia Ussaro is left disfigured by a gangster while helping Duca in his investigation into a prostitution ring. In *Traditori di tutti* Susanna Paganica will probably face a life sentence for the murder of Turiddu Sompani and Adele Terrini, hardened criminals who betrayed and killed her father during the Second World War.[30] In Scerbanenco's crime novels female characters are either presented as morally irreprehensible (as in the case, for instance, of the young teacher Matilde Crescenzaghi in *Traditori di tutti*) and as such somehow more likely to become victims; or they embody a model of modern, emancipated femininity (Livia Ussaro) that is seen as potentially dangerous and subversive. Scerbanenco's depiction of femininity mirrors anxieties about social and urban changes, for it is a disruptive force that challenges fixed gender roles and traditionally demarcated spaces. The threatening idea of femininity is more pronounced when the perpetrator is a woman. In *I ragazzi del massacro* both the victim and perpetrator are women, albeit of a very different kind: the young teacher Matilde Crescenzaghi embodies the values of integrity and human compassion, while her persecutor, Marisela Domenici, is an alcoholic and drug addict whose only pursuit in life is avenging the death of her partner, which she blames on Matilde. By raising concerns with the police about their son Ettore, who is one of her students, Matilde leads to the incrimination and temporary incarceration of Marisela and her partner. The latter, who already suffers from a number of health conditions, dies shortly after in prison. Years later Marisela takes revenge by meticulously arranging the murder of Matilde at the hands of her own students.

---

30 In *I milanesi ammazzano al sabato* the problematic ending involves a man, Amanzio Berzaghi, who becomes a murderer to avenge the death of his daughter at the hand of a group of criminals.

The extreme violence that permeates the novels is a further indication of the difficulty of making sense of the new Milan. People who have been left behind by economic growth and are less able to benefit from the new opportunities offered by the modern city are more likely to turn to crime or end up in dangerous situations. In another scene from *Traditori di tutti* Duca is once again reading the newspaper. The front-page headlines and the local news on the inside pages, which reports brutal crimes mostly involving vulnerable young people, trigger Duca's monologue about the reality of senseless violence in present-day Milan:

> Non portiamo più coltelli, sciabole, e spade, e allora ammazziamo con quello che troviamo a portata di mano, – disse Duca –, quando siamo in auto prendiamo il cacciavite dal cassetto del cruscotto e sfondiamo il collo di quello che ci ha sorpassato a destra. A casa, invece, nel sano ambiente domestico, tra gli utili arnesi casalinghi, scegliamo forbici e con cinquanta sessanta colpi, finiamo l'amico che non ci ha restituito del denaro prestato. (*TT*, p. 118)

> [We no longer carry daggers, swords and sabres, said Duca, so we kill with whatever comes to hand. When we're in a car, we grab a spanner from the toolbox, and crack the skull of the man who passed us on the wrong side. At home, however, in our cosy, domestic surroundings, we look through the household equipment, and choose a pair of scissors with which to stab (some sixty times) a friend who has failed to return the money we lent him.] (*DM*, p. 106)

Duca describes a corrupt society in which people kill for petty reasons or in a fit of temper, using whatever weapons are at hand – a spanner, a pair of scissors – ordinary objects with a practical, banal use. The fact that, as Barbara Pezzotti points out, Scerbanenco's murderers are 'mostly greedy, stupid people who become irrational for squalid and trivial reasons'[31] reveals that rapid post-war growth has enhanced individualistic and competitive orientations and has deepened the discrepancy between the rich and poor. Ginsborg writes that the boom 'lacked the dimension of collective responsibility'.[32] By neglecting the communitarian and public dimensions of economic transformation, post-war modernization ultimately reinforced Italian society's traditional emphasis on the family and self-reliance.[33] The

---

31 Barbara Pezzotti, *Politics and Society in Italian Crime Fiction: An Historical Overview* (Jefferson, NC: McFarland, 2014), p. 68.

32 Ginsborg, *A History of Contemporary Italy*, p. 240.

33 Giuliana Pieri points out that 'the impact of industrialization, as Ginsborg argues, emphasized and reinforced the individual or familial road to prosperity

characters-turned-criminals in the Milan of Scerbanenco operate in the type of environment that is dominated by a culture of individualism and economic interest. Through frequent urban descriptions infused by shadiness and desolation, Scerbanenco emphasizes the characters' isolation and moral corruptibility.

In the monologue quoted above Duca goes on to liken Milan to Marseille, Chicago and Paris, traditionally *noir* cities:

> C'è qualcuno che non ha ancora capito che Milano è una grande città, non hanno ancora capito il cambio di dimensioni, qualcuno continua a parlare di Milano, come se finisse a Porta Venezia o come se la gente non facesse altro che mangiare panettoni, o pan meino. Se uno dice Marsiglia, Chicago, Parigi, quelle sì che sono metropoli, con tanti delinquenti dentro, ma Milano no, a qualche stupido non dà la sensazione della grande città, cercano ancora quello che chiamano il colore locale, la *brasera*, la *pesa*, e magari il *gamba de legn*. Si dimenticano che una città vicina ai due milioni di abitanti ha un tono internazionale, non locale, in una grande città come Milano, arrivano sporcaccioni da tutte le parti del mondo, e pazzi, e alcolizzati, drogati, o semplicemente disperati in cerca di soldi. (*TT*, pp. 118–19)

> [There are still people who don't realize that Milan is a great cosmopolitan city. They have failed to notice that the scale of things has altered. They talk about Milan as though it ended at the Porta Venezia, and as though the people ate nothing but *panettoni* and *pan meino*. Mention Marseilles, Chicago or Paris, and everyone knows you're talking of a wicked metropolis, but with Milan, it's different. Surrounded as they are by the unmistakable atmosphere of a great city, there are still idiots who think of it in terms of local colour, looking for *la brasera*, *la pesa*, and *mangari* [sic] *il gamba de legn*. They forget that a city of two million inhabitants is bound to acquire an international flavor. There's precious little left nowadays of the old local colour. From all over the world, spivs and layabouts are converging on Milan in search of money.] (*DM*, pp. 106–07)

The contrast between the past and the current situation of Milan as a great cosmopolitan city that attracts people of every kind and has seen a rise in violent crime is emphasized here by references to popular Lombard recipes such as the *pan meino* and *panettoni* and other lost elements of the local lore (*brasera*, *pesa* and *gamba de legn*), which belong to tradition and some people insist on identifying with Milan.

---

but ignored the collective and public dimension of the economic and social changes' (Giuliana Pieri, 'Crime and the City in the Detective Fiction of Giorgio Scerbanenco', in *Italian Cityscape*, ed. by Lumley and Foot, pp. 144–55 (pp. 146–47)).

Urban descriptions in the Lamberti novels emphasize the unfathomable and unsettling aspects of metropolitan life, for example through their 'meteorological observations'.[34] Fog in particular has been a trademark of Milan as an industrial, bleak city in literary and cinematic representations, not only in Bianciardi's *La vita agra* but also, for instance, in Visconti's *Rocco e i suoi fratelli* and Antonioni's *La Notte* [*The Night*] (1961). In *I ragazzi del massacro* Duca looks out of the office window to discover that the streets of Milan are covered in a blanket of fog. It is nearly dawn and he has spent the night at police headquarters, interrogating the eleven students involved in the murder of their teacher Matilde, while at home his little niece is unwell and will die shortly afterwards of complications from pneumonia:

> Guardando oltre la finestra, nella nebbia e nella notte, d'un tratto Duca vide che i due fanali più vicini si erano spenti, la nebbia, per un momento fu solo una nera macchia d'inchiostro, poi si accese di qualche cosa di chiaro e di rosa: era il nuovo giorno che cominciava, e di attimo in attimo la nebbia si accendeva di rosa.[35]

> [Looking out of the window, into the fog and into the night, Duca noticed that the two nearest lights had gone out suddenly and the fog, which for a moment was just a black ink stain, was lit up by something clear and pink: it was the new day that was beginning; and with each passing moment the fog took on more and more of a pinkish glow.]

The break of the new day seems to suggest that hope is still possible even in the most difficult of times. It is, however, just a feeble light which struggles to plough through the thick fog that engulfs people and things. Fog becomes a clue to the mysterious side of the city, another embodiment of the Other. Its presence here emphasizes the emotional and moral isolation of the characters. Due to its flattening and de-individualizing effect, fog can also facilitate crime. In *I ragazzi del massacro* it conceals and somehow protects Marisella Domenici when, 'in quella sera di nebbia densa' [on that evening of dense fog],[36] she breaks into the school where Matilde teaches evening classes for disadvantaged young people from the area and kills her.

Scerbanenco's topographical accuracy functions to root the stories in the Milan of the 1960s. In *Venere privata* Milan is mentioned thirty

---

34 Giuliana Pieri, 'Milano nera: Representing and Imagining Milan in Italian *Noir* and Crime Fiction', in *Italian Crime Fiction*, ed. by Giuliana Pieri (Cardiff: University of Wales Press, 2011), pp. 132–50 (p. 137).

35 Giorgio Scerbanenco, *I ragazzi del massacro* (Milan: Garzanti, 1999 [1968]), p. 55.

36 Scerbanenco, *I ragazzi del massacro*, p. 212.

times; its streets and squares eighty-one times, some of them more than once.[37] *Traditori di tutti* features a long car chase sequence, which starts from Duca's flat in the via Imola 3, continues across Milan's city centre and then leads outwards towards the villages of the hinterland. The reader can trace the itinerary almost as if on a map thanks to the abundance of topographical details. Whilst the attention to details of site and setting, such as street names and real public buildings, is, therefore, the pre-condition for the verisimilitude intended to ground shared knowledge of the city,[38] accurate urban descriptions are counteracted by the abstract darkness that suffuses places. Milan is often portrayed at night when familiar places appear weirdly deformed and illegal actions take place more easily. In the extract below, Susanna Paganica has managed to hitch a lift into town from a passing car after murdering Turiddu Sompani and Adele Terrini. She asks to be dropped off in a deserted service area on the periphery of Milan, from where she intends to take a taxi to her hotel and then a second one to the airport, where she will board a flight bound to the United States: 'Era stato un passaggio pericoloso, ma anche qui non poteva farci niente, sola nello smisurato piazzale all'estrema periferia di Milano, nel dolce ma un po' freddo vento di fine aprile, ebbe paura' [It had been a dangerous ride, but she had had no choice. Only now, alone in this neat little square [*sic*] on the very edge of the city of Milan, did she realize that she was frightened. It was a mild night, towards the end of April, but there was a cool breeze blowing] (*TT*, p. 15; *DM*, p. 14). The description, which reflects Susanna's subjective perception of the place – the qualities of emptiness and vastness, the cool April wind that blows across the deserted square – exemplifies well the idea of the uncanny as an emotional and mental emanation, a quality ascribed to places rather than inherent in them. Marginal and neglected places like the above service area, an anonymous, transitory environment, are privileged sites for the resurfacing of feelings of uncanniness. As Vidler points out, it is in the 'darkest recesses and forgotten margins' of space that what has been repressed resurfaces more readily.[39] It is also interesting to note that the adjective *smisurato* [immeasurable] in the extract above, the analogous *sterminato* [endless] (used elsewhere) and the augmentative suffix -one, as in

---

37 Alessandro Mazzola, 'Giorgio Scerbanenco e Duca Lamberti: note su un incontro fatale', *Delitti di carta*, 6 (2006), 37–47.

38 Howell, 'Crime and the City Solution', p. 366.

39 Vidler, *The Architectural Uncanny*, p. 167.

'sterminati vialoni' [endless avenues],[40] all hint at places perceived as weirdly enlarged and therefore at the difficulty of assimilating Milan's new-scaled spaces.

Other examples may be provided of how, in the Lamberti novels, places appear weirdly out of proportion, strange and almost exotic. In the extract below from *I milanesi ammazzano al sabato*, Duca is on his way to meet Amanzio Berzaghi to tell him that his daughter, who was kidnapped by a criminal group, has been found dead. Duca's gloomy thoughts are projected onto the passing urban landscape framed by the car window: 'Le strade alle dieci e mezzo erano quasi deserte, l'Alfa percorse in tutta la sua lunghezza piazza della Repubblica, nella sua oscura vastità sahariana' [The streets at half past ten were almost deserted, the Alfa travelled the entire length of the Piazza della Repubblica, in its dark Saharan vastness].[41] Dark, immersed in a sort of haze that makes it difficult to distinguish its features, the Piazza here has elements of the eerie. Fisher argues that the weird and eerie share 'a preoccupation with the strange', that is, with the 'outside'.[42] The latter comprises everything that lies 'beyond our standard perception, cognition and experience'.[43] The Piazza is apprehended by reference to something else and foreign (the Sahara Desert), suggesting that the familiar has turned strange and existing reference points have shifted. In the following example from *Venere privata* the modern tower blocks that project themselves against the rural landscape of Milan's hinterland resemble 'new isolated cathedrals in the desert':[44] 'Era l'unica costruzione fra tutti quei campi, una torre grigio celeste a dodici piani, gigantesca e avveniristica, così isolata, e che pure rammentava i monumentali templi aztechi che sorgono ogni tanto in selvaggi deserti' [It was the only building among all those fields, a twelve-storey blueish grey tower, gigantic and futuristic, standing there isolated, and which yet was reminiscent of the monumental Aztec temples that rise up every now and then in wild deserts] (*VP*, p. 183). The extract provides a further example of the perception of the built environment as grotesque, disharmonious and out of place. The mismatch between the modern building and

---

40 Giorgio Scerbanenco, *Il Cinquecentodelitti*, ed. by Oreste del Buono (Milan: Frassinelli, 1994), p. 266.

41 Giorgio Scerbanenco, *I milanesi ammazzano al sabato* (Milan: Garzanti, 1999 [1969]), pp. 37–38.

42 Mark Fisher, *The Weird and the Eerie* (London: Repeater, 2016), p. 8.

43 Fisher, *The Weird and the Eerie*, p. 8.

44 Pieri, 'Milano nera', p. 142.

rural environment highlights the impact of industrialization and the urbanization of the outskirts. Lefebvre argues that the receding of the natural environment in contemporary societies due to urbanization and population growth is often experienced as bewilderment or nostalgia.[45] Here, the incorporation of the countryside into the city conveys inconsistency and disorientation. Once again the changing built environment evokes Otherness, as Duca likens the tower block to an Aztec temple springing up unexpectedly in a deserted area. The frequent association of places within the city with the desert points to the isolation encompassing the characters in the novels. Moreover, the lack of life once again conjures up an eerie feeling.[46]

The following extract from *Traditori di tutti* describing a car chase includes many of the elements of the urban uncanny as 'the slippage or mismatch between our expectations of the city [...] and the often surprising and unsettling experiences it can evoke':[47]

> E la cavalcata nella notte continuò, dopo piazza Cinque Giornate la Giulietta uscì dai bastioni, chi sa perché, e prese Viale Montenero, viale Sabotino, resi teatrali dall'ora notturna, dalla vuotaggine, dai lampeggianti gialli agli incroci, dall'ultimo trani aperto con l'insegna luminosa *Crota Piemunteisa* che tremolava, priva delle spente lettere *r u a*, e poi viale Bligny e viale Col di Lana, e insomma tutta la cerchia della semiantica Milano coi pezzi ancora residui e architettonicamente conservati o spesso ricostruiti, per i turisti, dei bastioni dai cui spalti, un tempo, pare, vigilavano prodi armigeri. (*TT*, pp. 53–54)

> [The little cavalcade rolled on through the night. After the Piazza Cinque Giornate, the Giulietta, for some reason, left the ramparts, and drove by way of the Viale Montenero and the Viale Sabotino, dramatically silent and deserted at this hour. At the crossroads, a solitary night-club was still open. Yellow light streamed from its doorway, and a flickering neon sign above it read *Crota ... Piemunteisa*, the letters *rua* having failed to light up. They then went along the Viale Bligny and the Viale Col di Lana, in other words they circled the whole of the old quarter of Milan, where many ancient buildings still stood, some heavily restored for the benefit of the tourists. On either side there were bastions and ramparts, once, no doubt, manned by valiant soldiers.] (*DM*, pp. 48–49)

45   He states: 'History is experienced as nostalgia, and nature as regret – as a horizon fast disappearing behind us' (Lefebvre, *Production of Space*, p 51).

46   As Fisher puts it, 'we find the eerie more readily in landscapes partially emptied of the human' (Fisher, *The Weird and the Eerie*, p. 11).

47   Lucy Huskinson, 'Introduction', in *The Urban Uncanny: A Collection of Interdisciplinary Studies*, ed. by Lucy Huskinson (London: Routledge, 2016), pp. 1–17 (p. 1).

In the night time the presence of blinking yellow traffic lights and a flashing neon sign that is missing a few letters make the deserted streets seem oddly 'theatrical'. Interestingly, here urban history makes one of its rare appearances in Scerbanenco's crime novels, which, as Burns points out, generally portray a Milan 'of the moment', devoid, that is, of historical depth.[48] The ancient buildings, however, are mainly a reconstruction for tourists and the ghosts evoked from the past contribute to eliciting an impression of artificiality and spatial estrangement. The old quarter, restored for the benefit of tourists, is emblematic of the de-realization of urban space in neo-capitalist societies. This is especially evident in the centres of major glocal cities, which have either become the domain of the rich who can afford luxury apartments or a recreational park for tourists.[49]

In Fruttero & Lucentini's *La donna della domenica* and *A che punto è la notte* Turin is also elusive and difficult to pin down. The city's inward character and tendency to secrecy[50] have inspired many contemporary crime writers, who have followed in the footsteps of *La donna della domenica* and its international success. Turin is an emblematic and, in some respects, anomalous Italian city. It was the seat of the Italian monarchy and the first capital of the country in 1861; in the course of the twentieth century it developed into a major industrial centre and the home of the Italian automotive industry, attracting immigrant workers from all over the country and especially from the more deprived South. In the public mind Turin is linked, like Milan, to the values of a work ethic and efficiency. As Pezzotti points out, however, Turin has also traditionally been seen as mysterious, a place associated with black and white magic, an original combination that has inspired Italian crime writers.[51] In *La donna della domenica* the impenetrability of Turin is best embodied by the aloofness of its dwellers and especially of its upper classes, to whom the book refers as 'l'ambiente' [the milieu or inner circle]: an exclusive environment with its own distinct etiquette and social norms which can only be accessed by right of birth. Fruttero & Lucentini establish a specular relation between the city, a fully-fledged character in the story, and its aristocratic milieu. Much like the latter, the city of Turin is

---

48 Burns, 'Founding Fathers', p. 33.

49 Rhodes, *Stupendous, Miserable City*, p. xvii.

50 Crovi describes it as 'attitudine al segreto' (Crovi, *Tutti i colori del giallo*, p. 143).

51 Pezzotti points out that 'industrialization, immigration, and magic are an unusual mixture that may provide a fertile ground for detective fiction' (Pezzotti, *Importance of Place*, p. 40).

conspiratorial and treacherous while pretending to be sober and detached. The Turinese setting provides the condition for the plot to take specific turns and for the characters to act in the way they do. It is the city itself which somehow evokes the solution of the murder case for the investigating hero, Inspector Santamaria. We read that 'l'idea venne al commissario la domenica mattina [...]. A dargli un aiuto nel suo solito modo negativo e circonlocutorio fu forse la città' [The idea came to the Inspector on Sunday morning [...]. Perhaps, in its usual negative and circumlocutory way, it was the city that lent him a hand] (*DD*, p. 429; *SW*, p. 354).

The main character is constructed in a way that helps the reader to navigate Turin, maintaining critical, and even ironic, distance. His moving across several urban-social milieux means we are able to form a multifaceted view of the city of Turin. Inspector Santamaria has a sense for social manners and the confidence to move within Turin's upper-class environment. A Sicilian immigrant, Santamaria fought in Piedmont in the Resistance; he is, therefore, as Franco Mannai suggests, both an insider and an outsider who discloses an insightful point of view on Turinese society.[52] His superiors entrust Santamaria with knowledge of Turin's high-society circles and appoint him to investigate the murder case of the architect Garrone, a bizarre individual who somehow gained access to that exclusive environment:

> In realtà, i suoi superiori non avevano idea di cosa fosse quell''ambiente' di cui gli attribuivano una così profonda conoscenza. Sapevano – oscuramente – che la differenza tra chi contava e chi no, a Torino, era molto più difficile da stabilire che a Roma o a Napoli o a Milano. Ma in pratica, la sola conclusione che ne traevano era che bisognava stare molto più attenti, moltiplicare le cautele, i riguardi, e al bisogno – per quanto a denti stretti – gli inchini: perché, a Torino, 'non si poteva mai dire'. (*DD*, p. 66)

> [Actually, his superiors had no idea what those 'circles' were, though they attributed to him a great knowledge of them. They knew – vaguely – that the difference between those who counted and those who didn't was much harder to establish in Turin than in Rome or Naples or Milan. But, in practice, the only conclusion they drew was that you had to be much more careful, multiply precautions, respect, and when necessary – though with gritted teeth – bowing and scraping: because, in Turin, 'you never can tell'.] (*SW*, pp. 53–54)

52   Franco Manai, '*La donna della domenica* and the Italian Detective Novel of the 1970s', in *Differences, Deceits and Desires: Murder and Mayhem in Italian Crime Fiction*, ed. by Mirna Cicioni and Nicoletta Di Ciolla (Newark, DE: The University of Delaware Press, 2008), pp. 83–98 (p. 91).

Santamaria's superiors share the idea that social relations within Turinese society are regulated by an unwritten code of conduct, something which seemingly does not apply to any other Italian city, and that therefore in Turin it takes extra caution and diplomacy to navigate the pitfalls of social life.

Massimo Campi is, at first, one of the primary suspects in the murder investigation, alongside his friend Anna Carla Dosio, an upper-class, sophisticated lady who entertains a brief, sentimental relationship with Santamaria. Through his lifestyle and personality the figure of Massimo Campi perfectly embodies the aristocratic aloofness that surrounds the city of Turin. A young dandy who belongs to one of the most influential families from the city's aristocratic milieu, Massimo believes that Turin is a dangerously masked city, deceitful in its provinciality and seemingly detached understatement. In his view, Turin is to blame for spreading a number of 'plagues' – that is, historical events and ephemeral trends that have originated in the city – to the rest of the country: he mentions the first automobile, the first unions, films, left-wing intellectuals and sociologists and the process of Italy's unification. Similarly, Massimo's apparent affability conceals a haughty sense of superiority and a condescending attitude which stem from his privileged social position. He is deceptive, just like the city of Turin. Santamaria cannot help but observe that he has a certain aura to him which resembles the aura of the city itself. To the attentive observer, he contends, the city and its inhabitants reveal an unexpectedly charming side or, as he puts it, 'lo *charme* d'impossibile definizione che stava sotto la crosta scontrosa della città, e che ogni tanto emergeva, irresistibile perché inaspettato' [that charm, impossible to define, which lay beneath the crusty surface of the city, which emerged every now and then, irresistible because unexpected] (*DD*, p. 167; *SW*, p. 139). The use of a foreign term to capture this idea is here a clue to an inherent quality of strangeness and impenetrability in the city.

La donna della domenica documents a changing urban landscape in which traditional socio-geographical boundaries are being redrawn as a consequence of industrialization and internal migration. Urban transformation is particularly evident in the areas of intensive apartment buildings for the lower-middle-classes, such as the Santa Rita neighbourhood, where the character of Oreste Regis lives. Regis works as a civil servant and has been an accomplice to Garrone's plan to blackmail an aristocratic widow, Ines Tabusso, something to which this chapter will return later. Regis is described as one of those people 'nati senza avvenire, per far numero, per figurare in statistiche di epidemie influenzali, di consumi, di trascurabili oscillazioni

98

elettorali' [born without a future, just to take up space, to figure in the statistics of influenza epidemics, of consumption of goods, of electoral trends] (*DD*, p. 458; *SW*, p. 379). He is a petit-bourgeois clerk and lives in a neighbourhood that mirrors the monotony of his existence in the uniformity of the modern apartment blocks that have been set down in a rigid grid, a specular reciprocity that calls up 'the uncanny effects of all mirroring'.[53] Santamaria meets Regis in his Santa Rita apartment, pretending to be the spokesman for a local group for the protection of urban green spaces and with the actual intent of interrogating him to elicit a confession. Regis is only waiting to complain about the recent construction frenzy that, in his view, has undermined the liveability of the neighbourhood. As he puts it:

Qui, comunque, siamo arrivati al punto di rottura, non è più ammissibile che questi mostruosi casermoni soffochino ogni possibilità di una vita sana, bella, armoniosa! Lei ha visto: questa non è più una via, è un tunnel, è un cunicolo. (*DD*, p. 457)

[Here, in any event, we've reached the breaking-point. It simply is not conceivable that these monstrous barracks should be allowed to stifle every possibility of beautiful, harmonious, healthy living! You can see yourself. This isn't a street anymore. It's a tunnel, an alley.] (*SW*, p. 377)

The monstrous, uncannily anthropomorphized barracks convey a sense of claustrophobia and suffocation as they loom over what is not a proper street anymore but a tunnel and a straight line. Their repetition is a figure of the uncanny. These buildings produce a specific form of spatial anxiety. They provide another example of how the built environment may foster uncanny experiences. They also point once again to rapid changes that challenge the conventional experience of urban spaces.

Likewise, in the following extract the emphasis on the geometry of functional architectures (implacable rows of buildings, minuscule trapezoidal terraces) suggests shapes inimical and unaccommodating to the human form:

[Regis] si sbracciava in ogni direzione, estendendo l'anatema a tutto il quartiere, di cui s'intravedevano all'ingiro i blocchi scaglionati in file implacabili. Sporgendo la testa, il commissario scorse sulla sinistra, così vicino che quasi lo poteva toccare, un minuscolo terrazzo trapezoidale messo di sghimbescio in una rientranza della facciata: sopra ci stavano a stento una sedia pieghevole e un tavolino di giunco. (*DD*, p. 457)

---

53 Vidler, *The Architectural Uncanny*, p. 221.

[He waved his arms in every direction, extending his anathema to the whole neighbourhood, whose great blocks could be seen all lined up in implacable rows. Sticking out his head, the Inspector glimpsed, to the left, so close he could almost touch it, a minuscule trapezoidal terrace set obliquely in an indentation of the façade: it could just contain a camp chair and a little wicker table.] (*SW*, pp. 377–78)

With its practical, utilitarian focus, this rational plan to shape the use of space and tackle demographic growth means that all the available space has been densely built up. Freedom of movement and the possibility of connecting with nature are compromised. One perceives, in Vidler's words, the 'haunting absence' of cities of the past.[54] The latter evoke the idea of a type of urban environment that facilitates socializing through pedestrian-friendly streets and squares. One may argue that the attraction to this traditional model is particularly strong in Italian culture, for the Renaissance city still works as a prototype of proportion and harmony, often in opposition to post-Second World War 'free-market orientated' cities.[55] Modernism, the leading movement in twentieth-century architecture and design, destabilized the principles of tradition and preservation of memory that had been at the heart of urbanism from at least the Renaissance onwards, promoting cities in which new momunemts, such as the skyscraper, embodied the value of functionality at the heart of modern life.[56] In the above passage, Regis also laments the loss of a closer, more harmonious connection with the natural environment.

Fruttero & Lucentini's depiction of Turin's old centre apparently celebrates the benign aura of authenticity of the older part of the city. On a closer look, however, it contains references to elements of 'disorder' as Massimo's walk in the old centre reveals unexpected insights into the transformation of this part of the city. There emerges once again a mismatch between preconceptions and the actual experience of the city. The latter is fraught with baffling and disorienting feelings:

[Massimo] se ne andò, tutto felice, fra le ghiotte bottegucce dove non aveva messo mai piede [...]. Tutto gli si ricostruiva soavemente intorno: droghieri in camice grigio, garzoni in grembiule bianco arrotolato alla vita, donnone con la sporta, suore bisbiglianti,

---

54   Vidler, *The Architectural Uncanny*, p. 183.

55   Richard J. Williams contrasts the latter type of city, particularly pronounced in English urbanism, with the allegedly more traditional, ordered European model (Williams, *The Anxious City*, p. 14).

56   Vidler, *The Architectural Uncanny*, pp. 179–80.

striminzite beghine, pensionati col mezzo sigaro, mamme che gridavano dagli ammezzati. A ogni cantonata sostava una prostituta grassa. Non era 'proletariato', questo, era ancora 'popolino', e Massimo, crogiolandosi nel suo sdoppiamento, vi si aggirava come in una festa in costume una volta tanto riuscita, insensibile ai fumi d'auto e motociclette, ai juke-box e ai dialetti meridionali che (il maestro di cerimonia non poteva aver pensato proprio a tutto!) sgorbiavano ogni tanto la composizione. (*DD*, p. 228)

[He went off, completely happy, among the seductive shops where he had never set foot [...]. Everything fell gently into place around him: grocers in white smocks, butcher-boys with aprons hitched up at their waists, housewives with shopping bags, murmuring nuns, withered church-mice, old men smoking half-cigars, Mammas yelling from balconies. At every corner a fat prostitute was stationed. This wasn't the 'proletariat': this was still the 'populace', and Massimo, reveling in his split personality, wandered as through a costume ball that had, for once, succeeded, insensitive to the fumes from cars and motorcycles, to the jukeboxes and the Southern dialects that (the master of ceremony couldn't think of every little thing!) occasionally marred the composition.] (*SW*, p. 188)

The pre-industrial scene that looks to Massimo like a costume ball staging the traditional figures of the 'populace' (artisans, grocers, women yelling at their children from balconies, prostitutes waiting for customers) turns out to be a simulacrum in a sort of slippage between reality and dream, as the old centre is changing as rapidly as the rest of the city. Massimo blames himself for having indulged in regret for the old days and in the sentimental celebration of an urban social order that probably never existed. The clues to new lifestyles and ways of mobility (the fumes from cars and motorcycles), cultural and leisure habits (the jukeboxes) and the 'jarring' presence of Southern immigrants all point to a defamiliarizing experience in which conventional and familiar categories are called into question. Furthermore, what Massimo sees appears messily human in form. The juxtaposition of different elements in Fruttero & Lucentini's description produce a montage-like effect, which is, according to Fisher, the clearest embodiment of the weird.[57]

In the extract quoted above, the act of walking enables one to see beyond superficial appearances, very much like the process of detecting. One may take this argument further and track an analogy between crime fiction and psycho-geographical enquiry, which

57   Fisher, *The Weird and the Eerie*, p. 11.

both rely heavily on walking. To begin with, they share the same object of analysis, that is, a city that has become more complex and enigmatic. The term psycho-geography, coined in 1950s Paris by the Situationist movement of Guy Debord, envisaged a set of theories and practices that were aimed at challenging traditional, established ways of moving around the city by promoting a playful urban experience.[58] Specifically, the Situationists encouraged a creative remapping of urban space through aimless drifting (the so-called *dérive*) and the practice of automatic writing in the lines of the Surrealist tradition, thereby accessing a more authentic experience of the city.[59] The communal search for alternative ways of apprehending and representing urban reality may explain why the act of walking features prominently in both psycho-geography and classical detective stories. Benjamin points out that both the *flâneur* and the detective record observations of urban scenes and grasp traces and hints disseminated across the urban fabric.[60] As Benjamin puts it, 'the joy of watching' makes of the *flâneur* an 'amateur detective'.[61] As shown in Bianciardi's *La vita agra*, walking may become an expression of non-conformism and even outright protest.

Roadworks are a further point of connection between *La vita agra* and *La donna della domenica*. Fruttero & Lucentini deem the frenzy of repair deafening and ubiquitous, hinting at Turin's relentless urban restructuring in those years. The improvement works, with their corollary of acoustic pollution and dust clouds, burden the characters in *La donna della domenica* with a sense of oppression and almost physical fatigue. This is particularly the case for those who have grown up elsewhere and have moved to Turin later in life, like Santamaria and other fellow police officers who are also originally from the South. The sensation of physical and mental effort conveyed by the seemingly ever-present roadworks suggests once again a loss of control over the rapidly changing urban landscape. Urban transformations are so central to the story in *La donna della domenica* that they may be seen as a trigger for the murder of the architect Garrone.[62] Having learnt about Tabusso's plan to turn her lawn into

---

58   Coverley, *Psychogeography*, p. 10.

59   Coverley, *Psychogeography*, p. 13.

60   Benjamin, *The Writer of Modern Life*, p. 72.

61   Benjamin, *The Writer of Modern Life*, p. 98.

62   Righini, too, observes that, in *La donna della domenica*, 'la trama gialla viene messa in moto proprio da un episodio legato all'ingigantirsi dello spazio urbano – siamo a Torino – a discapito della campagna. Il desiderio della signora

building plots and being aware of a building restriction that could block her application, Garrone begins to blackmail her. He demands that she choose his own building project over the official one, which has been drawn up by a distinguished architectural firm. Tabusso, who is described as a 'vecchia torinese con l'acqua alla gola, sopraffatta da nuove genti, nuovi costumi, nuove leggi, nuovi vizi' [old Turinese lady with her back to the wall, bullied by new people, new customs, new laws, new vices] (*DD*, p. 502; *SW*, p. 415), somehow persuades herself that the only way out of her predicament is to kill Garrone. Manai has observed that the figure of Tabusso exemplifies the tension between Turin's past and present, or between old and new money: on the one hand the aristocracy and on the other the middle- and upper-class business people who are becoming the new predominant actors on the Turinese scene.[63]

As noted earlier, modern crime fiction calls into question a unitary and absolute knowledge of the city by proposing an alternative perspective based on the shared viewpoint of the characters. The interacting points of view of characters who, in *La donna della domenica*, are representatives of different urban social groups create a dynamic sketch of Turin's evolving social geography. Similarly, Fruttero & Lucentini's subsequent novel *A che punto è la notte* stages a choral ensemble of characters who perform different functions and are based in various areas of the city. It still features Inspector Santamaria as the detective, this time dealing with the assassination of Don Alfonso Pezza, the unusual priest of the Church of Santa Liberata. Don Pezza is surrounded by a group of equally shady individuals, such as the Fiat engineer Vicini and the retired Fiat worker Priotti. Don Pezza's murder triggers a series of events that connect even more characters together, including Monguzzi and Rossignolo (who work in a publishing house and are arguably a caricature of Fruttero and Lucentini themselves); Thea Guidi and her mother, who belong to a wealthy Turinese family; and the Mafia associate Graziano Scalisi.

Tabusso di lottizzare il proprio appezzamento collinare per rivenderlo come terreno edificabile la spinge all'omicidio di due persone [...]. Allo stesso tempo, ponendola in relazione con lo scatenarsi della violenza omicida, i due autori sottolineano la negatività di questa speculazione urbanistica' [the crime plot is set in motion by an episode linked to the spread of the urban agglomeration – we are in Turin – to the detriment of the countryside. Mrs Tabusso's desire to divide up her hilly plot to sell it as building land leads her to murder two people [...]. [B]y placing it in relation to the outbreak of murderous violence, the two authors underline the negativity of this urban speculation] (Righini, 'Città degli incubi', p. 147).

63   Manai, '*La donna della domenica*', p. 93.

Fruttero & Lucentini's second Turinese crime novel was published in 1979, a period of economic recession and socio-political turmoil in Italy, which may account for the crepuscular atmosphere of the story, alluded to in the title and in the recurring references to corrupted Babylon.[64]

In *A che punto è la notte*, the narrative focus moves significantly to suburban Turin and the municipalities of the urban belt. The story has the same trajectory. The novel is framed by Turin's modern peripheries: it begins with the description of the Brussone housing project developed in the hinterland during the 1960s, while the final police chase takes place in a disused industrial area awaiting redevelopment, still in the outer city. The emphasis on the precariousness of the housing projects and urban interventions that were carried out only a decade before and the general sense of incompleteness and urban decay bear witness to Turin's abrupt development in the aftermath of the boom. The spread of a 'burgeoning periphery' was the result of the rapid rise in population following the arrival of hundreds of thousands of immigrants, which 'put pressure on Turin's infrastructure'.[65] Graziano's and Thea's car journey offers a pretext for Fruttero and Lucentini to take the reader on a tour through the urban belt, where neon-lit, semi-abandoned furniture workshops, run-down motels and shabby night clubs remind us once again that 'the uncanny erupt[s] in empty parking lots around abandoned or run-down shopping malls, in [...] the wasted margins and surface appearances of postindustrial culture':[66]

La Porsche correva tra gli innumerevoli misteri della periferia. Alti edifici nudi, resi più simili gli uni agli altri da differenze irrisorie, bordavano lunghi viali senza fine, ormai identici in tutte le città del mondo. [...] una vittoria dell'anonimo, del piatto e uniforme plurale. (*PN*, p. 100)

[The Porsche went fast across the many mysteries of the periphery. Bare, tall buildings, made more similar to each other by negligible differences, bordered long endless avenues, now identical in every city in the world. [...] a victory of the anonymous, of the flat and uniform plural.]

64   The title refers to an obscure oracle from Isaiah 21.11: 'The burden of Dumah. He calleth to me out of Seir, Watchman, what of the night? Watchman, what of the night?'.

65   Mary Louise Lobsinger, 'Architectural Utopias and *La Nuova Dimensione*: Turin in the 1960s', in *Italian Cityscapes*, ed. by Lumley and Foot, pp. 77–89 (p. 79).

66   Vidler, *The Architectural Uncanny*, p. 3.

In their replicability, the anonymous buildings embody the figure of the double with its effect of disorientation. These modern developments are almost interchangeable and replaceable. The impersonality of buildings and peripheral urban areas here hint at the levelling effect of economic growth and rapid urbanization that have sacrificed distinctive local features. The same, Fruttero & Lucentini contend, applies to every city in an increasingly globalized world. As national economies grow more interconnected after the end of the Second World War, and mass tourism became an established reality, the geography of global capitalism has tended to flatten out spatial differences: what Fruttero and Lucentini describe as a victory for uniformity.

The post-industrial landscape of suburban Turin is a disorderly juxtaposition of various architectural and industrial remnants from different epochs. Again, like in a sort of montage, the new stands next to the old, the elegant next to the shabby. What Fruttero & Lucentini describe as 'horizontal archaeology' conveys the apparent loss of coherence and legibility of the urban landscape:

Tra i compatti spicchi delle abitazioni cominciavano ad apparire basse cancellate e tetti aguzzi di fabbriche e manifatture, e ogni tanto un rettangolo d'erba marrone nel quale becchettava il collo smisurato e schematico di una gru. La città si dilatava, ricoprendo i vecchi confini coi paesi della cintura, e ciò che restava era una specie di archeologia orizzontale, gli strati uno accanto all'altro, ben riconoscibili, la diroccata cascina barocca, poi la stazione Esso, poi la ciminiera ottocentesca, poi la casa operaia dei primi del secolo, poi la villetta 1920 col giardino e i pesci rossi, poi di nuovo una cascina, una stazione Chevron, un casello daziario abbandonato, e così via in cerchi sempre più ampi. (*PN*, p. 101)

[Between the compact segments of the houses, the low gates and pointed roofs of factories and manufactures began to appear and every now and then a rectangle of brown grass being pecked at by the huge and angular neck of a crane. The city expanded, covering the old borders with the villages of the belt; and what remained was a kind of horizontal archaeology, the layers next to each other, easily recognizable, the ruined Baroque farmhouse, then the Esso station, then the nineteenth-century chimney, then the workers' house from the beginning of the century, then the cottage from 1920 with the garden and goldfish, then again a farmhouse, a Chevron station, an abandoned customs' toll booth – and so on in ever widening circles.]

The landscape appears unevenly cluttered with traces of previous industrial endeavours. The description conveys the sense that rapid, haphazard urbanization has turned what was once countryside into an ugly, inhospitable place, the almost complete absence of vegetation (a few faded blades of bleached grass are all that remains) emphasizing this negative impact. The desolate, unkempt landscape conveys feelings of neglect and lack of care. Worries about the changing relationship to the natural environment bear witness to the fact that post-war development privileged growth over the preservation of the historic patrimony and environment; and took place in a country, Italy, deeply concerned with its past and traditions and generally reluctant to implement innovation. A country, to put it in Volponi's words, 'altalenante e sfuggente, scrimine tra sviluppo e ritardo' [oscillating and elusive, suspended between development and delay] (*MC*, p. 186). Paul Ginsborg points out that between 1957 and 1964 the number of new houses being built in Italy increased enormously, and often haphazardly, with the conservation of green areas frequently overlooked in the planning process.[67] Building speculation also played a central role in unregulated urban sprawl at the expense of the countryside.[68] It is also interesting to note how the gendered element of the language ('la città si dilatava') in the extract, like the example discussed above in relation to Scerbanenco, denounces anxiety about unregulated urban sprawl. As in the Lamberti novels, it betrays a male-biased conception of the expansion and fluidity of urban spaces, which challenge a sense of (masculine) rational order and mastery.

Dangerous City

As the city expands and becomes more complex, it also becomes less controllable. Urbanization and domestic immigration bring about the fear of penetration by criminals. The correlation between crime rates and the size of the city where these are recorded has been the focus of a number of sociological studies.[69] Edward Glaeser and Bruce Sacerdote identify three main peculiarities of the big city that may explain why the incidence of crime is higher in dense urban areas: these enjoy greater access to economic resources and therefore higher pecuniary returns, a lower probability of arrest and the presence of a higher number of crime-prone individuals.[70] Italian

---

67 Ginsborg, *A History of Contemporary Italy*, p. 246.

68 Ginsborg, *A History of Contemporary Italy*, p. 246.

69 Edward L. Glaeser and Bruce Sacerdote, 'Why Is There More Crime in Cities?', *The Journal of Political Economy*, 107 (1999), 225–58 (p. 226).

70 Glaeser and Sacerdote, 'Why Is There More Crime?', p. 227.

cities are no exception and the connection between urbanization and crime provides a fertile ground for detective stories. Scerbanenco and Fruttero & Lucentini show that crime follows the geography of industrialization by proliferating in the newly urbanized areas of Milan and Turin and by taking advantage of the improved road and motorway networks. The stretching out of Milan and Turin to absorb adjacent settlements also means more interstitial spaces where illegal activities may take place. At the same time, as cities are increasingly interconnected in the geography of global capitalism, criminal groups find new international markets.

The remainder of this chapter is dedicated to a more detailed discussion of the geography of crime in the examined novels. Scerbanenco and Fruttero & Lucentini address the connection between urban development and evolution of criminality not only in terms of how the latter concretely mirrors the growth of the city, but also at a more subtle level. On the one hand, criminal organizations show the efficiency of modern industry; on the other, criminal acts are often engendered by the frustrated aspirations of the characters who are not able to succeed in the competitive environment of the big city and are therefore more likely to be lured into illegal rackets. As John Foot observes, this is particularly the case for 'those who arrived in the cities during the boom in search of work – for whom *exclusion*, not integration, was often the dominant experience'.[71]

Urbanization and Crime

When in *Venere privata* Alberta Radelli is found dead in Metanopoli, her wrists cut so as to disguise the murder as suicide, Duca observes that 'oggi ci si svena nei nuovi centri del petrolio, dell'industria pesante, schiavi in fondo, anche in questo ultimo atto di volontà, della spietata marcia verso il futuro' [nowadays one cuts one's wrists in the new centres of oil, of heavy industry, fundamentally slaves, even in this last act of will, to the ruthless march towards the future] (*VP*, p. 75). Metanopoli was created between 1955 and 1960 in San Donato Milanese, in the suburbs of Milan, by Enrico Mattei, founder of the multinational oil company Eni,[72] as a complex of offices, factory buildings and blocks of flats for factory workers; it was to represent an ideal model of the modern industrial town, providing housing and

---

71 Foot, *Milan since the Miracle*, p. 23.
72 Eni SpA or Ente Nazionale Idrocarburi [State Hydrocarbons Authority].

other amenities for Eni employees.[73] It is, therefore, emblematic that Alberta Radelli finds her death here, close to the industrial complex which is a famous example of the entrepreneurial spirit of the boom years. To Duca it goes to show the social deracination produced by the widespread culture of profit, as if Alberta has here relinquished her own will to this new idol.

Crime draws on the opportunities opened up by economic growth and develops around the new centres of power. Inspector Santamaria, however, cautions against taking too simplistic a view of the new metropolitan criminality and compares the belief that in recent years a generation of ruthless criminals has replaced a more dignified, respectable *malavita* [criminal underworld] to certain unrealistic reveries of the past in which memories are transfigured and sensory perceptions become more intense:

> I criminali – pareva a lui – erano sempre stati violenti e sempre 'nuovi', cioè un passo più avanti della polizia. [...] Rimpiangere la malavita 'di una volta' era un po' come rimpiangere il gusto delle albicocche dell'infanzia o le estati interminabilmente serene di un passato meteorologico immaginario. (*PN*, p. 116)

> [Criminals – it seemed to him – had always been violent and always 'new', that is, always one step ahead of the police. [...] Regretting the 'once-upon-a-time' underworld was a bit like regretting the taste of childhood apricots or the endlessly serene summers of an imaginary meteorological past.]

While it would clearly overstate the case to suggest that crime undergoes a sort of anthropological mutation in those years, it is undeniable that the new socio-economic circumstances of post-war Italy effect a certain evolution of crime. Marco Paoli identifies a number of elements that concur to shape new forms of criminality in post-war Italian society, such as the involvement of the Mafia in the North of the country, the shift away from traditional values that causes a widespread lack of orientation and the political mistrust that accounts for the social unrest and violence of the Years of Lead.[74] The texts examined here, and especially the Lamberti novels, offer an insight into organized criminal activities that may be considered modern in terms of their organizational methods and transnational scale. They show the international ramifications of crime due to

---

73 Marco Biraghi, Gabriella Lo Ricco and Silvia Micheli, *Guida all'architettura di Milano, 1954–2014* (Milan: Hoepli, 2013), pp. 20–21.

74 Paoli, *Giorgio Scerbanenco*, p. 99.

the increasing interconnectedness of Western societies after the Second World War. As for Fruttero & Lucentini, it may be argued that while *La donna della domenica* encompasses many of the stylistic features of the traditional *giallo*, such as the enclosed space of the murder and the detective's psychological enquiry, undertaken within the well-defined circles of a conservative urban society, *A che punto è la notte* features a more complex criminal organization with transboundary interests. The criminal plan around which the story revolves betrays in-depth business knowledge. Over the course of the novel, it emerges that Fiat executive Musumanno is indeed the mastermind of the criminal scheme. Generally speaking, however, the international dimension of crime pertains more to Scerbanenco's fiction, which reflects the reputation as a global industrial centre that Milan achieved in the 1960s. Despite the fact that Turin's population grew exponentially in the post-war years, exceeding one million inhabitants,[75] in Fruttero & Lucentini's view the city has never risen above its small-town mentality. 'Il vecchio nucleo provinciale di Torino' [the old, provincial core of Turin] (*DD*, p. 168; *SW*, p. 140], as Santamaria puts it, stubbornly resists change.

Scerbanenco's *Traditori di tutti* and Fruttero & Lucentini's *A che punto è la notte* are especially illustrative of the urban tendency towards crime, for they show most clearly that urban growth fosters the development of criminal activities. In *Traditori di tutti* a series of connected murders occur along the *strade provinciali* [provincial roads] and *navigli* [canals] that connect Milan to the municipalities of the hinterland, Buccinasco, Banco Romano and Ca' Torino. Susanna Paganica kills Turiddu Sompani and Adele Terrini by pushing the car in which they lie asleep into the waters of the Alzaia Naviglio Pavese at the point of intersection between a country road 'ancora commoventemente campagnola' [old, unsurfaced towpath] (*TT*, pp. 8–9; *DM*, p. 8) and a more recently developed *strada statale* [state highway] heading to Milan.[76] Susanna has chosen the spot carefully, taking into account the less frequented, peripheral location but also the proximity of the road links that enable her to hitch-hike a ride and organize her escape after the murder. A similar fate awaits Giovanna Marelli and Silvano Solvere, whose car plunges fatally into the water

---

75 Vanessa Maher, 'Immigration and Social Identities', in *Italian Cultural Studies: An Introduction*, ed. by David Forgacs and Robert Lumley (Oxford: Oxford University Press, 1996), pp. 160–77 (p. 166).

76 The English translation does not include the observation, stressed here, that this old towpath is still 'touchingly rural'.

of the Naviglio Grande, near Ronchetto sul Naviglio, while they desperately attempt to escape from a shootout. The novel's primary focus on the suburbs is symptomatic of the expansion of Milan from the centre outwards. The arms-trafficking investigated by Duca relies on a system of meeting places and delivery and collection points which are again mainly located in the suburbs. Examples of these criminal hubs are the Trattoria Binaschina, a restaurant that provides a front for illegal activities and is situated along a country road outside Milan, and Ulrico Brambilla's butcher's shops, which are the transit points for the smuggling of illegal arms. The chain of butcher's shops has recently opened new branches in Banco Romano and Ca' Torino, expanding from the city centre to the suburbs. The criminal organization trading arms is based in Milan but has branches in Genoa, France and the Alto Adige region, where the weapons are distributed to local terrorists.

In *A che punto è la notte*, we learn that a group of *mafiosi* have been relocated to the suburbs of Turin from the South of the country, following a court order known as a *soggiorno obbligato*. This was a Fascist policy reintroduced in 1956 which prescribed the forced resettlement within the national territory of criminals affiliated with a Mafia group. The policy had the twofold purpose of cutting the criminals' ties with their places of origin and of keeping them under law enforcement.[77] In this sense, the development of crime follows patterns of modernization not only within the city but also on a national scale, since one may assume that the decision to relocate these serious offenders to the cities of the North betrays a perception of Northern Italy as the virtuous, productive half of the country. In other words, it expresses the idea that such an environment may exert a positive influence on these individuals' deviant tendencies as well as cutting off their links with organized crime in the South.[78] Such a measure was not without problems and controversy. A common argument,

---

[77] On this topic see also Alessandro Coletti, *Mafie: Storia della criminalità organizzata nel Mezzogiorno* (Turin: Società Editrice Internazionale, 1995); and Romano Canosa, *Storia della criminalità in Italia dal 1946 ad oggi* (Milan: Feltrinelli, 1995).

[78] As Fruttero and Lucentini put it, the *soggiorno obbligato* involves 'l'idea di allontanare quei criminali dal loro *habitat* in Sicilia e in Calabria, costringendoli a vivere nei piccoli comuni attorno alle metropoli del nord, dove l'ambiente li avrebbe domati, se non addirittura redenti' [the idea of removing those criminals far from their native habitat in Sicily and Calabria, forcing them to live in small towns around the northern metropolises, where the environment is meant to tame them, if not quite redeem them] (*PN*, p. 340).

especially among those whose agenda involves blaming the South for the problems of the country, has been that the *soggiorno obbligato* ultimately accelerated the Mafia's infiltration in the North, enabling them to re-build a network for their activities. Nevertheless, research has shown that Mafia transplantion may be due more broadly to the emigration of people from territories where mafias are widespread. No entrenchment or direct correlation exists with the *soggiorno* policy.[79] It is also interesting to note that the social geography of cities like Turin and Milan tended to reproduce national imbalances. Mary Louise Lobsinger observes that the polarity between affluent central areas and more deprived suburban areas mirrored the uneven growth at the national level.[80] If it is true that crime follows the geography of industrialization, the same may be said about de-industrialization in *A che punto è la notte*. The final pages of the novel are set in an abandoned foundry that once belonged to Fiat and has been left unused following a series of corporate spin-offs (*PN*, p. 566). The crime group has set up its headquarters here in order to carry out its money-laundering plan without arousing attention. In a way that evokes other descriptions of neglected, cluttered urban environments which we find elsewhere in the book, the foundry is surrounded by 'tetti di fabbriche, capannoni, piccole officine, depositi, silos di cemento, sparsi villini, lontani falansteri, gobbe di tennis coperti, come balene arenate' [factory roofs, warehouses, small workshops, depositories, cement silos, scattered cottages, distant phalanstères and the swollen domes of covered tennis courts, like beached whales] (*PN*, p. 507).

Scerbanenco's *Venere privata* explores the issue of organized and irregular prostitution in the city of Milan. In the novel, prostitution takes place in central as well as outer areas of the city, showing how 'the absence of any definable red-light district in the city [of Milan] makes the whole urban area available for trade'.[81] *Venere privata* tells the story of two young women, Alberta and Livia, who have been experimenting with occasional prostitution, partly out of a material need to earn extra money and partly for purposes of sociological research (Livia is indeed a former student of sociology). One day Alberta is approached by an elegant old man who persuades her to follow him to a photography studio

79   Federico Varese, *Mafias on the Move: How Organized Crime Conquers New Territories* (Princeton, NJ: Princeton University Press, 2011), p. 37.

80   Lobsinger, 'Architectural Utopias', p. 81.

81   Foot, *Milan since the Miracle*, p. 13.

to have some nude photographs taken. The man turns out to be a member of an international network dedicated to exploiting young women and the decision to follow him costs Alberta her life. Duca's plan to find the man who has approached and murdered Alberta involves using her friend Livia as bait: she will walk with affected nonchalance, like 'una signorina che cerca qualcuno o qualche cosa, un negozio, o che aspetta l'ora di un appuntamento' [a young lady looking for someone or something, a shop perhaps, or waiting for an appointment] (*VP*, p. 160), in the areas between the Piazza della Scala, Piazza San Babila and Piazza San Carlo, waiting for the man to make an appearance. As is also shown by the following example, the streets and landmarks of Milan feature prominently in the novel in connection with the theme of prostitution. In other words, through the issue of prostitution Scerbanenco gives prominence to the topography of Milan:

> In quel tratto di viale che dall'Arco del Sempione mira al Castello Sforzesco, anche appena passate le dieci del mattino, vi sono sul bordo dello stradone accattivanti figure femminili [...] che sanno di operare in una grande metropoli dove non vi sono provinciali limiti di orario o conformistiche divisioni tra notte e giorno. (*VP*, p. 58)

> [In that stretch of avenue which leads from the Arco del Sempione to the Castello Sforzesco, even after ten in the morning, there are captivating female figures on the edge of the road [...] who know they work in a large metropolis where they are not subject to provincial notions of time or traditional divisions between night and day.]

No matter what time of day or night, in the big city there are always people around and therefore potential clients. The relevance of the topic of prostitution in novels such as *Venere privata* and (as mentioned earlier) in *La donna della domenica* may to some extent be a reflection of the debate sparked in Italian society by the Merlin Law of 1958, which was the result of the ten-year battle fought by Senator Lina Merlin against the exploitation of prostitutes.[82] When the bill was finally approved after ten years of political negotiation, it appeared to be a heavily revised version of Merlin's original proposal, which was to maintain the legality of prostitution and offer assistance and provision to former prostitutes, while reinforcing the punitive measures against their customers. The final version

---

82 In *La donna della domenica* the prostitutes who work the hills and woods around Turin often meet their clients within the property of Tabusso.

of the new legislation failed to recognize and guarantee the basic rights of prostitutes.[83]

Clues to the evolution of metropolitan criminality may also be found in the new connotations acquired by specific urban places in the post-war period. One example, also seen in Chapter 1, is Milan's Stazione Centrale. 'A place of exchange and the settling of accounts',[84] as Foot puts it, the station provides, for example, the main transit point for an illegal trade in diamonds in Scerbanenco's short story 'Stazione centrale ammazzare subito'. The members of the criminal organization meet and exchange the diamonds at the Stazione Centrale before blending into the crowds of people arriving into or leaving the station. Milan's *tangenziale* or *circonvallazione* [ring road] is another place that features prominently in crime stories set in the Northern capital: a trend that once again follows the example of Scerbanenco.[85] As Giuliana Pieri points out, the ring road separates 'both physically and metaphorically' Milan city centre from outer areas and acts as a gateway that allows the action to move into and out of these boundaries, thereby covering the territory of the whole city.[86] The fact that, more generally, Scerbanenco's novels contain frequent references to the modern road network bears witness to the major road improvements and sharp increase in mobility of the post-war years. In *Venere privata* Alberta and Davide travel at high speed on the Autostrada del Sole, the motorway linking Milan and Naples that was inaugurated in 1964, since they have decided on a whim to have lunch in Florence and arrive back in Milan in time for the *aperitivo*, embracing the hedonism of the boom years. Elsewhere, criminals use thoroughfares and motorways to escape the authorities who are tracking them. In the short story 'Basta col cianuro' [Enough of Cyanide], a smuggler is arrested by the police on a motorway as he flees from the criminal organization that is chasing him. In 'Piccolo

---

83 According to Molly Tambor, 'what Merlin framed as a liberating reform became a protective, moralizing law which upheld the isolation and maintained the status of prostitutes as second-class citizens' (Molly Tambor, 'Prostitutes and Politicians: The Women's Rights Movement in the Legge Merlin Debates', in *Women in Italy, 1945–1960: An Interdisciplinary Study*, ed. by Penelope Morris (New York: Palgrave Macmillan, 2006), pp. 131–46 (p. 131)). On the same topic, see also Sandro Bellassai, *La legge del desiderio. Il progetto Merlin e l'Italia degli anni cinquanta* (Rome: Carocci, 2006).

84 Foot, *Milan since the Miracle*, p. 7.

85 Pieri, 'Milano nera', p. 138.

86 Pieri, 'Milano nera', pp. 138–39.

Hôtel per sadici' [A Small Hotel for Sadists], two killers attempt a similar escape, driving from Milan to Rome.[87]

When discussing the link between urbanization and crime, one should also take into account the social and anthropological implications of Italy's post-war economic growth. In this chapter we have seen textual examples of crimes that are engendered by certain kinds of obstacle that prevent the characters from achieving their goals and aspirations. Post-war economic development emphasized individual initiative and achievement, championing an idea of success as the attainment of money and social and professional recognition. In the novels examined in this chapter the predominance of this individualistic culture transpires through characters who resort to illegal means to achieve their ends since they are unable to gain access to material goods legitimately. As Burns observes, in Scerbanenco's Milan 'everyone aspires to move ahead and upwards'.[88] The Lamberti novels show that the opportunities offered by modern urban life are not within everyone's reach and that frustrated desires and aspirations may develop into crime. Criminal acts are, indeed, often committed by underprivileged people who aim to afford the material lifestyle and luxury goods available in the city. Prostitution is a clear example of this: in Scerbanenco's crime stories women are either forced into the sex trade by a man whom they trust or they decide to become prostitutes out of financial difficulties that would make it impossible for them to live in an expensive city like Milan. In other instances, characters turned criminal may already enjoy a comfortable lifestyle and yet aspire to greater wealth and professional and social prestige, as shown by the criminal plot at the very top of the industrial world in *A che punto è la notte*.

A further way in which crime evolves lies in its ability to share some of the organizational methods of modern industry. When the criminal organization of *Venere privata* moves its activities from the city centre to the suburbs of Milan in order to attract less attention, Duca observes that 'si sono decentrati anche loro, come le grandi fabbriche' [they, too, have been decentralized, like large factories] (*VP*, p. 178). He is suggesting that the crime syndicate has adopted the principles of modern business management, particularly its strategy of delocalization. Duca also notes that the crime group is

---

87   Giorgio Scerbanenco, 'Basta col cianuro', in *Milano calibro 9*, pp. 26–39; and 'Piccolo Hôtel per sadici', in *Milano calibro 9*, pp. 171–86.

88   Burns, 'Founding Fathers', p. 33.

organized 'esattamente come un ufficio importazione-esportazione' [exactly like an import-export office] (*VP*, p. 169). Similarly, the illegal trade in 'Stazione centrale ammazzare subito' is reminiscent of the Fiat production lines in its methodical organization and operational efficiency.[89] Criminal and capitalist worlds come symbolically to coincide in the scene of Vicini's murder in *A che punto è la notte*. As mentioned above, at least two Fiat executives, Musumanno and Vicini himself, are implicated in the financial fraud which Santamaria unravels. The following passage, which describes the scene of the murder, explicitly compares criminal and industrial systems through the image of the gun that is found next to Vicini's body in the basement of the Fiat headquarters in Turin:

> L'arma, una Beretta cal. 9 corto, dopo i rilievi era stata provvisoriamente posata su uno stretto tavolo bianco, fra un telefono e gli altri oggetti tolti dalle tasche del morto. Nera, metallica, *funzionale*, non contrastava affatto col paesaggio *asettico* del centro elaboratori, occupava anche lei il suo *esatto* spazio aziendale. (*PN*, p. 487)

> [After forensic evalutation the weapon, a Beretta cal. 9 short, had been provisionally placed on a narrow white table, between a telephone and the other objects removed from the dead man's pockets. Black, metallic, *functional*, it did not contrast at all with the *aseptic* landscape of the computer centre; it, too, occupied its *proper* place in the company setting.]

The gun that has just fired the fatal shot has its own legitimate place in the business setting, for it shares with it the same parameters of efficiency and cold, tactical precision.

So far the role of the periphery in the link between urbanization and violent crime has only been hinted at. What follows will look in more detail at the representation of suburban areas in our novels, scrutiny which generally confirms their shared image of bleak and dangerous areas. In so doing, it will refer closely to Foot's study of the modern periphery. While Foot focuses on the case of Milan, his deliberations may be extended to other Italian cities, for the negative reputation of outer urban areas is a nationwide phenomenon.[90] Foot shows that these stereotypes rely on a static view of the urban environment. Intriguingly, the periphery holds a special place in the imagery evoked by the uncanny and eerie, for it is perceived as Other.

---

89   Scerbanenco, 'Stazione centrale ammazzare subito', p. 102.

90   Foot, *Milan since the Miracle*, p. 135.

Periphery

As seen above, *A che punto è la notte* gives special prominence to suburban Turin. The novel opens with the description of the Brussone residential neighbourhood developed during the 1960s, presenting it in terms of architectural failure:

> Vent'anni prima, dopo molti viaggi-studio nei paesi scandinavi e in Inghilterra, un gruppo di architetti e urbanisti aveva deciso di costruire all'estrema periferia di Torino un quartiere modello, dove due o tremila cittadini fra i meno abbienti potessero vivere, per una somma alla portata dei loro guadagni, in mezzo alla natura. Per questo esperimento era stata prescelta la zona di una vecchia cascina (subito demolita) denominata 'Il Brussone', e su quei campi e prati e orti tra la Dora e la Stura erano sorte case 'a misura d'uomo', ossia a tre piani, di mattoni e calcestruzzo a vista, senza ascensori e con terrazzetti chiusi da alte grate di cemento, dietro le quali gli inquilini avrebbero dovuto stendere ad asciugare la biancheria, come facevano i loro omologhi flagellati dai venti artici. (*PN*, pp. 7–8)

> [Twenty years earlier, after many study trips to Scandinavian countries and to England, a group of architects and urban planners had decided to build a model neighbourhood on the outskirts of Turin where two or three thousand from amongst the poorest citizens could live, for a sum within the range of their earnings, in the midst of nature. For this experiment the area of an old farmhouse (immediately demolished) called 'Il Brussone' was chosen and on those fields and meadows and vegetable gardens between the Dora and the Stura rivers were built houses 'on a human scale', i.e., three storeys, brick and exposed concrete, without lifts and with terraces closed by high concrete grates, behind which the tenants would have to hang their laundry out to dry, just like their northern counterparts scourged by Arctic winds.]

The neighbourhood of Brussone incorporates Modernist ideals of simplified, purpose-oriented architectural forms. It takes inspiration from a Northern European model of minimality and efficiency that does not fit into the landscape of Turin's urban belt: the result is a striking mismatch and a failed attempt to embody an ideal of modern living intended to meet the needs of those residents who have limited economic means. Its current state of neglect and decay betrays the many shortcomings of the project. We read, for instance, that 'ciuffi d'erba giallastra, calve radure, informi gibbosità e tumuli di aiuole sconfitte' [tufts of yellowing grass, razed clearings, shapeless mounds and the tumuli of conquered flower beds] are all that remains of the blooming meadows imagined by the urban planners (*PN*, p. 8). Objections to functionalism in architecture often point precisely to the need to build 'contextually', that is, to take into account historical and local contexts.[91]

Fruttero & Lucentini's portrayal of the Brussone neighbourhood is also interesting from the perspective of the alleged lack of history of the periphery. It dwells on the Brussone street toponymy, repeating like a refrain that 'in via dei Rododendri non c'era nessun rododendro. [...] nel viale degli Ontani non c'era nessun ontano, come non c'era nessun ranuncolo in via dei Ranuncoli' [in the Via dei Rododendri there was no rhododendron. [...] in the Viale degli Altani there was no alder, just as there was no buttercup in the Via dei Ranuncoli] (*PN*, pp. 7–8). On the one hand, Fruttero & Lucentini here suggest that the project feels contrived, for the street names that evoke the soothing presence of flowers belong to a desolate concrete landscape. On the other, they hint at the memorability of places. De Certeau points out that place names which refer to the history of an urban community inspire feelings of identification and attachment, feelings which make those places emotionally relevant and ultimately habitable.[92] Unlike street names that refer to meaningful historical events or figures who fulfil the role of identity-building,[93] the Brussone toponyms sound empty and artificial. Brussone has no character and resembles other, similar places on the urban periphery: it is replicable, like 'un pezzo di viale cittadino trapiantato tale e quale a venti chilometri da Torino' [a piece of city avenue transplanted as it is to a place twenty kilometres from Turin] (*PN*, p 131), and aseptic, with 'viali sempre più larghi, aggiornati, indispensabili, come elenchi telefonici, in cui non mancava niente tranne la vitalità di un errore, la suggestione del superfluo' [ever wider avenues, fully modernized, indispensable, like telephone directories, in which nothing was missing except for the vitality of an error, the suggestion of the superfluous] (*PN*, p. 418).

Foot argues that such representations of the periphery rely on a dual model which opposes the city centre as the custodian of identity and tradition to outer urban areas, often dismissed as the product of unregulated urban growth.[94] This view fails to acknowledge that boundaries within the city are constantly redefined and that the periphery is itself fluid: peripheral areas may, for example, come

---

91 Ellin, *Postmodern Urbanism*, p. 4.

92 De Certeau, *Practice of Everyday Life*, pp. 106–09.

93 Botolv Helleland, 'Place Names and Identities', in *Names and Identities*, ed. by Botolov Helleland, Christian-Emil Ore and Solveig Wikstrøm (= *Oslo Studies in Language*, 4 (2012)), pp. 95–116) < https://www.journals.uio.no/index.php/osla/article/view/313/438> [accessed 21 September 2018].

94 Foot, *Milan since the Miracle*, p. 145.

to be perceived as more central and upmarket due to processes of gentrification and the creation of faster road links to the centre.[95] According to Foot, the abstract dual model of the city is responsible for the idea of the periphery as an 'anti-city' or 'non-city'.[96] On the one hand, this reputation stems from the supposed lack of history and traditional urban features such as squares and monuments in the modern suburbs. On the other, it draws on the allegedly poor architectural quality and bleakness of modern building developments and denounces the role of building-speculation practices.

These arguments reverberate in Fruttero & Lucentini's description of Brussone. In the following example the lack of a clear identity of the modern periphery is reflected in the mismatch between modern highways and ring roads and the surviving fields and trails through pasture land nearby:

> Fra tutti gli antichi paesi della cintura, la città, scoppiando, aveva piantato le sue schegge, disseminato i suoi brandelli. Sentieri da pascolo in terra battuta correvano accanto a superstrade a quattro corsie, tortuose carreggiate comunali e provinciali si dilatavano in grandi arterie di circonvallazione [...]. In quella aggrovigliata trama di snodi e raccordi [...] orientarsi era diventato un problema anche di giorno e senza nebbia. (*PN*, p. 52)

> [Among all the ancient towns of the urban belt, the city, bursting, had planted its splinters, scattered its shreds. Dirt paths through pastures ran alongside four-lane motorways, winding municipal and provincial carriageways expanded into large ring roads [...]. In that tangled web of junctions and connections [...] orienting oneself had become a problem even during the day and without fog.]

The extract contains several interesting elements. The image of the city spreading out into the countryside is a violent one, described like an explosion that scatters around splinters and shreds. The concrete jungle embodies the out-of-control growth of the city and the resultant feelings of bewilderment and disorientation as the boundaries between city and countryside blur. Foot also identifies architectural disorder as a fundamental trope that has shaped the discourse about the periphery.[97] Once again, one may find here the idea of the periphery as Other, an uncanny outgrowth of the city that is perceived as incongruous and out of place.

---

95 Foot, *Milan since the Miracle*, p. 136.

96 Foot, *Milan since the Miracle*, pp. 140–42.

97 Foot, *Milan since the Miracle*, p. 143.

The fear of losing oneself in the city brings to mind Freud's account of his own experience of losing his way in the unfamiliar Italian town of Genoa. It may be regarded as one of the uncanny experiences par excellence and a further indication of the ways in which the built environment may evoke this peculiar emotion. Freud recounts how he feels increasingly uncomfortable as, while trying to find his way, he keeps inadvertently coming back to the same street in a disreputable part of town where he begins to attract attention.[98] Repetition is a prominent theme of the uncanny: here, it points again to the return of what had been forgotten and repressed. In *La donna della domenica* Anna Carla walks along the River Po, suddenly to find herself in an unfamiliar part of Turin. She is deep in thought and does not immediately realize that she has walked farther away than she had intended. Her pensive, uneasy mood as she mulls over the argument she had the night before with her friend Massimo finds a symbolic counterpart in the bleak landscape she soon encounters as she walks out towards the periphery:

> Continuò lungo l'argine: a destra aveva le acque basse e grigie del fiume, sorvegliate da lontane figure di pescatori; a sinistra un vasto e accidentato prato con alti mucchi di rifiuti, profilati contro un orizzonte di rigide strutture e neri tralicci che infittivano, in direzione di Chivasso, lungo un'arteria di grande traffico coi lampioni già incongruamente accesi. Lo squallore era calligrafico, perfezionistico, arrivava alla pianta d'acacia solitaria e morente, alla scatoletta di sardine arrugginita tra le ortiche del sentiero. (*DD*, p. 25)

> [She walked on along the bank: to the right was the low, grey water of the river, punctuated by distant forms of fishermen; on her left, a vast and uneven field with high piles of rubbish, standing out against a horizon of stiff structures and black pylons which grew denser towards Chivasso, along a busy highway with its street-lights already incongruously burning. The squalor was over-refined, perfectionist; it included the solitary, dying acacia, the rusting sardine can among the nettles on the path.] (*SW*, p. 20)

The extract brings to mind similar descriptions of the periphery that may be found in *A che punto è la notte* (for instance, in the absence of vegetation) and Scerbanenco's novels (city waste and pollution). These are the undesirable products of urbanization, the underside of economic development that ought to have remained hidden from view and instead come to light: the Freudian return of the repressed.

---

98   Freud, 'The Uncanny', p. 144.

The extract also suggests that familiar urban features gradually fade away as Anna Carla moves out of the city centre. As she looks around, all she can see are a big road clogged with traffic, black pylons and some structures whose purpose is not immediately clear. The only human presence, that of some faraway fishermen, is incongruous and disquieting:

> Dall'acqua aveva ora cominciato a salire un'umidità nebbiosa, dal cielo scendeva una cappa d'un giallo sporco e freddo. Non si viene da sole in un posto così, pensò con disagio. Tornò indietro, ma sforzandosi di non correre, per non sentirsi ancora più stupida. (*DD*, p. 26)

> [From the water a misty humidity had begun to rise, from the sky a kind of lid of cold yellow dirty air descended. You don't come to a place like this alone, she thought uneasily. She turned back, forcing herself not to run, so she wouldn't feel still more stupid.] (*SW*, p. 21)

Anna Carla feels unsafe. While the passage should be read through Fruttero and Lucentini's ironic style, which in this case makes fun of the upper-class lady who feels lost outside her elegant central neighbourhood, it still tells us something about women's freedom of movement in the city. Anna Carla has crossed an invisible boundary and instinctively rushes back, because this is no place for a woman to go alone. The periphery emerges again as impersonal and soulless, a place where it is easy to become lost and which is potentially dangerous, especially for women.

In order to find a periphery that is genuinely frightening, however, we must turn to Scerbanenco's Lamberti novels. As Foot has pointed out, the Milanese periphery has outgrown the city centre since the boom years.[99] In the 1950s and 1960s several new neighbourhoods, such as Comasina, Quarto Oggiaro, Gratosoglio and Gallaratese, were developed to accommodate the hundreds of thousands of unskilled immigrant workers who moved to Milan in those years. These modern peripheries were an addition to the older ones that had developed during the first industrial revolution of the early 1900s. Already in the 1950s Milan's municipal boundaries stretched from Monza in the North to Pavia in the South.[100] Some of the newly developed suburbs became soon infamous as crime-ridden areas and ghettos for Southern immigrants, especially Comasina and Quarto Oggiaro in Milan and La Falchera, Mirafiori Sud and Le Vallette in

99   Foot, *Milan since the Miracle*, p. 5.
100   Foot, *Milan since the Miracle*, p. 5

Turin.[101] It is easy to see how these areas, which became associated with poverty, marginalization and crime, fuelled the imagination of the writers who in those years were writing about crime and the city.

While Scerbanenco makes no real distinction between the city centre and peripheries, for in his novels these are equally unsafe, it is true that the suburbs enable criminals to act more discreetly and to escape the city more easily if necessary.[102] To put it simply, what happens in the periphery is less traceable. In *I ragazzi del massacro* Duca refuses to believe that the students who have killed their teacher Matilde have done so because they were after some fun or were driven by some uncontrollable impulse. He rejects this idea on the basis of the fact that 'da piazzale Loreto al Parco Lambro hanno tutti i posti che vogliono per organizzare certe festine senza correre quasi nessun pericolo di essere presi' [from the Piazzale Loreto to Parco Lambro they have all the places they want to organize certain parties without running any appreciable danger of being caught].[103] In other words, these students, who come from deprived, unsafe urban areas (Parco Lambro in particular being a historical hot spot for drug-dealing),[104] may find other ways to vent their impulses. Duca believes they have been spurred on by someone else, most likely an adult with a proper motive. We know that he is right and that Marisela Domenici masterminded the murder plot. While the periphery affords more opportunities for illicit activities, it also allows criminals to keep a strong connection with the wider city thanks to the enhanced road networks. Maintaining this connection is crucial, for a limited access to the resources offered by the city means less business and a higher risk of being caught. This is why, in *I ragazzi del massacro*, Duca is able to figure out that Marisella and Carolino (the student she has kidnapped) must be hidden somewhere in the periphery or in some place not far from Milan:

> Un rifugio come questo, non esiste in una città, al massimo alla sua estrema periferia, molto più facilmente in campagna, anche vicino alla città, ma non in un paese, un paese piccolo è il luogo più pericoloso che esista per nascondersi.[105]

---

101   Foot, *Milan since the Miracle*, p. 40.

102   As Pieri comments, 'the lumpenproletarian zones of the city are captured by Scerbanenco as they shift from the city centre to the new peripheries, which became the perfect setting for the new violent and often pointless crimes of the new industrial city' (Pieri, 'Milano nera', p. 134).

103   Scerbanenco, *Ragazzi*, p. 81.

104   Vincenzo Ruggiero and Nigel South, *Eurodrugs: Drug Use, Markets and Trafficking in Europe* (London: Routledge, 2016 [1995]), p. 76.

105   Scerbanenco, *Ragazzi*, p. 195.

[A hiding-place like this does not exist in a city, at best on its extreme periphery, but much more easily in the countryside, perhaps also close to the city, but not in a village, a small village is the most dangerous place to hide.]

The issue of the social and anthropological implications of economic change comes to the fore more starkly with the characters who come from the suburbs as areas that have allegedly failed to forge a positive sense of community and identity.[106] The students of *I ragazzi del massacro* come from socially disadvantaged families who live in the peripheral areas of Milan. The files that Duca examines at the police headquarters on the night of the interrogation contain detailed information about their family situations, with parents who are alcoholics, drug addicts or at best simply neglectful. That being said, Scerbanenco also restores aesthetic dignity to the periphery as a privileged setting for his crime stories. In *Traditori di tutti*, for example, one reads that 'Ca' Tarino fa parte di Romano Banco, che è una frazione di Buccinasco, che è un comune vicino a Corsico, che è vicino a Milano, praticamente è sempre Milano' [Ca' Tarino is an area of Romano Banco, which is part of the commune of Buccinasco, adjoining that of Corsico. Both are outlying suburbs of Milan. Corsico, indeed, is almost an integral part of Milan] (*TT*, p. 148; *DM*, p. 132). Scerbanenco recognizes the periphery as integral to Milan's identity and in this sense rejects a superficial binary opposition between centre and periphery.

Like Bianciardi and Volponi, Scerbanenco and Fruttero & Lucentini document the difficulty of apprehending dramatic social and spatial transformations. They do so by focusing on aspects of the built environment that evoke feelings of disorientation and bewilderment. Scerbanenco depicts an urban landscape of deserted streets, anonymous buildings and places that appear distorted in the darkness of the night. These urban descriptions convey social disorientation in the Milan of the boom and hint at the shortcomings of the post-war development strategy in tackling the collective dimension of socio-economic changes. The rise of mindless violence on the streets of Milan, which most directly affects the urban poor and more vulnerable, is a further indication that these people have been failed by economic growth. Scerbanenco's Milan is dark and violent. His Lamberti novels accentuate the sensation of unease through problematic endings, a feature which seemingly questions the very

---

106   Foot, *Milan since the Miracle*, p. 137.

possibility of enduring social justice. Fruttero & Lucentini's Turin is ambiguous and deceptive, familiar and yet strange. In both *La donna della domenica* and *A che punto è la notte* the multiple perspectives brought by characters who are inspired by real Turinese types form a composite picture of the changing urban landscape in the 1970s.

Urban space becomes the locus where feelings of anxiety and lack of direction are projected. The writers bring to the fore the enigmatic, unfathomable aspects of urban space which reveal a darker side to the process of modernization, its contradictions beyond the reassuring narrative of progress. The notion of the uncanny helps, on the one hand, to illuminate the issue of rapid changes that affect customary ways of life, shifting the boundaries of the familiar and unfamiliar; on the other, it helps to shed further light on Italy's unresolved past. In the analysis in this chapter the theme of the past emerges in different ways: for example, through its negation in Scerbanenco's portrayal of a Milan of the present, almost completely devoid of references to the past, and through the conflict between old and new Turin in *La donna della domenica*. This conflict is perfectly embodied by the figure of Tabusso: a wealthy aristocratic woman whose declining fortune tells us that she is about to make room for younger, more dynamic social figures. The perception of urbanization and industrialization as rupture is revealing of controversial attitudes towards the past more broadly. In *A che punto è la notte* modern and traditional values clash in the descriptions of the bleak suburban setting where recently built housing developments look dilapidated and underused, familiar urban features have grown fainter and it is easy to feel disoriented and lose one's way. In these descriptions one may perceive the nostalgia for more traditional urban models.

This chapter then explores the link between rapid urbanization and the evolution of crime by providing examples of how, in the selected writings, crime mirrors the growth of the city and follows the geography of industrialization. Particular attention is given to the representation of the periphery as a geographical and anthropological entity that occupies a specific uncanny and eerie imagery. The novels of Scerbanenco and Fruttero & Lucentini generally represent the suburbs as desolate and architecturally unpleasant, places that have failed to forge a sense of community and where criminality may take root more easily. In the Lamberti novels city centre and peripheries are equally dangerous but, in the latter, the negative aspects of urbanization are somehow exacerbated. In Fruttero & Lucentini's novels, and especially in *A che punto è la notte*, the periphery lacks history, identity and coherence with the rest of the city. As seen above, the idea of the periphery as a place that does not meet certain standards of good living and is potentially dangerous is generally measured against a hegemonic and ideal model of the city. The periphery is, in fact, a relative concept: on the one hand, it is constantly being reshaped and, on the other, it is defined subjectively. For instance, for the rich Anna Carla, who enjoys a privileged position in Turin's urban society, the periphery is what lies just outside her elegant neighbourhood. The periphery is also potentially more dangerous for her as a woman. By establishing it as the setting where their stories unfold, Scerbanenco and Fruttero & Lucentini assign equal dignity to centre and periphery, even though the representation of the latter is not devoid of stereotypes.

While Milan and Turin share some significant traits as major hubs of the so-called Northern Industrial Triangle, comprising Lombardy, Piedmont, and Genoa, in the novels examined in this chapter they are different in terms of the types of crime that are committed and the criminals who operate within their territory. Milan is arguably the most cosmopolitan of Italian cities, has historically filtered innovations from abroad and has been at the centre of the main historical movements and events of twentieth-century Italy, constantly re-inventing itself.[107] Milan is a city that has traditionally taken pride in its hard-working mentality or, as John Foot puts it, the 'American qualities of dynamism, profit and attraction'.[108] It seems, therefore, apt for Scerbanenco to draw on the tradition of the American hard-boiled to portray an urban environment in which the culture of personal gain has won the upper hand over human compassion and solidarity and violence is commonplace. Luca Crovi refers to this as the mythology of murder 'Milanese-style'.[109] In comparison to Milan, Turin is seemingly more inward-looking and conservative. This does not come as a surprise, since the identity of Turin has largely been shaped by the presence of the Italian monarchy and subsequently of the Italian flagship car manufacturer Fiat. The overall picture is, of course, more complex. Robert Lumley, for instance, points out that in post-war Turin urbanization and industrialization led to a more cosmopolitan cultural society and a greater interest in innovation.[110] Nevertheless, it may be argued that Turin's more pronounced resistance to change, compared to Milan, is reflected in Fruttero &

107 Foot, *Milan since the Miracle*, p. 3.

108 Foot, *Milan since the Miracle*, p. 4.

109 Crovi, *Tutti i colori del giallo*, p. 106.

110 Robert Lumley, 'Turin after Arte Povera: A New City of Art?', in *Italian Cityscapes*, ed. by Lumley and Foot, pp. 100–13 (p. 102).

Lucentini's kind of locked-room murder and in criminal intrigues which are hatched within the upper-class environment, as in the example of *La donna della domenica*. The novels by Scerbanenco and Fruttero & Lucentini lend themselves to an analysis of the differences between the *noir* and the traditional detective story, two sub-genres of the crime fiction tradition. It has been pointed out, for instance, that the traditional *giallo* is more conventional in its displaying of the detective's investigation that leads up to the solution of the case, while the *noir* shakes up established norms by giving a complex representation of reality and by rejecting the happy ending or final restoration of order.[111]

---

111   Vermandere, Jansen and Lanslots, 'Introduzione', pp. 9–10. Righini has pointed out that the *giallo* may also be considered to be more 'static' in that the space in which the events unfold is usually smaller and subject to definite limits (Righini, 'Città degli incubi', p. 143).

3. The Northern Italian Province in Natalia Ginzburg's *Le voci della sera*

Introduction: The Idea of Province

Many works of literature produced in the time period under scrutiny here, such as the ones examined in the previous two chapters of this book, may fall under the rubric of urban fiction, since they are inextricably tied to the city in which they are set. On the one hand, as we have seen, this points to the fact that the process of post-war urbanization captures the imagination of Italian writers and provides them with the material for their books; on the other, it reminds us that historically big cities have attracted writers and artists, providing a fruitful environment for them to establish connections and aspire to recognition and success in their chosen field. Nevertheless, there also exists a longstanding, fecund tradition of works of literature and art which gravitate to the rural, provincial and small-town environment and make the unique kind of atmosphere and experiences evoked by these territories into their stylistic hallmark. In the European literary tradition this strand is arguably best epitomized by nineteenth-century writers such as Gustave Flaubert, Honoré de Balzac, Marcel Proust and Franz Kafka,[1] whose works revolve around the province or feature young, ambitious characters who come from small-town and rural realities and project their aspirations onto the big city, pursuing the possibilities of social advancement and redemption that the metropolis seems to afford. It is interesting to note that even these prototypical novels inspired by provincial life tend to reproduce the dichotomy between the provinces, often a point of departure, and the

---

1   Marina Spunta, 'Escaping the World and Returning to the "Province" in Claudio Piersanti's Fiction', in *The Poetics of the Margins: Mapping Europe from the Interstices*, ed. by Rossella Riccobono, Cultural Identity Studies (Oxford: Lang, 2010), pp. 33–53 (p. 52).

city as a real or imaginative destination which evokes promises of success and salvation. Italy, too, has developed a tradition of literary works that are tinged with the peculiar nuances of provincial life: the mixture of melancholic, sentimental yearning for this intimate and allegedly authentic world and the sense of non-belonging, which is exacerbated by the more conservative, conventional mindset that one may often find in small-town environments. Amongst the Italian authors who have engaged with the *provincia* in the period examined in this book, one may recall Goffredo Parise, Piero Chiara, Lucio Mastronardi and Natalia Ginzburg. It is precisely on Ginzburg that this chapter will focus.

It is useful, first of all, to ask ourselves what we mean by 'provinces'. The term itself was born in, and is still associated with, the colonial context: in ancient Rome it indicated the Empire's possessions outside Italy.[2] *Provincia* therefore indicates a territory that is secondary and peripheral in relation to a more powerful centre, upon which it depends politically and economically and which is also considered culturally dominant, as it claims to define the fashions and values of a given time. Against this broad backdrop it is important also to bear in mind that in its modern specification the notion of 'province' takes on specific meanings in different national contexts.[3] In Italy, moreover, *provincia* is technically an administrative division into which regions are organized. Whatever the differences and variations, at the core of the notion of the province there is always a hierarchical way of seeing and conceptualizing the Other. This analysis privileges precisely the socio-cultural implications of the *provincia* meant in this way. In the Italian context, *provincia*, and particularly the adjective *provinciale* denoting villages, small towns and their inhabitants, commonly carry a derogatory nuance, 'with associations of backwardness and insularity'.[4] When someone is described as a *provinciale*, this generally entails a judgement of that person as simpleminded, perhaps slightly uneducated, naïve and generally not versed in the ways of the world. One reason for these enduring stereotypes may be that, generally speaking, change happens more slowly in the provinces. While one

---

2   Ceserani, 'Dalla piccola città', p. 3.

3   Marcello Flores points out that in England provincialism does not refer to a sense of geographical distance from London or other main cities, but rather to social and cultural backwardness, by identifying those groups of people and places (working-class neighbourhoods as opposed to the countryside and small towns and villages) which are provincial in the sense that they stand opposite to the lifestyle and social conditions of the conservative elite (Flores, 'La provincia', p. 14).

4   Spunta, 'Escaping the World', p. 34. See also Ceserani, 'Dalla piccola città', p. 4.

should avoid simplistic oppositions, especially in the era of mass communication, in which places are much more interconnected than in the past, the province still remains somewhat peripheral to the cultural ferment of the big city. According to Carl Amery, the delay in assimilating changes may be explained by the fact that in small-town environments social conventions are more fixed and difficult to modify and people tend to belong to roughly the same social groups for their entire lives, whereas in big metropolitan areas these kinds of affiliation are more fluid and fleeting.[5]

In order to interrogate the extent to which post-war socio-spatial changes are perceived and conceptualized in the *provincia*, and therefore to give a more comprehensive picture of the post-war development in Italy, this chapter will switch the focus of the analysis from the urban novels discussed thus far to a work that presents a provincial setting, specifically, Natalia Ginzburg's *Le voci della sera*, written in 1961 and set in a small town in Northern Italy. As discussed below, the exact place name of the town is not given and, in a side note at the beginning of the book, Ginzburg actually warns the readers that the places and characters portrayed in the novel are fictional. Nevertheless, the presence of other toponyms and geographical features clearly points to the Piedmontese countryside near Turin, that is, to the places of Ginzburg's childhood, as the author herself confessed in a later interview.[6] The analysis of *Le voci della sera* will be complemented by some incursions into other novels by Ginzburg, chiefly *Lessico famigliare* [*Family Lexicon*] (1963), as well as into Lucio Mastronardi's *Il maestro di Vigevano* [*The Teacher of Vigevano*] (1962), which provides some useful points of comparison to enrich the discussion in this chapter.

Central to Ginzburg's oeuvre – and *Le voci della sera* is no exception – is family life. Her books narrate minutely how the lives of the members of a family and their relationships to one another evolve over the course of the story, which in *Le voci della sera* spans two generations. In *Lessico famigliare* Ginzburg recounts the story of her own family. Here, peculiar idiomatic words and expressions that make up the

---

5   Carl Amery, 'La provincia come categoria sociologica', *L'Asino d'oro*, 1 (1990), 21–28 (pp. 23–24).

6   Ginzburg was born in Palermo, where her father was a university lecturer, and moved with her family to Turin at the age of three. She lived in Turin until 1952, when she moved to Rome to live with her second husband, Gabriele Baldini. At a later stage Ginzburg herself confessed that those locations portrayed in *Le voci della sera* are the places of her childhood in the Piedmontese countryside. See Elena Clementelli, *Invito alla lettura di Natalia Ginzburg* (Milan: Mursia, 1986), pp. 75–76.

titular family lexicon provide a sort of secret code shared by the members of the family, one which bonds them by identifying them as members of that particular affective microcosm and by activating memories relating to the family environment. Much like *Le voci della sera*, *Lessico famigliare* spans the decades which go from the author's childhood to the end of the Second World War and the post-war years until the beginning of the 1960s. While *Le voci della sera* presents some of the themes and motifs that recur in Ginzburg's oeuvre as a whole, it may be argued that these are somehow intensified, in particular the ultimate insufficiency of human relationships, the loneliness that arguably contradicts the idea of the small town as a safe, comforting place and the oppressiveness of conventions that seem more difficult to overcome in a provincial environment. It is interesting to reflect on how the provincial setting affects, influences and shapes such themes addressed in the book. In this regard, it is also useful to question the notion of margin and the related preconceived ideas which have been associated with the province as a territory that is peripheral to the real centres of political, economic and cultural power. It is worth noting that in Italy this idea also applies nationwide to the North–South divide. This is discussed in the next chapter, where enduring representations of the Italian South as subaltern are explored.

The Italian provinces therefore encompass territories that have more often than not been deemed marginal in geographical, economic and cultural terms.[7] Such definitions are clearly given in relation to and, crucially, from the point of view of a legitimized centre, which in the Italian context may be identified with the wealthy urban society of the North and the capital Rome, that is, the hubs of political and economic institutions, as well as of the media and communication industries that have become increasingly influential since the 1950s. David Forgacs has shown that the rhetoric of the margin as a spatial and cultural category has been central to the construction of the Italian nation and identity since the unification of the country in 1861.[8] While this may be true for all modern nations, there are some peculiarities pertaining specifically to the Italian case. The so-called

7   As Spunta puts it, the *provincia* 'is normally seen as synonymous with marginal, minor, peripheral – both spatially and culturally' (Spunta, 'Escaping the World', p. 34).

8   David Forgacs, *Italy's Margins: Social Exclusion and Nation Formation since 1861*, Cambridge Social and Cultural Histories (Cambridge: Cambridge University Press, 2014), p. 1. Forgacs argues that 'margins are not simply there, like a fact of nature. They are produced by particular ways of seeing and organizing social space' (Forgacs, *Italy's Margins*, p. 1).

Southern Question, for instance, refers to a complex set of socio-economic circumstances and processes that have unfolded through the centuries. Born within the Italian post-Unification context, this notion revolves around the perception of persistent backwardness and poverty in the South, which are deemed responsible for widespread organized crime and political clientelism in the region. It is clearly a notion that reflects the point of view of the dominant classes in the North. Moreover, while the South may be the most blatant example of cultural and geographical marginalization within the Italian context, other areas of the country have also traditionally been regarded as peripheral in relation to the major industrial centres of the North. This is the case, for example, for the rural areas of the North-East, whose main contribution to the economic growth of the post-war years was to supply large numbers of unskilled, cheap workers to the cities of the Industrial Triangle.[9] The focusing of the lens of our investigation on provincial and 'peripheral' areas across the Italian Peninsula is therefore crucial in helping us to illuminate and unravel discursive practices that have shaped the divide between modern and traditional, centre and margin, relevant and less relevant in post-war Italian society.

In so doing, it is also important to bear in mind that, quite paradoxically, the *provincia* is very central to Italian national identity, to the point where some argue that it best epitomizes the Italian character. This is due to the history of the Italian nation, the delayed achievement of its territorial unity and therefore to the patchwork of urban centres which for centuries, all across the Peninsula, have exercised institutional power over their jurisdiction. As Carl Levy points out, '[s]ince the Italian nation-state was a relatively recent development, arising from the fortuitous combination of European diplomacy, Piedmontese initiative and nationalist conspiracy, older varieties of vibrant localistic or regional identities were suppressed but never completely eradicated'.[10] The creation of the Italian nation-state reflected the rational, deliberate calculation of the Piedmontese elite; it was not the expression of the heartfelt desire of all Italians for a unified nation. Quite the contrary, local interests and identities were

---

9 Forgacs, *Italy's Margins*, p. 2. Ginsborg reports that 'in the period 1955–61, the Veneto lost over 237,000 of its inhabitants, mainly to the industrial cities of Lombardy and Piedmont. No other region, not even those of the South, suffered so great an exodus in these years' (Ginsborg, *A History of Contemporary Italy*, p. 233).

10 Carl Levy, 'Introduction: Italian Regionalism in Context', in *Italian Regionalism: History, Identity and Politics*, ed. by Carl Levy (Oxford: Berg, 1996), pp. 1–30 (p. 3).

safeguarded and continued to provide a greater sense of belonging even after the unification of the country had been achieved. Hence, if we look at the Italian *provincia* through the lens of repression, which is a central thread in this work, we may find that the preconceived, derogatory notions commonly associated with it simply conceal the very centrality of provincialism in the Italian national character. Present-day Italy is still largely characterized by local and regional affiliations;[11] arguably, this situation was all the more noticeable in the post-war years, when the unification of the country was still a relatively recent achievement and Italy had just come out of a civil war.

It may seem obvious to claim that provincial cities did not partake with the same intensity in the post-war process of modernization that we have seen taking hold more immediately and noticeably in the major Italian cities, perhaps more dramatically in Milan. The rest of the country certainly underwent substantial transformations, too: villages and towns were not left untouched by the wave of modernization but they did not undergo an equal renewal, at least architectonically, although in many cases they still expanded at the expense of the surrounding countryside. Nevertheless, with the diffusion of the radio and, even more, of television from the middle of the 1950s onwards, which gradually reached into every corner of Italian society, there was potentially no home, street or neighbourhood across the country which was left unaware of the social and economic revolution that was underway. Television projected glittering images documenting the wealthier, more comfortable standard of living enjoyed by urban dwellers of the North, which proved particularly alluring to the people living in the South and in other, less industrialized areas of the Peninsula.[12] Commenting on this new interconnectivity between places, in *Se una notte d'inverno un viaggiatore* (1979) Calvino writes:

> Non ci sono più città di provincia e forse non ci sono mai state: tutti i luoghi comunicano con tutti i luoghi istantaneamente, il senso d'isolamento lo si prova soltanto durante il tragitto da un luogo all'altro, cioè quando non si è in nessun luogo.[13]

---

11   Spunta, 'Escaping the World', p. 41.

12   Paul Ginsborg writes that 'for the young, who were to constitute the majority of the first migrants [to the North], the lure of the city was irresistible. In the evenings, in the piazzas of the southern villages, their talk was of nothing else. The television of the local bar transmitted images from the North, images of a consumer world, of Vespas, portable radios, football heroes, new fashions, nylon stockings, mass-produced dresses, houses full of electrical appliances, Sunday excursions in the family FIAT' (Ginsborg, *A History of Contemporary Italy*, pp. 221–22).

13   Italo Calvino, *Se una notte d'inverno un viaggiatore* (Turin: Einaudi, 1979), p. 17.

[It is all very well for me to tell myself there are no provincial cities any more and perhaps there never were any: all places communicate instantly with all other places, a sense of isolation is felt only during the trip between one place and the other, that is, when you are in no place.][14]

Prefiguring the hyper-connectivity of today's world, Calvino argues that there is no such thing as a provincial town, since in our networked age all places are ultimately linked to one another through the continuous flow of information and the physical movement of people for work or leisure. In this context, the sites of transit that guarantee such interconnectedness acquire a particular prominence.

Crucially, the boom was not merely a metropolitan phenomenon. As Paul Ginsborg notes:

> The geographical location of Italy's industrial production expanded beyond the narrow confines of the Industrial Triangle. If Lombardy and Piedmont still remained the epicentres, industrial Italy now spread southwards towards Bologna and eastwards along the whole of the Val Padana, to reach the Adriatic at Porto Marghera and Ravenna.[15]

This model of 'diffused industrialization' meant that several industries developed outside the leading economic centres of Lombardy and Piedmont. These industrial districts usually specialized in a specific trade and linked a city with the surrounding countryside.[16] Small but economically dynamic centres helped to propel post-war economic development, thanks especially to the presence of firms operating in traditional fields of production, which in those years became increasingly profitable due to the expansion of the market both at home, with the accrued purchasing power of larger sections of the Italian population, and abroad.[17] The relatively small-scale

---

14 Italo Calvino, *If on a Winter's Night a Traveller*, trans. by William Weaver (London: Vintage, 2002 [1981]), p. 17.

15 Ginsborg, *A History of Contemporary Italy*, pp. 215–16.

16 As Ginsborg writes, 'the terms "diffused industrialization" (*industrializzazione diffusa*) and the "urbanized countryside" (*la campagna urbanizzata*) became widely employed to describe this model of economic growth. City and countryside were linked in industrial districts, usually specializing in a single field of production: textiles at Prato, ceramics at Sassuolo, hosiery at Carpi, footwear at Ascoli Piceno, and so on. The dynamic growth of these districts began with the "economic miracle" but was only to reach its apogee in the 1970s' (Ginsborg, *A History of Contemporary Italy*, p. 234).

17 This type of economy, centred on small firms and workshops, mainly trading in traditional manufacturing sectors such as clothing, textiles, footwear, metalwork, leather goods and furniture, is typical of the so-called 'Third Italy',

production of high-quality products favoured by many of these firms contributed to creating the 'Made in Italy' label as a synonym for luxury fashion, design and exclusivity. An example is the shoe-making industry in Vigevano, portrayed by Lucio Mastronardi in his trilogy of novels *Il calzolaio di Vigevano* [*The Shoemaker of Vigevano*] (1959), *Il maestro di Vigevano* [*The Teacher of Vigevano*] (1962) and *Il meridionale di Vigevano* [*The Southerner of Vigevano*] (1964), although at the time in which he wrote the industry was still largely labour-intensive, poorly equipped and reliant on the entrepreneurial skills and initiative of single individuals.[18] A further point to consider is that industrial plants are often located outside metropolitan areas, in their hinterland or in areas which are convenient for the proximity of road and communication links and this was also the case with some of the new factories that sprang up as a result of the economic boom of the late 1950s. Major steelworks and petro-chemical plants were located in the South in an effort to create new jobs in traditionally deprived territories, although these attempts had controversial results or proved to be entirely vain in that they did not foster local development.[19]

The sense of economic dynamism and increased wellbeing could not be felt in the same way everywhere in provincial Italy, not only in the South, but in the richer North itself. Some rural areas of Lombardy, Piedmont and the Veneto remained economically deprived.[20] Post-war Italian cinema has engaged directly with this somewhat forgotten, or deliberately concealed, side of the Northern provinces. The number of regional documentaries that were

---

which comprises the Centre and North-East of the country. It represents an 'industrialization [...] very distinct from that taking place in the great centres of Lombardy and Piedmont. With one or two notable exceptions, like Porto Marghera and Ravenna, it was characterized by small firms employing less than fifty people – and often less than twenty' (Ginsborg, *A History of Contemporary Italy*, p. 234).

18   As described, e.g., in *Il maestro di Vigevano*. This is even more the case in *Il calzolaio di Vigevano*, set in the pre-war and war years, in which the main characters are all employed in the shoe industry, work extremely long hours and live in very modest conditions.

19   This was partly due to the phenomenon of clientelism that often determined the areas in which such industrial plants were to be built. Moreover, the fact that they were more 'capital- than labour-intensive industries' ended up contributing very little to the economic development of the surrounding areas (Ginsborg, *A History of Contemporary Italy*, p. 230).

20   Ginsborg, *A History of Contemporary Italy*, p. 233.

produced in those years bears witness to the fact that, perhaps for the first time, huge numbers of Italians from all over the Peninsula came into contact and therefore became more familiar with regional differences, as we shall also see in the next chapter, which examines post-war Italian travel writing. Through the analysis of some of these regional documentaries Clarissa Clò argues that the connections and similarities between the North and South of Italy at the time have often been overlooked. More specifically, Clò shows how these documentaries were often censored by the post-war Christian Democrat governments (in a way that was eerily reminiscent of the efforts of the Fascist regime to suppress minorities and marginal voices in order to homogenize the country), for they conveyed an unfavourable and detrimental image of the North, its peripheries and poorer areas, an image that was not consistent with the idea which official propaganda sought to consolidate of this part of Italy, namely of an area rapidly transforming into one of the most advanced regions in Europe.[21] More or less hidden pockets of poverty continued to exist in communities throughout the country. New forms of urban poverty and precariousness in the rich Northern cities are well documented in Bianciardi's *La vita agra*, as is seen in Chapter 1.

The following analysis focuses on how the issues and controversies connected with the multifaceted notion of *provincia* discussed in this introduction come into play in Ginzburg's *Le voci della sera*. It does so by concentrating on three major themes which emerge from the book: that is, the city–province dichotomy, social norms and conventions (with a special focus on gender) and, finally, human relationships. The 'spatial relevance' of the analysis is perhaps more evident with the first of the three topics. The two remaining themes will, however, also be discussed from a spatial perspective to establish how the provincial environment in which the story is set interacts with socially codified attitudes and (gender) stereotypes on the one hand and with the more intimate, emotional dimension of human connections on the other.

City and Province in *Le voci della sera*: A Contextualization

It is widely known, not least because it is also told in *Lessico famigliare*, that Ginzburg belonged to the group of intellectuals who founded the Einaudi Publishing House in Turin, a group which included the

21   Clò, 'Visions of Italy', pp. 49–50.

likes of Cesare Pavese, a friend of Ginzburg's, and her first husband, Leone Ginzburg. She was, therefore, connected with the most prominent figures on the Turinese literary and cultural scene and one might argue that she was herself a clear example of an 'urban intellectual'. Ginzburg lived practically all her life in major cultural centres: Turin as a child and then an adult, becoming a protagonist in the thriving intellectual community gravitating towards Einaudi and subsequently Rome and London, where she moved to follow her second husband, the literary critic Gabriele Baldini. Hence the fact that she chose to set *Le voci della sera* in a provincial, tranquil and rather uneventful setting is all the more notable. Whilst the author's side note at the beginning of the book warns that 'in questo racconto, i luoghi e i personaggi sono immaginari. Gli uni non si trovano sulla carta geografica, gli altri non vivono, né sono mai vissuti, in nessuna parte del mondo' [the places and characters in this story are imaginary. The first are not found on any map, the others are not alive, nor have ever lived, in any part of the world], one may easily detect in these places, as in the characters' regular excursions to the nearby city, the Piedmontese countryside and Turin itself. An important clue is, of course, the fact that memory and real-life experiences are major sources of inspiration in Ginzburg's oeuvre, the clearest example arguably being *Lessico famigliare*, which builds on the themes and on the family ambiance of *Le voci della sera*.[22] The choice of not providing a name for the town at the centre of the latter novel may also suggest that Ginzburg intends to render the experience of the characters in the story universal, relatable to anyone living in the similar provincial centres that are so commonly found in Italy. Ginzburg does, however, mention the names of other nearby places, such as Castello, Cignano and Borgo Martino. These, again, are fairly common, standard toponyms that may potentially be found elsewhere in Italy and have the effect of activating a shared experience which allows Italian readers to empathize with the characters in the novel and shape a sufficiently accurate image of those places in their imagination.

---

22   In this regard, Luigi Fontanella writes that 'while in *VS* places and characters were fictitious yet always filtered through Ginzburg's biography, here in *LF* they become equipped with their own names. The whole contributes to form a narrative orchestration permeated by *nostalgia and fiction*: the binomial that is at the root of Ginzburg's narrative canon in these texts' (Luigi Fontanella, 'Natalia Ginzburg Between Fiction and Memory: A Reading of *Le voci della sera* and *Lessico famigliare*', in *Natalia Ginzburg: A Voice of the Twentieth Century*, ed. by Angela M. Jeannet and Giuliana Sanguinetti Katz, Toronto Italian Studies (Toronto: University of Toronto Press, 2016), pp. 32–45 (p. 37)).

The novel centres on the vicissitudes of the De Francisci family, a well-off, yet modest and reserved family, whose ups and downs intertwine with those of the other characters who live in the same provincial town, including Elsa, the young female narrator of the story. The figure of the female narrator recurs in other novels by Ginzburg and appears in many ways to be an alter ego of the author. Before the war De Francisci father, who is nicknamed Balotta, started from scratch a textile-manufacturing plant that went on to become very profitable, making him rich. Despite profits continuing to grow and Balotta becoming a sort of reference point within the local community, where he is regarded with respect and admiration, the De Francisci remain true to their humble origins and reject a wealthier lifestyle. This sober way of living – family meals are unpretentious, consisting of simple ingredients, and the De Francisci children have a limited wardrobe of clothes that are regularly mended – is consistent with Balotta's political views. A Socialist who remains coherent with his beliefs throughout the Fascist regime and Second World War, Balotta is reminiscent of Ginzburg's father, himself a promoter of an austere lifestyle as well as a Socialist who helped some of those, like Filippo Turati, who were persecuted by the Fascist dictatorship by hiding them in his house. The example of Balotta, moreover, reminds us of the trajectory of another prominent Italian industrial family, the Olivetti, family friends of Ginzburg's (Adriano Olivetti married her sister) and major protagonists in the post-war economic growth, who championed progressive, humane reforms in Italian industry. Balotta and his wife Cecilia have five children – Vincenzino, Mario, Gemmina, Raffaella and Tommasino (if one wanted to draw further analogies with Ginzburg's biography, one should recall that she had the same number of siblings) – and have also raised a distant orphan relative of theirs, Fausto, who becomes known to everyone as 'Purillo' because of the type of hat, a beret, that he invariably wears.[23] During the course of the story, which spans the pre- and post-Second World War years, the De Francisci interact with other characters, who in turn take centre stage in this scene of provincial life and whose personality traits take shape gradually through the minute description of their activities, mental processes and nuanced emotions, which are skilfully captured by Ginzburg. Up to a certain point in the novel, the reader is led to believe that the female narrator, Elsa, is external with regard to the narrated facts, embodying a seemingly omniscient narrator who observes and reports back in a neutral, unbiased way.

---

23   In Northern Italian dialect, *purillo* is the short strip of stiff cloth sewn in the middle of a beret. By extension, in the novel it indicates the type of hat itself.

As in a sort of coup de théâtre, however, we soon discover that she is also very much a part of the story and that she is in a relationship (which is initially kept secret) with the youngest of the De Francisci siblings, Tommasino.

Elsa and Tommasino meet secretly in the city, where Tommasino has rented a pied-à-terre. As mentioned, it is not specified which city this is, but from a number of clues we can guess that it is Turin. For instance, in the following description of one of the regular walks Elsa and Tommasino take when they meet up in the city, the park with the castle and the river that flows alongside it undeniably remind us of the Parco del Valentino, with its namesake *castello* and the River Po, which runs along the park's eastern side. The quietly flowing river provides a counterpart to Tommasino's taciturn disposition, as we apprehend that he is prone to gloomy states of mind:

> Camminiamo interminabilmente, in silenzio, nel parco, sul fiume. Ci sediamo su una panchina; c'è dietro a noi, nel mezzo del parco, il castello, con le sue torrette rosse, le guglie, e il ponte levatoio: e da un lato la veranda a vetri del ristorante, deserta a quell'ora, ma con due camerieri che aspettano ugualmente fra i tavoli, col tovagliolo sotto il braccio. E c'è il fiume, davanti a noi, silenzioso, con le sue acque verdi, con le barche legate alla riva, col casotto dell'imbarcatoio piantato su palafitte, la scaletta di legno dove batton le onde. (*VS*, p. 739)

> [We walked interminably, in silence, in the park, along the river. We would sit down on a bench; behind us in the middle of the park was the castle with its red turrets and spires and the drawbridge: and on the side there was the glassed-in veranda of the restaurant, deserted at that hour: two waiters would be there expectantly all the same, among the tables, with napkins under their arms. There was the silent river in front of us, with its green waters, and the boats moored to the bank, the shelter of the landing-stage built on piles, the wooden steps against which the waves lapped.] (*VE*, pp. 113–14)

Since initially Elsa and Tommasino are unwilling to disclose their relationship, Elsa explains her frequent trips to the city with the various errands that she actually runs for her parents and her Aunt Ottavia, an avid reader who finishes at least one book per week and always requires new ones from the 'Selecta' public library in the city. Initially, the reader is therefore led to believe that these chores are the only reason Elsa goes to the city twice a week; that she also sees Tommasino when she is there is revealed only later in the book. Since these very first allusions to her city escapes, however, it seems clear that Elsa enjoys these trips also, and perhaps primarily, as a welcome change, a way to leave behind the mundane preoccupations and routine of small-town life, albeit only temporarily. Another clue that she has always been curious to explore the world beyond her hometown is the fact that she attended university and graduated in Italian Literature in the city (a further resemblance to the author, since Ginzburg did indeed enrol in the *Facoltà di Lettere* in Turin, though she never graduated). After completing her studies, Elsa returns to her hometown and seemingly blends in with the rituals of provincial life again, performing what is expected of her. Nevertheless, her aloofness and the general reserve she maintains in her interactions with other characters in the novel suggest uneasiness and dissatisfaction, the fact that she believes there must be more to life. Whether this 'certain something' may be found somewhere in her own environment, in the big city or elsewhere completely remains unanswered in a book that generally exposes and debunks the illusions nursed by its characters.

In the city Elsa and Tommasino walk for long hours, sometimes reaching the peripheries where the city blends into the countryside. On such occasions it looks as if the appeal of home, albeit controversially, remains strong for them, like a sort of umbilical cord that has not been entirely severed or a mysterious force that pulls them back: 'Camminiamo, interminabilmente, sul fiume. Lui si guarda intorno, dice: – Ma qui è proprio campagna. Veniamo in città, ma poi andiamo sempre in cerca della campagna, non è così?' [We walked interminably by the river. He looked about him and said, 'But this is quite country. We come to the town, and then we always go to look for the country, is it not so?'] (*VS*, p. 739; *VE*, p. 114). After Elsa and Tommasino officialize their relationship and he becomes a regular guest at her parents' house, the two continue to go for their walks. Now that they are an officially engaged couple and can, therefore, be seen together (a sign of the fairly rigid conventions that prevail in this provincial milieu, which are examined more closely later in the chapter), they do not need to hide in the city anymore but can opt for walks in the nearby countryside. Tommasino compares these walks to the urban ones they used to enjoy and praises the beauty of this rural scenery against the constrained green that nevertheless provides a valuable respite in urban environments: 'Andavamo, io e il Tommasino, a passeggio per la campagna. [...] È più bello qui che al parco. Abbiamo fatto tante camminate, per quel parco, per la città. E invece era più bello qui, no?' [Tommasino and I used to go for walks in the country. [...] It is nicer here than in the park. We have had so many walks in the park and through the town. In contrast it is nicer here. Yes? No?] (*VS*, p. 764; *VE*, p. 150). Here, the common notion of the *provincia* as something that exists only in relation to the city and is almost an extension or satellite of it, a notion of which the book is, nonetheless, not entirely devoid, is rejected as Tommasino claims the superiority and self-sufficiency of the countryside as a place of unspoiled natural beauty that affords a real sense of peace and contentment. It is also interesting to note that the extract hints additionally at Elsa's discontent: a feeling which tinges the pages of the entire book and which, to different extents, all the characters seem to experience at one point or another. It is all the more striking that Elsa feels this way, since she has finally convinced Tommasino to formalize their engagement, seemingly fulfilling her most intimate aspirations. Why she is not happier, she cannot herself explain. The surrounding environment therefore evokes different feelings in the two characters, in an interplay between emotions and space that speaks of the unique kind of experience elicited by places 'on the margins', which are symbolically and geographically distant from the big city.[24]

Le voci della sera also contributes to a composite picture of the Italian provinces by hinting at the fact that, in the years under scrutiny, the latter often gave impetus to the economic development of the whole country. Specifically, we can see that people with entrepreneurial skills and resourcefulness like Balotta start new economic activities, creating new jobs and benefiting their territory. The prominent place that Balotta's enterprise has gained within the local community is reflected, for instance, in the following passage: 'Tutto il paese vive in funzione della fabbrica. La fabbrica produce stoffe. Manda un odore che riempie le strade del paese, e quando c'è scirocco arriva quasi fino alla nostra casa, che pure è in aperta campagna' [The whole neighbourhood lives by the factory. The factory produces cloth. It emits a smell which permeates the streets of the town and when the scirocco blows it comes pretty well up to our house, which is, however, in the country] (*VS*, p. 674; *VE*, p. 20). In a way that is reminiscent of Volponi's description of the *fabbrica* in *Memoriale*, discussed in Chapter 1, here the factory becomes a focal point, the centre from which all human activities seem to radiate, therefore somehow dictating the rhythms of life in town. Within the context of the post-war model of diffused industrialization, specialized trades or single, leading companies became in many cases the trademark of a city or territory. Specific Italian cities and towns therefore became inextricably associated with the name of the company that was located there. Ginsborg, for instance, mentions the example of Pordenone, which 'became the company town of Zanussi', a major manufacturer

---

24   See, e.g., Doreen Massey, *Space, Place, and Gender* (Cambridge: Polity, 1994).

of home appliances, to the extent that its 'inhabitants identified the transformation of their own fortunes with those of the firm'.[25] The centrality of Balotta's factory in Ginzburg's provincial microcosm is exemplified by the smell of industrial processing which, on those days on which the Scirocco blows, engulfs the whole town and reaches as far as the countryside where Elsa's family live. It is not, however, simply a matter of the physical, imposing presence of this building. More subtly, and more importantly, the power relations within the factory are mirrored in the social and economic structures of this provincial microcosm and the ways in which people within it relate to one another. In the face of the increased social mobility in post-war Italian society, new divisions and inequalities crystallized quickly, generated by contradictory processes of modernization.[26] Whilst social discrepancies are often more striking in a big city, it is more difficult for individuals in smaller provincial cities to change their status, for here social structures are generally more rigid and people's roles and positions within their social group and the wider community more fixed. Hence, once new class divisions have been established in a small-town environment, they are more likely to be perceived as unchanging. While it is true that the De Franciscis do not take advantage of their position of wealth and privilege, remaining committed to a humble, unsophisticated lifestyle, it is clear from the way in which the other characters in the novel relate to and talk about them that they are considered to be the town's most respected family. In Italy, as in other Western societies, success is often measured in terms of individual power and prestige. One may argue that, in many ways, the post-war years simply increased this individualistic orientation, privileging profit over much-needed social reforms.

Mastronardi's Vigevano novels also bear witness to a social landscape which has been profoundly transformed by economic growth, once again showing how the boom was not an exclusively metropolitan phenomenon. Mastronardi narrates how Vigevano has been home to a thriving footwear industry since the pre-war years and how, in the wake of the boom of the 1950s and 1960s, the sector flourished further, employing a substantial portion of the local population. Despite increased economic wellbeing, old inequalities have deepened and new ones have emerged. Mastronardi provides a clear example of a writer who has turned to marginal existences and neglected areas within the richer Northern provinces. As

25 Ginsborg, *A History of Contemporary Italy*, p. 215.
26 See John Foot, *Modern Italy* (Basingstoke: Palgrave Macmillan, 2014).

already noted in the Introduction, these images of enduring poverty and underdevelopment have the effect of demystifying official representations of the Italian North as a whole as one of the most prosperous regions in Europe and of the South as the only part of the country that, in the boom years, still lagged behind due to issues dating back to Unification and beyond. The figure of Antonio Mombelli, the titular *maestro* of Mastronardi's book, who lives on the verge of poverty, well exemplifies how the public sector was underfunded and, in many ways, still backward in the post-war years. He struggles to make ends meet, despite giving private classes outside his working hours to supplement his income. The occasions for socialization in a popular central café illustrate the class divide in the city. The habitual clientele fall into categories that are socially and economically determined and interactions reproduce these divisions. Antonio's entourage include other teachers and people from the lower middle class, like the journalist Pallavicino from the minor local paper *L'informatore*, who writes about the town's football team. At a different table one may find an important industrialist with one of his employees reduced to a sycophant.[27] Every evening at the same time another industrialist and his wife show up in their fancy car.[28] The opulence these people exhibit contrasts starkly with the frugality of Antonio and his friends.

From the analysis so far, it appears that *Le voci della sera* rejects a clear-cut distinction between the urban and provincial, insomuch as neither of them is ultimately judged as more desirable or prevails over the other. The novel does not reproduce traditional ways of portraying these two environments as antithetical and complementary, for example by presenting the excitement of vibrant city life as an antidote to tedious and predictable village life, or instead the tranquillity and safety provided by the latter as a soothing balm for the chronic overstimulation to which urban dwellers are subjected. While these connotations are not entirely absent in the novel (for example, the city is a discreet space where the two lovers can go unnoticed; it is more heterogeneous and adventurous), we are not left with the impression that the characters' predicament depends entirely on the environment in which they live. On the contrary, moving to the city would hardly make them feel more fulfilled. Moreover, the nodal themes of the book, such as affectivity and familial relationships, are addressed with a similar sensibility in other novels by Ginzburg

---

27 Lucio Mastronardi, *Il maestro di Vigevano* (Turin: Einaudi, 1962), p. 19.

28 Mastronardi, *Il maestro di Vigevano*, p. 20.

that present an urban setting. At the same time, Ginzburg hints at the economic dynamism of the Italian province, in spite of the rigidity of class structures and the limited social mobility that are often a feature of these territories. If we look more closely at issues such as social conventions and gender roles, and how they play out in a provincial environment as opposed to an urban and allegedly more progressive one, we realize that the picture is more complex still. The environment in which the novel takes place is more than a mere setting: it appears to give an impulse to the events in specific ways and to shape the social and emotional worlds of the characters, as discussed in the next two sections.

Social Conventions and Gender Roles: Are the Provinces More Traditional?

It is a fairly established belief that attitudes which are more rigidly conservative are more commonly found in provincial settings than in metropolitan ones, since the latter are, at the very least, repositories of a wider array of world views, often diverse and conflicting, due to the greater number of people who live there. The following analysis of how this idea plays out in *Le voci della sera* is particularly interested in taking into account the gendered point of view offered by the female author as well as by the main character and narrator, Elsa. The female perspective is, indeed, essential if one is really to show how dominant values are inscribed in space at the expense of subjects who are considered subordinate. The discussion on gender in this section will also address some of the peculiarities of Ginzburg's oeuvre, showing how her views on women's issues and feminist ideals are controversial and not wholly sympathetic. A particular interest lies in examining the interplay between social conventions, gender and space by analysing how the more or less explicit norms that regulate the characters' social behaviour are a reflection of the specific type of built environment described in the novel and vice versa. In so doing, this chapter asks questions such as the following: does *Le voci della sera* confirm the belief that the city affords a more liberated, progressive lifestyle, whereas the role of traditions that are defended and advocated by the established authorities and introjected into one's own cultural imprinting is greater in small, 'marginal' towns? If so, which stance does the novel take? To what extent do social expectations and assumptions translate into conditioning that shapes human relationships and existential trajectories in the novel (whether the characters reject or, conversely, embrace them, willingly or unconsciously, as part of their 'cultural baggage')? Do these expectations disproportionately affect male or female characters?

After the end of the Second World War Italian society witnessed increasing polarization around the two main political parties, the Christian Democrats and the Italian Communist Party. While the former either governed directly or were continuously part of coalition governments from 1944 to 1994, a huge consensus also formed around the PCI (a major political force for decades) and, more broadly, around progressive Socialist ideas that sought to minimize the role of religion in public life.[29] At the time when Ginzburg was writing, the process of secularization that was to transform Italian society radically and irreversibly had certainly started, yet the social presence of the Catholic Church, which remains a feature of Italian society to the present day, was still very strong. The Christian Democrats embodied ideals and delivered policies that were inspired by Catholic values, seeing women essentially as wives and mothers.[30] The traditional patriarchal order and issues around the legitimacy of men legislating on spheres that primarily concerned women's rights and wellbeing were hardly questioned. To be more precise, feminist ideas were starting to circulate in Italy at the time, but feminism was yet to become the organized mass movement that would achieve many path-breaking victories, most notably the promulgation of the divorce and abortion laws in 1970 and 1978 respectively. Feminism as a well-defined political force with a revolutionary impact developed in Italy in the so-called 'long 1970s', which is to say the years from 1968 to 1983.[31] In the post-war years, in Italy as in other Western countries, it was still largely accepted that women belonged in the domestic sphere as housewives and mothers. Unlike in other European countries, however, the employment rates of Italian women in the period between the 1950s and 1970s did not increase substantially, while their traditional role within the family was somehow strengthened over the same period of time, also due

---

29   See, e.g., Gianfranco Baldini, 'Christian Democracy: *The* Italian Party', in *The Oxford Handbook of Italian Politics*, ed. by Jones and Pasquino, pp. 173–83 (p. 173).

30   On women's changing socio-economic roles in post-war Italian society and women's politics in the same period, see, e.g., Perry Willson, *Women in Twentieth-Century Italy*, Gender and History (Basingstoke: Palgrave Macmillan, 2009).

31   Maude A. Bracke, *Women and the Reinvention of the Political: Feminism in Italy, 1968–1983*, Routledge Research in Gender and History (New York: Routledge, 2014), p. 2. Italian feminism stemmed from a transnational movement, 'commonly referred to as "second-wave feminism", the phenomenon of radical women's activism between the early 1960s and the late 1970s in various countries that gave rise to a repertoire of new political agendas, practices and theory' (Bracke, *Women and the Reinvention of the Political*, p. 2).

to the impact of emigration and the influence of Catholicism, with its idealization of motherhood.[32] Ginzburg's stance in connection to issues addressed by the feminist movement, such as the legalization of abortion, arguably reflects her complex religious views. We know that she was religious, but also that she was constantly interrogating her faith and experiencing self-doubt.[33] Ginzburg resisted what she perceived as dogmatism, be it of a religious or political kind, but she held traditional values. In terms of abortion, for example, Ginzburg supported women's right to have a choice on matters concerning their own bodies, but considered this choice highly problematic and traumatic due to what she saw as the inviolability of the life that was forming inside these bodies.[34]

Interestingly, it has been pointed out that Ginzburg rejected a 'feminine style' – a label that ought to be taken as such, for it inevitably encompasses a variety of individual and unique approaches to writing – in favour of a more objective, and therefore more stereotypically male, approach that dissects the inner world of the characters in her books with precision and detachment, using a clear, economical language.[35] Arguably, this choice also speaks of Ginzburg's documented fear of being labelled, and therefore somewhat dismissed, as a woman writer rather than a writer *tout court*, which may also be related to her centrality in the Einaudi milieu.[36] Women writers have only become part of the literary canon relatively recently; indeed, their work has traditionally had ascribed to it, usually by male critics, a set of somewhat derogatory stylistic features and concerns, such as a distinct sentimentalism, and has often been disregarded.[37] Ginzburg's interest

---

32   Bracke, *Women and the Reinvention of the Political*, p. 3.

33   Judith L. Pastore, 'The Personal is Political: Gender, Generation, and Memory in Natalia Ginzburg's *Caro Michele*', in *Natalia Ginzburg*, ed. by Jeannet and Katz, pp. 89–98.

34   Pastore, 'The Personal is Political', p. 96.

35   Alba Amoia, *20th-Century Italian Women Writers: The Feminine Experience* (Carbondale, IL: Southern Illinois University Press, 1996), p. 63.

36   Rebecca West claims the following: 'Ginzburg had an ambivalent and uneasy relation to feminism […]. Like other women more or less of her generation who wished to write (Elsa Morante, Anna Maria Ortese, Alba De Céspedes, Maria Luisa Spaziani), she did not welcome the label "woman writer", preferring instead to make her way in the primarily male literary universe as a "writer" *tout court*' (Rebecca West, 'Introduction', in *Natalia Ginzburg*, ed. by Jeannet and Katz, pp. 3–9 (p. 3)).

37   See Sharon Wood, *Italian Women's Writing 1860–1994*, Women in Context (London: Athlone, 1995); and Adele Bardazzi and Alberica Bazzoni (eds), *Gender and Authority Across Disciplines, Space and Time* (Basingstoke: Palgrave Macmillan, 2020).

in the intimate, everyday sphere of family and affective relationships has meant that she has not escaped the categorization of 'woman writer', with the more or less negative connotations that this entails.[38] While she indeed chooses an objective narrative style, she is also particularly interested in the inner world of the women who are the protagonists of her books, as is the case in *Le voci della sera* but also, for instance, in *Sagittario* [*Sagittarius*] (1957), a short novel that depicts an exclusively feminine microcosm formed by the female narrator of the story, her mother, sister and an eccentric woman, Scilla, whom the narrator's mother befriends.

In terms of gender relations in *Le voci della sera*, and how they relate to space, it is worth pointing out again that Elsa and Tommasino escape to the city for their secret meetings. The city clearly grants them the anonymity and freedom that they cannot have in their hometown, where everyone knows who everyone else is. The necessity to meet elsewhere is also revealing of ingrained social conventions in small-town environments. When Elsa asks Tommasino why they pretend they do not know each other when they meet in their home town, he replies: 'Per la tua reputazione. Non devo comprometterti, visto che poi non ti sposo' [It is for your reputation. I must not compromise you, seeing that I am not going to marry you] (*VS*, p. 739; *VE*, p. 114). From the moment in which we discover that Elsa and Tommasino are lovers, it is difficult to dismiss a lingering feeling about the direction that things between them will take, namely that they will eventually separate. While this is arguably also due to the pessimism which generally informs Ginzburg's writings and her view of relationships – anyone who is at least partially familiar with her oeuvre would be aware of this – there is an additional reason why one is inclined to think that the relationship between Elsa and Tommasino is ill-fated. Indeed, from the beginning it is clear that the latter does not adhere to a traditional, acceptable and therefore more secure idea of romantic involvement, which in those years was still expected to follow a clearly established pathway to official engagement and marriage. Elsa and Tommasino instead meet secretly in his city apartment and are unwilling to officialize their involvement until Elsa realizes that she does not want to live in a relationship without expectations anymore. It should be noted that, in *Le voci della sera*, romantic relationships generally give way to alienation and discontentment

38   West, 'Introduction', p. 4.

over time, even when they follow the more established trajectory of marriage and children, which is the path that all the Balotta siblings, with the exception of Tommasino, have followed. These couples remain together (apart from Vincenzino and Cate, who eventually divorce) even though their marriages are unhappy, or so we are led to believe. This view suggests a broader disillusionment with relationships *per se*, a topic that will be discussed more closely in the next section of the chapter. Against this backdrop, one may even argue that, paradoxically, in refusing to comply with social requirements and expectations that are imposed from on high, and therefore to be categorized according to one of the labels available, the relationship between Elsa and Tommasino is the only one in the novel which conserves a degree of purity and spontaneity, despite the fact that it will eventually lead to a separation. Symptomatic of a certain provincial narrow-mindedness and penchant for gossip is also the fact that after the breakup between Elsa and Tommasino people in the small town come up with their own stories, usually denigratory, to explain the end of the relationship. Some argue that Tommasino had an affair, others that Elsa did; others still claim that the De Franciscis are in financial trouble and that, as the accountant responsible for looking after their finances, Elsa's father had found it out. There are even those who claim that Elsa is a drug addict.

Relationships in the book are illustrative of the conservatism in the Piedmontese provincial milieu portrayed by Ginzburg, where marriages often consolidate relations between local families and recognized members of the community. Vincenzino, for instance, marries Cate, a girl from the nearby village of Borgo Martino. Precisely because she is a local, she is automatically assigned virtues by his family which they consider to be very important in a wife: kindness, purity, humbleness and good health. Cate is indeed said to be 'chiara, semplice, pulita' [a clean, simple, honest woman] (*VS*, p. 703; *VE*, p. 63) and again, a few pages later, 'sana, semplice, [...] una buona ragazza' [healthy, honest and a good girl] (*VS*, p. 709; *VE*, p. 71). The humble simplicity, cited twice, seems to be particularly valued in a future wife. All these attributes and dispositions, seen as valuable and desirable, are ascribed to Cate by Vincenzino and his family simply by virtue of the fact that she comes from their same territory and is therefore one of their own. This tendency to judge people according to their ancestry and place of birth is revealed perhaps even more starkly by the way in which the De Francisci react to the marriage of Mario with Xenia, a Russian who has escaped from Moscow during the Revolution and whom he meets on a business trip to Munich.

Balotta and Vincenzino welcome the news and the bride, on their return from Germany, with undisguised mistrust and open hostility:

> Il vecchio Balotta era sconsolato. Pensava che il Mario avrebbe sposato una delle figlie del suo vecchio amico, l'avvocato Bottiglia. E invece ora avevano davanti questa sconosciuta, emersa da chissà qual vita oscura, e che parlava in francese, lingua che lui e sua moglie non sapevano affatto. (*VS*, p. 703)

> [Old Balotta was very much put out. He thought that Mario should have married one of his old friend the advocate Bottiglia's daughters. And instead they now had with them this unknown woman, emerging from who know what obscure life, who spoke French, a language which he and his wife did not know at all.] (*VE*, p. 63)

By contrast with the simplicity and transparency assigned to Cate as qualities, the foreigner Xenia appears to carry an obscure history and past which cast a shadow over her personality. The allusion to the fact that she speaks no Italian but only French, a language that Balotta and his wife do not understand, reinforces the feelings of diffidence because it makes communication more difficult. Men (since it is the men who normally choose their wives) are expected to marry childhood friends or local women. Balotta himself 's'era scelto la Cecilia in un vicino sobborgo, scegliendola perché era bionda, povera e sana' [had chosen Cecilia from some neighbouring hamlet, choosing her because she was blonde, poor and healthy] (*VS*, p. 709; *VE*, p. 71). These three attributes of Cecilia's are very reminiscent of the above descriptions of Cate and also speak of a tendency on the part of men in the novel to objectify women in relation to their needs, which in this case include finding a woman who is 'sana', is therefore likely to bear children and who has all the qualities of a good-natured, mild-mannered wife. The adjective 'povera' also merits additional comment, in terms of the secure economic dominance and therefore broader power in the relationship that it seems to secure for the male partner.

Indeed, the female characters in the novel overwhelmingly adhere to the gender stereotype of woman as mother and housewife. They all go on to be married and have children, following what was very much the norm at the time. Elsa represents the exception to the rule, but this does not make her happier, nor does it transform her into a sort of champion of female self-determination and empowerment. On the contrary, the fact that her engagement with Tommasino is terminated is ultimately seen as a failure. At the point at which the story ends, we leave her rather disconsolately still living with her parents and on track to end up like her aunt, the 'old maid' Ottavia, on whom more later. Balotta's wife Cecilia may be seen as the classic example of the woman who stands behind the succesful, self-made entrepreneur who has created a prosperous family business, even though the old-fashioned Socialist Balotta is about as distant as one can be from the stereotype of a conceited, arrogant, successful businessman. While he is clearly very attached to his wife (after her death he is never the same again and basically loses interest in life), he also often scolds her to put her in her place. Cecilia is portrayed as a good woman, if a little fatuous and light-minded, as is often the case with the figure of the mother in Ginzburg's novels (one needs only to think of the portrait Ginzburg gives of her own mother in *Lessico famigliare*, which resembles closely that of Elsa's mother in *Le voci della sera*). Balotta is the undisputed head of the family, an ill-tempered, authoritative man who reminds us of Ginzburg's father in *Lessico famigliare*.

One exception to this predominant characterization of women in the novel is Raffaella, another of Balotta's children. She is presented, at least initially (for things change during the course of the novel, as illustrated below), as 'un ragazzaccio sguaiato' [a boisterous hobbledehoy] (*VS*, p. 710; *VE*, p. 73). It is interesting that she is assigned masculine traits in a slightly derogatory way (here through the perspective of Cate, Vincenzino's wife, who is at the river with Raffaella and a little annoyed with her because, in her view, she plays dangerously with her children), while she is, in fact, a strong, independent young woman who is less concerned with finding a husband and starting a family than with joining the Resistance during the Second World War. Raffaella's joining up with the partisans in the mountains is perhaps the only moment in the novel at which a woman leaves the domestic sphere to which female characters are normally relegated and claims her active role in the making of history. The Second World War was indeed a turning point, paving the way for the steadily increasing participation of women in the labour force, in Italy as well as in other countries. Raffaella will go on unexpectedly to marry Purillo, taking everyone amongst her family and friends by surprise, and therefore to adapt herself to the lifestyle of a middle-class housewife, looking after the house and her baby son Pepè.

Nevertheless, women in the story are not merely background characters who stay in the shadow of their husbands and are powerless with regard to their own destiny. Within the narrow limits of the horizon shared by everyone else in the novel, men included, albeit to different extents – since everyone's destiny seems somehow to be predetermined by the very fact of having being born into a certain family and social condition (or at least this is what the people inhabiting this provincial microcosm apparently take for granted) –, women do take small steps to improve their circumstances, in as much as this is possible. Men can still somehow broaden and improve their lives, not only through work (Vincenzino constantly comes up with new ideas and plans for developing the family business) but, potentially, also by moving somewhere else and exploring the world outside their home-town environment (after breaking up with Elsa, Tommasino contemplates the idea of taking up a job opportunity in Montreal, then moves to Liverpool for a few months to look after the company's interests there, only to come back and presumably stay). In short, men may freely move and exercise their initiative outside the home, in the public sphere, while women are mostly confined to the private and domestic domain, something which makes their room for manoeuvre considerably narrower. Within the undeniable limitations entailed by being women in a conservative, male-dominated society, however, female characters show remarkable resilience and the will to make things better for themselves, whether by meticulously overseeing all aspects of their daily lives and routines, like Xenia, or by eventually separating from their husband and going their own way, like Cate. It is Xenia who decides that Mario and she should move into the Villa Rondine; it is Xenia who decorates the house and personally selects the furniture, upholstery and drapery, as well as the housekeepers whom she instructs in great detail as to how she likes things done. More importantly, she creates her own workroom in the house, where she spends most of her time painting and carving works of art. All things considered, one may argue that Xenia has shaped for herself the kind of life that suits her best, especially since she is essentially an introvert who rarely leaves her studio or garden to go into town. Cate provides another interesting example of a female character who takes her destiny into her own hands. From the melancholy of the early years of her marriage with Vincenzino, whom she marries without love and with an eye to the financial stability that will come from it, she gradually becomes more confident and independent. She adjusts and finds her way to navigate married life. For example, she decides regularly to visit her mother in nearby Borgo Martino, something that she initially avoids because she is afraid it might irritate her husband. Afterwards, she becomes a mother herself and this occupies her completely. She then goes on to have a number of affairs until she separates from Vincenzino (who respects her decision and lets her go) and starts a new life in Rome. She is not happy, though: she appears to cling emotionally to the past since she keeps asking, 'Ma perché abbiamo sciupato tutto, tutto?' [Why is everything ruined, everything?] (*VS*, pp. 723, 725; *VE*, p. 92).

The private space of the house and family, which has traditionally been considered the female domain, as clearly emerges from the analysis of the lives of female characters in *Le voci della sera*, was to become one of the main issues at the core of the political agenda of Italian feminism in the 1970s. Some feminist activists and thinkers claimed that, since women had been relegated to the domestic sphere for centuries and even millennia, the political dimension of the private – that is, the ways in which power relations are perpetuated within the family and shape its structure and functions – had to be researched and addressed.[39] This issue, however, sparked controversy and divisions within the feminist movement itself, for advocating the need for a politicization of private issues meant accepting that the State regulate, in however supportive and permissive a way, matters such as abortion, which according to some feminists pertained solely to women as the only ones who could legitimately claim control over their own bodies.[40] In *Le voci della sera* female characters show no awareness of feminist issues. Quite the contrary: it is more or less accepted and taken for granted that the women in the novel will establish themselves as housewives and mothers, attending to the needs of their husbands and children. As will be pointed out later, Ginzburg considers the (patriarchal) family an important bulwark of order and security in an otherwise chaotic, unpredictable world. Interestingly, the only unmarried woman in *Le voci della sera*, Aunt Ottavia, is a featureless character without strong personality traits (except for her passion for books mentioned above) and mainly characterized by her silence, for she hardly speaks at all in the novel unless invited to express her opinion. She can be conveniently placed in the living room with one of her books in her lap in order to make sure that Elsa and Tommasino are not alone during their meetings in the house, but without bothering them: 'Non ti dà mica noia la zia, basta metterla lì con un libro, non si sente nemmeno' [The Aunt does not worry you at all; it is enough to provide her with a book, and one hears nothing more from her] (*VS*, p. 779; *VE*, p. 171). The main attributes of Aunt Ottavia are her quietness and silence: she is barely noticeable. As already noted, while Elsa presents an exception to the

39   As Bracke puts it, 'feminists in the 1970s *prioritized* the private sphere as an area where, it was felt, liberation was to occur as a precondition for wider change'. She goes on to show how 'this rethinking of the "private sphere" was a response to the transformation of the legal framework affecting the personal lives of individuals and families and led to a destabilisation of the very notions of public and private' (Bracke, *Women and the Reinvention of the Political*, p. 22).

40   Bracke, *Women and the Reinvention of the Political*, p. 22.

stereotype of devoted fiancée and wife, since she is involved in a non-conventional relationship with Tommasino, she is also dissatisfied with this arrangement and hopes that one day Tommasino will agree to marry her. There is no indication in the novel that the end of her engagement with Tommasino somehow prompts her to reflect on her own situation and possibly to re-imagine her future.

It would be mistaken to argue that the situation of women in *Le voci della sera* is entirely dependent on the fact that they live in a provincial, inward-looking environment, even though, especially in the years in which Ginzburg was writing, this type of environment was usually slower to absorb social changes. Other novels by Ginzburg which are, for example, set in Turin – a city that, while it has traditionally been somewhat secluded and, some may argue, *provinciale*, has also been the place where some of the most significant political and economic events in modern Italian history have originated, as well as a vibrant hub for intellectual ideas and activities – also depict traditional social and gender relations. In cities, as well as in the rest of the country, the situation of post-war Italian women changed only gradually through a process that was still fraught with controversy. As Bracke puts it:

> As notions of the 'modern' woman were at the heart of a modernisation project, women were affected in specific ways: positively, for instance in new education opportunities, and negatively, by the increasingly intense projection of ideal womanhood in public discourse. Such ideal images involved the dedicated housewife, the loving mother and the efficient double-burden carrier.[41]

Since, in the post-war years, leadership positions were occupied exclusively by men, and considering that modernity was accompanied by the survival of traditional mindsets as regards social relations and gender roles, we can see how the enduring models and stereotypes which belonged to the patriarchal society and religion provided an obstacle to female emancipation. Historically, it is in the big city that innovative ideas take hold more readily and translate into new approaches and ways of thinking, activist practices and consciousness-raising movements. The second wave of Italian feminism, which achieved unprecedented popularity and success in the 1970s, was no exception. The fact that city life presents more opportunities for female emancipation, however, has its downside. Indeed, metropolitan life has traditionally been regarded as a threat to the respectability of women, since controlling their behaviour proves

---

41   Bracke, *Women and the Reinvention of the Political*, p. 11.

far more difficult in an urban environment.[42] On the contrary, rural villages and smaller provincial towns have traditionally provided 'safety and continued respectability for women'.[43]

While traditional social and gender relations are, therefore, not merely ascribable to the provincial environment in which *Le voci della sera* takes place, it may be argued that the *provincia* acts as a sort of magnifier of the themes and motifs that always accompany Ginzburg's representation of relationships. Due to the historical fragmentation of the Italian nation and its problematic path to unity, provincialism and the strong sense of attachment to one's own local community have always been constitutive of the Italian character, to the point that it may be suggested that the provinces are 'the most revealing locus of (Italian) identity'.[44] The sentiment of a sort of hypertrophy and ubiquity of the Italian province reverberates in *Le voci della sera*, especially in the last conversation that Elsa and Tommasino have before their separation. Here Tommasino introduces the interesting idea of a sort of collective vital energy that has already been drained by all the other people who have lived in their hometown even before Elsa and Tommasino were born:

> – Perché ho sempre avuto l'impressione, – disse, – che abbiano già vissuto abbastanza gli altri prima di me. Che abbiamo [sic] già consumato tutte le risorse, tutta la carica vitale che era disponibile. Gli altri, il Nebbia, il Vincenzino, mio padre. A me, è rimasto niente. – Gli altri, – disse, – tutti quelli che hanno abitato in questo paese, prima di me. Mi sembra di non essere io, che la loro ombra. (*VS*, p. 771)

> [It is because I have the feeling, – he said, – that they have already lived enough, those others before me; that they have already consumed all the reserves, all the vitality that there was for us. The others, Nebbia, Vincenzino, my father. Nothing was left over for me. – The others, – he said, – all those who have lived in this village before me. It seems to me that I am only their shadow.] (*VE*, p. 160)

Tommasino explains his indolence and lack of motivation by the fact that there are no vital resources left, that the 'carica vitale' to which he refers is not renewable but fixed and limited in time and has already been consumed. The collective strength and stamina have been exhausted and he has been left with none to sustain himself, to

---

42 Leslie Kern, *Feminist City: Claiming Space in a Man-Made World* (London: Verso, 2020), p. 11.

43 Leslie Kern, *Feminist City*, p. 11.

44 Spunta, 'Escaping the World', p. 34.

the point where he feels like an empty shell, a shadow of the people who have come before him. Tommasino clearly feels that everything has already been said and done by other people in his community, that his path (working in the family business, ideally settling down and starting a family) has already been established; and he lacks the willpower to envisage his life differently. In Tommasino's view there is, therefore, a clear connection between a lack of vitality and the provincial milieu in which he lives, which leaves no room for unconventional life choices, no possibility for self-determination outside the habitual, customary line of conduct. In this sense, the province as the Italians' core identity also seems a destiny that cannot be escaped. Tommasino goes on to blame *il paese*, so small with its handful of houses and yet so heavy, like a burden of which he seems unable to free himself: '– Come può pesare, un paese! – disse. – Ha un peso di piombo, con tutti i suoi morti! Come mi pesa questo nostro paese, così piccolo, un pugno di case! Non posso mai liberarmene, non posso dimenticarlo!' [How a place can get one down! – he said. – It has a weight of lead, with all its dead. This village of ours, it just gets me down; it is so small, a handful of houses. I can never free myself from it, I cannot forget it] (*VS*, p. 772; *VE*, p. 161). 'Il paese' has become for Tommasino a state of mind. He hopes that by leaving and taking up the job opportunity in Montreal he will have the chance to recover at least some of the lost energy and enthusiasm. Towards its end, the novel therefore suggests that only by broadening one's own limiting circumstances and embracing opportunities in the wider world may one live a fulfilling life. It is significant, however, that Tommasino will end up staying in his hometown, going on with his usual life.

The provincial setting of the novel arguably accentuates the pessimistic tinge of Ginzburg's oeuvre as a whole, presenting an oppressive, confining environment that limits the characters' possibilities to develop their aspirations and enrich their lives. This section of the chapter has especially focused on gender relations and how they are mirrored through the way in which this environment is structured and organized. Space is a social phenomenon: the reflection and, in Lefebvrian terms, the product of the society that inhabits it and moulds it in specific ways through its system of norms, rules, values and attitudes. Systems of privilege and oppression are, therefore, reflected and in turn shaped by the organization of the built environment. In *Le voci della sera* women are bound to the private, domestic domain of the household and therefore have limited freedom of movement compared to men, who leave the house to work and enjoy the freedom to travel further afield if they wish to. Accordingly, the built environment largely accommodates and facilitates men's needs and is instead experienced by women 'through a set of barriers – physical, social, economic, and symbolic',[45] which are there precisely to maintain and reproduce those traditional gender roles. The chapter so far has, therefore, shed some light on how axes of discrimination which rely on culturally defined binaries such as male–female and centre–margin intersect in space in ways that mirror a society's dominant values.

Loneliness, Familial Ties, Impossibility of Close Relationships

The last section of this chapter centres on the theme of affectivity in *Le voci della sera*. As previously, the interest lies in analysing whether the patterns and themes surrounding human relationships in the novel are somehow shaped by the environment in which these unfold and therefore whether the setting is instrumental in bringing to the fore issues that Ginzburg intends to illuminate in relation to human connections and intimacy. In particular, attention is paid to the issue which may be the real key to interpreting *Le voci della sera*, that is, the inherent degree of misunderstanding that informs human interaction and, therefore, the ultimate impossibility of authentic, mature, fulfilling relationships, not only between men and women but also between family members and generations. Ginzburg's oeuvre tells us that one may only have ephemeral glimpses into human contacts which are truly genuine and spontaneous, devoid of any conditioning and superstructure. Perhaps the best example is provided by the idioms and expressions which form a sort of secret language shared by the family members in *Lessico famigliare* and automatically foster a deep sense of group belonging among them. It is important to note that, in Ginzburg's view, there is also a generational issue, since in her novels it is especially younger people who seem unable to cultivate healthy, stable relationships, whereas the older generation (Ginzburg's parents in *Lessico famigliare* arguably providing the clearest example of this) show more resilience and the ability to understand what is really important in life, perhaps because they are more used to hardship. This generational theme is arguably foregrounded more distinctly in *Caro Michele* [*Dear Michael*] (1973), to which this discussion will briefly return.

45   Kern, *Feminist City*, p. 14.

A central point to bear in mind is the fact, which has already been highlighted, that living in big cities usually offers the opportunity to expand one's kinship network and that this network is also considerably more prone to changing and renewing itself than its counterpart in small-town environments, where contacts and relationships remain fairly stable throughout a person's life. Symptomatic of such a state of affairs is the fact that people who live in small towns often find their lifelong partners within this existing and longstanding circle of connections and acquaintances. Certainly this is the case for Elsa and Tommasino, who, as Elsa recalls in the following passage, used to play together as children:

> Disse: – Però vorrei essere andato lontano, in qualche luogo all'estero, e averti conosciuto per caso, in una strada qualunque, ragazza mai vista prima. Vorrei non sapere niente di te, niente dei tuoi parenti, e non incontrarli mai. – E invece, – io dissi, – siamo cresciuti nello stesso paese, e abbiamo giocato insieme, bambini, alle Pietre. Ma a me, questo, non mi disturba. Non me ne importa niente. Dissi: – Non me ne importa, e anzi m'intenerisce perfino un poco. E da quando tu esisti per me, quel nostro paese là è come se fosse diventato una terra sconosciuta, grandissima, e tutta piena di cose imprevedibili, drammatiche, emozionanti, che possono succedere in qualunque minuto. (*VS*, pp. 757–58)

> [He said: – But I should have liked to have gone far away, somewhere abroad, and to have got to know you by chance, in some street or other, a girl one had never seen before. I should like to know nothing about you, nothing of your relations and not to meet them ever. – Instead, – I said, – we have grown up in the same village, and played together as children, at Le Pietre. But that does not worry me at all. To me it is of no significance. I said: – It is of no significance to me. And since you have come to exist for me, our village there has become an unknown land, very big and all full of unforeseeable dramatic things that stir the emotions and can happen at any moment.] (*VE*, p. 140)

The extract presents, in the form of a dialogue signalled by the verbs 'disse' and 'dissi', the different viewpoints of Tommasino and Elsa on their social milieu and how this has shaped their rapport throughout their lives, first as childhood playmates and then as lovers in their adulthood. The novel often makes use of direct speech, a narrative device that very much belongs to Ginzburg's peculiar style and literary voice and that in many cases translates into a continuous, slightly neurotic chattering which resembles more of a monologue. In short, Elsa defends the comforting aura of safety and familiarity evoked by the lifelong friendships and connections which people are normally able to form in smaller provincial towns, while Tommasino sees in this limited kinship circle a contraction of possibilities.

Different places shape the characters' experience and their relationships in specific ways. The province, the city and the abstract elsewhere, possibly a foreign country where, according to Tommasino, things may be different: all these places seem to afford varied possibilities and degrees of fulfilment and self-realization, more or less imagined or ephemeral. The studio flat that Tommasino has rented in the city comes to symbolize a space of freedom from the conformity and conventions of the provincial home town, where people are seemingly trapped in unhappy relationships because of external expectations and ways of living that are widely accepted as normal. Initially, while they live their relationship in a rather casual, carefree manner, both Elsa and Tommasino share the view of a greater freedom granted by the city. As the story proceeds, however, Elsa becomes increasingly discontented with this arrangement, longing for something more stable and secure. The studio flat in the Via Gorizia therefore turns out to be only an illusionary escape from the responsibilities of adult life and from the constrictions of society. Tommasino, who continues to pay the rent for the apartment even after he and Elsa stop meeting there, clings to a romanticized idea of it as a space of freedom, authenticity, spontaneity and real human connection – all aspirations which a conservative social milieu like the Italian provinces of the 1960s tended to inhibit:

> Vuoi che andiamo là, in via Gorizia, un momento? – disse. – L'ho tenuta sempre, quella stanza, ho pagato sempre l'affitto. Ci andavo, sai, qualche volta, mentre tu eri, con tua madre, dalla sarta, o nei negozi di biancheria. Andavo là, mi riposavo un poco, e qualche volta mi facevo il caffè. Sentivo un gran silenzio, una gran pace. (*VS*, p. 769)

> [Would you like to go up there in the via Gorizia for a little while? – he asked. – I have kept that room on all the time and paid the rent. I went there, you know, sometimes while you were with your mother at the dressmaker's or the draper's. I went there and had a little rest and sometimes made some coffee. I felt a great silence there, a great peace.] (*VE*, p. 156)

Again the text states: '– Prima, – lui disse, – quando ci trovavamo là in quella stanza, in via Gorizia, io avevo sempre voglia di raccontarti quello che pensavo. Era bello, era una gran libertà, un senso di pieno respiro' [Formerly, – he said, – when we were up there in that room in the Via Gorizia, I always had the wish to tell you everything I was thinking about. It was fine; there was a great freedom, a sense of breathing fully] (*VS*, pp. 767–68; *VE*, p. 154). The qualities and associations the room evokes for Tommasino are telling: freedom, silence, stillness, peace, a sense of expansion and the possibility of breathing fully and deeply – in short, the possibility of truly being oneself outside social conventions and expectations. This sense of personal freedom translates into a more sincere, heartfelt way of connecting with others. Tommasino recalls that he was always keen to open up and share his thoughts and emotions with Elsa while they were still seeing each other in this carefree way, without expectations.

After the engagement is officialized and the couple begin to spend more time in their home town and with Elsa's parents, Tommasino gradually withdraws into himself and loses the pleasure of opening up with Elsa. The same apparently happens to other characters in the novel; and one may argue that, by having the courage to reject established attitudes and values and eventually to go their separate ways, once again Tommasino and Elsa are the only ones who face the suffering inherent in the human condition and in human relationships without deceiving themselves. Tommasino believes that most of the people he knows have buried their uneasy, painful thoughts just below the level of awareness, becoming oblivious to their own discontent, and that their relationships therefore harbour a similar sense of dissatisfaction. He confesses to Elsa that he has done the same during the months of their engagement and that this is the reason why he has lost his willingness to communicate openly and honestly with her:

> Ho sotterrato tanti miei pensieri. Gli ho scavato una piccola fossa. […] Stiamo quasi sempre zitti, ora, insieme. Ce ne stiamo quasi sempre zitti, perché abbiamo cominciato a sotterrare i nostri pensieri, bene in fondo, bene in fondo dentro di noi. (*VS*, pp. 766–67)

> [I have driven a great many of my thoughts underground. I have dug out a little grave for them. […] We are almost always silent, because we have begun to drive our thoughts underground, right at the bottom, right at the bottom inside ourselves.] (*VE*, p. 153)

The provincial environment seems to have a repressive effect on people and their relationships. This kind of imprinting is so ingrained that, according to Tommasino, even moving somewhere else would turn out to be in vain, since one carries one's conditioning and expectations along with one. Thus the only way the relationship might have enjoyed a different fate is if Elsa and Tommasino had met as complete strangers:

> – Se tu fossi stata, – disse, – una ragazza di un altro paese! Se ti avessi trovato a Montreal, o non so dove, se ci fossimo incontrati, e sposati! Ci saremmo sentiti così liberi, così leggeri, senza queste case, queste colline, queste montagne! […] Ma se anche ti portassi ora con me, a

Montreal, – disse, – sarebbe come qui, non sapremmo inventare niente di nuovo. Là continueremmo forse ancora a parlare del Vincenzino, del Nebbia, del Purillo. Sarebbe uguale, come essere qua. (*VS*, p. 773)

[If only you had been a girl, – he said, – from another village! If only I had found you in Montreal or somewhere, if only we had met there and married! We should have felt so free, so unburdened, without these houses, these hills, these mountains. [...] But even if I took you with me to Montreal now, – he said, – it would be just like it is here; we should not be able to create anything new. We should probably still go on talking about Vincenzino and Nebbia and Purillo. It would be exactly the same as being here.] (*VE*, pp. 161–62)

As they discuss their situation while walking in the park and along the river in the city, the dialogue between Elsa and Tommasino is punctuated by spatial impressions. What particularly stands out are the crowds of people cheering and enjoying themselves (there is a fair in the park and a boat race on the river) and the music and festive decorations, which provide a jarring background to the two characters' sombre emotional state:

Camminavamo per il parco, sul fiume. C'era la folla, chiasso e musica, e avevano installato, sui prati dietro al castello, un Luna Park. Accanto a noi la gente passava, passava, si radunava sulla balaustra di pietra che s'affaccia sul fiume, e si gettava giù sulla scarpata erbosa, con grida e fischi, perché c'erano, quel giorno, le regate. Passavano sul fiume barche e barche, con bandierine che sventolavano. Anche il casotto dell'imbarcatoio, piantato su palafitte, era pieno di gente, e sul tetto sventolavano bandierine. (*VS*, p. 767)

[We were walking in the park by the river. There was a crowd, noise and music, and they had set up a Luna Park on the lawns behind the castle. People kept passing by us, or gathered together by the stone parapet which faces the river, and threw themselves on the grassy bank with cries and whistles, for the regatta was on that day. Many boats were going up and down the river, with little flags fluttering in the wind. The shelter, too, on the landing stage, built on piles, was full of people, and little flags fluttered in the wind on its roof.] (*VE*, p. 154)

The multitude of people, things (funfair, boats, flags) and audio and visual stimuli (music, loud cheering, colours) in the surrounding environment contrasts with the feelings of emptiness and despair that Elsa and Tommasino are probably experiencing while examining their relationship.

Ginzburg's oeuvre suggests that suffering is existential and inextricably bound to the human condition. It also points to the fact that this universal truth becomes more clearly manifest in relationships when one's hopes of alleviating one's loneliness give way to disillusionment, the inability to communicate and estrangement. The universal, existential nature of suffering implies that, as an experience, it is shared by all human beings, regardless, for example, of where they live, be it in a vibrant cosmopolitan city or a quieter provincial town. Accordingly, in all Ginzburg's novels the characters face very similar challenges and predicaments to those one may find in *Le voci della sera*. That being said, the analysis in this chapter also highlights the fact that in small provincial centres conventions and social conditioning tend to affect existential choices and trajectories to a greater extent than in big cities and that, therefore, in this regard urban dwellers enjoy a greater degree of freedom and arguably more opportunities for self-realization. Mastronardi's *Il maestro di Vigevano* lends itself to similar reflections.

Antonio Mombelli has a wife and a son. Most of the time he adheres idly to the rituals of its provincial town, while feeling very much as if his life were slipping away. He takes a stroll with his wife in the town centre in the evening and at weekends regularly joins a group of colleagues and acquaintances – always the same faces and conversations – at a café in the main piazza for an espresso and a game of cards. Antonio's complicated relationship with his wife and son, and especially the blaming and lack of love in his marriage, provide the storyline alongside his sense of estrangement and inability to fit into his social environment (signalled, for instance, by the fact that his school colleagues appear to be pettily concerned with the possibilities of career advancement, however tiny). The difficulties in human interaction and the ultimate impossibility of authentic, fulfilling relationships therefore link Mastronardi's and Ginzburg's novels, both of which arguably point to the idea that such feelings are perceived more acutely in environments that are inward-looking and conservative. However, it is important to note that, however controversially, other writers have assigned prominence to the province as a place where apparently banal individual stories 'on the margins' enable psychological identification and therefore become representative of the universal human condition. For instance, Rossella Riccobono argues in relation to Pier Vittorio Tondelli, and especially his last novel *Camere separate* [*Separate Rooms*] (1989), that 'by charging it with stories and affection ("affetti, storie, racconti") the Italian province is given the same significance and centrality as the well-known artistic or fashionable European capitals'.[46]

---

46 Rossella Riccobono, 'Introduction', in *The Poetics of the Margins*, ed. by Riccobono, pp. 1–16 (p. 8).

Another controversial issue, moreover, is the fact that the sense of limited opportunities and discontentment evoked by the conservative milieu of *Le voci della sera* is somehow at odds with the centrality of the theme of the traditional family in Ginzburg's writings: that is, the sort of family typical of the patriarchal social order, in which the man, as husband and father, is the main or sole wage earner and therefore the undisputed head of the household. Ginzburg appears to be nostalgic for this model of family and social structure, as emerges clearly from the portrayal of her own family and father, an authoritative and domineering figure, in *Lessico famigliare*. As mentioned above, this sentiment also informs Ginzburg's depiction of different generations and the relationships and conflicts between them. Arguably, generational conflict is also symptomatic of the boom years as a time in which Italian society was caught between modern and traditional pulls: while younger generations enjoyed the benefits of increased possibilities and economic wellbeing, they were also somehow disorientated. *Caro Michele* was born out of this society. In the novel the crisis of male-dominated social structures is met with concern, as it appears to bring about a lack of values and purpose and a general sense of loneliness among the characters.[47] Some have explained this conservative stance by the suffering and hardship Ginzburg experienced during the Second World War and therefore by her anxieties about social unrest and political instability. One should remember that her husband Leone Ginzburg, a militant anti-Fascist, was jailed by the Fascist authorities and killed in 1944. According to Judith Laurence Pastore, these particular anxieties would explain why 'the fusion of the personal and the political creates in many, if not all, of [Ginzburg's] mature texts a longing for the remembered order and security associated with a dominant father figure'.[48] The contradiction is at least partially resolved if we consider that Ginzburg's world view is essentially pessimistic: while she longs for traditional values which have been lost, she does not believe that the stable, reassuring social order of male dominance can ease the pain and suffering which are intrinsic to human existence. The same reason also explains why the places where Ginzburg's characters live only partially affect their fortunes. For instance, we are left with the impression that Tommasino would not find real happiness should he move to a different country. There is an implicit sense of rupture in Ginzburg's novels between the Italy of the past, where powerful but

47   Pastore, 'The Personal is Political', p. 91.
48   Pastore, 'The Personal is Political', pp. 90–91.

largely benevolent father figures prevailed, and the Italy scarred by Fascism, war and civil war, in which models of masculinity seem also to have been undermined. This links to Tommasino's comments above about previous generations having exhausted all available 'carica vitale'. The younger generation – male and female – thus seem to be irreparably damaged. This feeling perhaps lies behind Tommasino's displacement of his emotional and moral energy towards elsewheres constructed in the imaginary, whether that is the impermanent space of the room in Via Gorizia or Montreal.

The chapter presents a notion of the provinces which challenges the idea of the big city as the only locus that enables a real or 'canonical' urban experience. This way of thinking overlooks the dynamism of smaller centres and the fact that secondary or provincial cities evoke their own unique kind of experience. More specifically, the chapter shows that in the context of post-war Italy smaller urban centres helped to propel economic development, for instance through their peculiar model of diffused industrialization. At the same time, the analysis of *Le voci della sera* suggests that certain codified types of behaviour are more ingrained and resistant to change in a provincial town like the one described in the novel than in the big city. One reason for this may be the stronger influence of familial ties and kinship networks, which are more stable and less subject to change in a small city than in the big city environment, where networks and interactions are usually more fleeting. Moreover, the weight of local and known histories, as seen, for example, in the vicissitudes of the De Francisci family, generates a sense of their inevitable reproduction into the future. A similar feeling of immobility seems to characterize gender relations in the novel. An important point, however, is that male characters are significantly more passive. They travel, work, develop ideas and theories, but all because that pathway has been laid out for them and it is expected that, as middle-class, wealthy men, they will take these opportunities. On the other hand, the female characters have to take the initiative actively and independently if they are to achieve even apparently minor change, such as new house décor or freedom of movement locally.

It is also argued that derogatory views of the provinces as something that needs to be concealed and derided may disguise the very centrality of the *provincia* in the Italian national identity due to Italy's history and its traditional fragmentation or 'tribalism'. One may argue that, in *Le voci della sera*, this 'denied centrality' is revealed by the fact that some of the themes and stylistic features of Ginzburg's work are somehow magnified in this tale of the Northern Italian province. While a pessimistic outlook on life and relationships tinges all Ginzburg's oeuvre, this tendency is arguably all the more central to *Le voci della sera*. The relationship between Elsa and Tommasino, and more broadly the existential trajectories of the other characters in the novel, are all seen and presented through this despairing lens. In this regard Ginzburg somehow condemns the characters to 'peripherality' in terms of their disconnected emotional worlds, the impossibility of establishing meaningful connections, their solitude and inability to communicate clearly. In this sense, in *Le voci della sera* the provinces remain marginal and peripheral in that they seem to foster atomization and do not enable fulfilling love and affective relationships, but only unfulfilled life trajectories.

4. Post-War Italian Travel Writing:
Piovene, Ortese, Arbasino

Introduction: New Conceptions of Journeying

The ambiguous place that travel writing occupies within Italy's literary tradition may largely be ascribed to the hybrid nature of the genre and its kinship with other forms of writing, such as journalism and the essay.[1] The marginality of travel literature links this genre to crime fiction, which, as seen, has also struggled to attain literary dignity within the Italian cultural panorama. Both forms of writing have indeed been considered less important than more canonical and allegedly prestigious forms of writing.[2] Theodore Cachey argues that the uncertain status of travel writing within the Italian literary canon may be linked to the centrality of the idea of 'placelessness' in the Italian literary tradition since at least Dante's and Petrarch's vernacular practices.[3] The relevance of displacement means that 'the entire tradition comprises a literature of travel, and more precisely a literature of exile/pilgrimage',[4] and that therefore there is no need for a specific travel category. This chapter focuses on post-war Italian domestic travel writing, that is, on travel accounts written by Italian

---

1   Joanne Lee, 'Alternative Urban Journeys: Italian Travel Writing and the *Contromano* Series', *Studies in Travel Writing*, 16 (2012), 203–14 (pp. 205–06) <http://dx.doi.org/10.1080/13645145.2012.682820> [accessed 7 February 2017].

2   Remo Ceserani and Pierluigi Pellini, 'The Belated Development of a Theory of the Novel in Italian Literary Culture', in *The Cambridge Companion to the Italian Novel*, ed. by Peter Bondanella and Andrea Ciccarelli (Cambridge: Cambridge University Press, 2003), pp. 1–19 (p. 16).

3   Theodore J. Cachey, 'An Italian Literary History of Travel', in *L'Odeporica/ Hodoeporics: On Travel Literature*, ed. by Luigi Monga (= *Annali d'Italianistica*, 14 (1996)), pp. 55–64 (pp. 55–56).

4   Cachey, 'An Italian Literary History of Travel', p. 56.

authors travelling in Italy, a specific category of travelogues that in the context of the genre may be considered even more marginal, for it has received very little critical attention until recent years.[5] Even among literary critics, there is a tendency to identify travel literature relating to Italy with the work of foreign authors. This means that the internal perspective of Italian writers has often been overlooked.[6]

From the Renaissance onwards, and particularly with the tradition of the Grand Tour, which enjoyed a great vogue in the seventeenth and eighteenth centuries, Italy became a privileged destination for international travellers as a major centre of classical culture. The Italian journey was considered almost an obligatory stage in the education of the European elite in a cultural context that was largely dominated by the study of the Classics.[7] The travel accounts of the Grand Tour have shaped the image of Italy as a sort of open-air museum, drawing on the wealth of its historical and cultural patrimony. This mode of viewing has informed the foreign gaze on Italy but also the way in which Italians see themselves.[8] This predominant perspective accounts for the enduring idea of Italy as the *Bel Paese*, one which conveys the view of a country frozen in the atemporality of its architectural and natural beauties. The dominant way of looking at Italy in travel writing remains largely reifying and travel narratives of the Italian Peninsula continue to be largely associated with the tradition of the Grand Tour and with the point of view of foreign travellers, more specifically, the point of view of the foreign male traveller of means, since travelling for leisure and education has traditionally been a privilege of the male elites.[9]

5   See Luca Clerici, 'Alla scoperta del Bel Paese: i titoli delle testimonianze dei viaggiatori italiani in Italia, 1750–1900', in *L'Odeporica/Hodoeporics*, ed. by Monga, pp. 271–303.

6   Sharon Ouditt and Loredana Polezzi, 'Introduction: Italy as Place and Space', *Studies in Travel Writing*, 16 (2012), 97–105 (p. 98) <http://dx.doi.org/10.1080/13645145.2012.682807> [accessed 7 February 2017].

7   Jeremy Black, *Italy and the Grand Tour* (New Haven, CT: Yale University Press, 2003), p. 2.

8   As Ouditt and Polezzi put it, 'many of the images of Italy and of Italian culture produced by international travellers were incorporated into construction of national identity' (Ouditt and Polezzi, 'Introduction', p. 97).

9   While there are certainly examples of women travel writers who are active as early as the age of the Grand Tour, these are considerably fewer in number than their male counterparts. As has been pointed out, this can be related to the idea that men and women occupy the public and domestic spheres respectively. Fortunati, Monticelli and Ascari, for example, point out that while men have always been free to embrace travel as adventure and intellectual exploration,

Nevertheless, Italian authors, too, have produced a large repertoire of written accounts documenting their journeys in Italy. Their travelogues began to appear as early as the eighteenth century.[10] It can be argued that the evolution of Italian travel literature went hand in hand with the tradition of foreign travel writing. Italian domestic travel accounts failed for a long time to provide a real alternative to the dominant image of Italy codified by foreign travellers and in some cases even retraced the latter's itineraries. In other instances, however, they included places off the beaten track of the Grand Tour.[11] Travel accounts by Italian authors flourished in the aftermath of the unification of Italy in 1861.[12] In particular, more comprehensive accounts began to emerge that took into consideration wider portions of the national territory as a reflection of the intellectual curiosity that accompanied the newly born nation and in response to the improvements in the road network.[13] Abbott Antonio Stoppani's book *Il Bel Paese* [*The Beautiful Country*] (1875) and Edmondo De Amicis's *Cuore* [*Heart*] (1886) are arguably the foremost examples of the new quest for discovery and the educational mission with which this was often invested.[14] Both

----

the role of women in relation to travel has traditionally been associated with the domestic sphere and therefore with the return home, along the lines of the archetypical figure of Penelope (Vita Fortunati, Rita Monticelli and Maurizio Ascari, 'Introduction', in *Travel Writing and the Female Imaginary*, ed. by Vita Fortunati, Rita Monticelli and Maurizio Ascari (Bologna: Patron, 2001), pp. 5–16 (p. 8)). Susan Bassnett also points out the gendered nature of travel as quest and adventure, mainly deriving from the fact that men 'moved more freely in the public sphere' (Susan Bassnett, 'Travel Writing and Gender', in *The Cambridge Companion to Travel Writing*, ed. by Peter Hulme and Tim Youngs (Cambridge: Cambridge University Press, 2002), pp. 225–41 (p. 225)).

10   Clerici's survey of Italian domestic travel writing in his *Il viaggiatore meravigliato* opens with Antonio Vallisneri's *Lezione accademica intorno l'origine delle fontane* (1714).

11   Clerici, *Viaggiatore*, p. xxviii.

12   Ouditt and Polezzi, 'Introduction', pp. 100–02.

13   Clerici, *Viaggiatore*, pp. xx–xxi.

14   Valtorta, Hill and Minghelli claim: '*Il Bel Paese* aimed to teach of the natural beauty of Italy [...]. The famous *Cuore* taught young people love of country, respect for family and the authorities, and the spirit of sacrifice, brotherhood, and obedience through stories whose protagonists were children from different regional and social backgrounds' (Roberta Valtorta, Sarah Patricia Hill and Giuliana Minghelli, 'Photography and the Construction of Italian National Identity', in *Stillness in Motion: Italy, Photography and the Meanings of Modernity*, ed. by Roberta Valtorta, Sarah Patricia Hill and Giuliana Minghelli (Toronto: Toronto University Press, 2014), pp. 27–56 (p. 28)).

Abbott Stoppani and De Amicis are crucial figures in the development of modern Italian reportage and journalism.[15] The emergence of Italian landscape photography in the first half of the twentieth century, chiefly through the activities of the Italian Touring Club[16] and the Alinari brothers, provided an additional boost to the establishment of a genuinely Italian travel imaginary. These photographs challenged the reductive rhetoric of the Grand Tour by capturing differences and variety across the Peninsula. It has been pointed out, however, that they still betray the persistence of a foreign, reifying gaze in their reflection of the political agenda of the Northern Italian elite who led Italy's unification process.[17]

Italy's political unification at the end of the nineteenth century gave the first significant impulse to the development of the national road network and rail system. It is, however, the boom years that witnessed a proper revolution in mobility thanks to substantial improvements carried out to the railway and road systems, for instance with the construction of *autostrade* [motorways], and to unprecedented motorization. These innovations fostered a change in the perception of distances within the country. As Ernesto Galli Della Loggia puts it, it seemed as if, in those years, Italy became smaller: 'Grazie ad una imponente motorizzazione di massa, mutarono anche le proporzioni geografiche del paese. Ricoperta di autostrade e di distributori di benzina, l'Italia si rimpicciolì, e mentre cambiava il senso dello spazio cambiò anche la sua misura' [Thanks to an impressive mass motorization, the geographical proportions of the country also changed. Covered by motorways and petrol stations, Italy shrank and as the sense of space changed, so did its size].[18] In the 1950s and 1960s the journey increasingly featured in Italian literature and cinema as a recurring trope for the discovery

---

15 According to Guagnini, De Amicis represents 'l'esempio di un tentativo di nuovo approccio al reportage' [the example of a newly attempted approach to reportage] (Elvio Guagnini, *Il viaggio, lo sguardo, la scrittura* (Trieste: Edizioni Università di Trieste, 2010), p. 37).

16 The Touring Club Italiano was founded in 1894 by a group of cyclists with the aim of promoting the values of cycling and travel. It soon proved popular, boasting 16,000 members by as early as 1899. It went on to produce a wide variety of maps and guidebooks that have become familiar household items.

17 As Valtorta, Hill and Minghelli put it, these photographs reveal the 'persistence of an old, picturesque image of Italy, born from the intersection of foreign and elite perspectives' (Valtorta, Hill and Minghelli, 'Photography', p. 43).

18 As quoted in Torriglia, *Broken Time*, p. 117. Torriglia does not name the actual source.

and appropriation of the national territory but also as a metaphor for self-discovery.[19] Journeying provided the occasion to investigate phenomena of modernization across the Peninsula, as shown by the many writers and intellectuals who committed themselves to documenting the country's changing geography.[20] In those years journeying also carried other meanings. If, on the one hand, the rise of the socio-cultural phenomenon of the *villeggiatura* [holidays spent away from the city] in the newly developed vacation resorts points to greater leisure time and economic wellbeing, on the other the 1950s and 1960s also saw masses of poorer Italians (especially from the South of the country) being forced to leave their homes for economic reasons. Many headed towards what Piovene has described as 'un aldilà fisico, il Nord, un paese straniero, dove si troverebbe la felicità' [an otherworldly place, the North, a foreign country where happiness would be found] (*VI*, p. 663). As Donna Gabaccia points out, post-war mass internal migration did not represent an entirely new phenomenon, for Italians have been among the most mobile people in the world since the Middle Ages.[21] What was new was the fact that Italian migrants moved in huge numbers to the North of the country instead of overseas, as had overwhelmingly been the case up to that point (and can be seen again today).[22]

This chapter explores three examples of post-war Italian travel literature, including, first, Ortese's collection of travel pieces *La lente scura*. Ortese is best known for her works of fiction, which were

---

19 This happened to the point that the journey provided 'a new cultural image of the country' and became an 'icon' (Torriglia, *Broken Time*, pp. 118–19).

20 As well as the three texts analysed in this chapter – Anna Maria Ortese's *La lente scura*, Guido Piovene's *Viaggio in Italia* and Alberto Arbasino's *Fratelli d'Italia* – examples include Mario Soldati's series of reports from the Po Valley, produced by Italy's public broadcasting company RAI at the end of the 1950s; Rocco Scotellaro's *Contadini del Sud* [*Peasants of the South*] (1954); and Ernesto De Martino's fieldwork in Southern Italy. De Martino's *Il mondo magico* [*The World of Magic*] (1948) and *Sud e Magia* [*South and Magic*] (1959) represent an effort to document the survival of the beliefs and practices of Southern peasant culture threatened by the diffusion of modern lifestyles. Films that feature some representation of the journey include Roberto Rossellini's *Viaggio in Italia* [*Journey to Italy*] (1954); and Michelangelo Antonioni's *Cronaca di un amore* [*Chronicle of a Love Affair*] (1950) and *Le amiche* [*The Girl Friends*] (1955).

21 Donna R. Gabaccia, *Italy's Many Diasporas*, Global Diasporas (Seattle: University of Washington Press, 2000), pp. 1–3.

22 As Gabaccia observes, the boom 'changed the character of Italy's international migrations and ended the country's long history as one of the world's most important exporters of labor' (Gabaccia, *Italy's Many Diasporas*, p. 160).

awarded prestigious literary prizes. She won the Viareggio Prize in 1953 with the collection of short stories *Il mare non bagna Napoli* [*The Sea Does Not Bathe Naples*] and the Strega Prize in 1967 with her novel *Poveri e semplici* [*The Poor and the Simple*]. For most of her career Ortese also worked as a journalist and reporter, publishing her articles in numerous newspapers and magazines. She was accustomed to moving around since, as a child, her father's employment by the Italian government had meant that the family had had to relocate frequently in Italy and abroad (they lived in Tripoli from 1924 to 1928). Ortese's restless approach to travel may, therefore, in part reflect this experience. The troubled road to publication of *La lente scura* may be seen as symptomatic of the uncertain status of travel writing within the Italian literary canon and book market. Ortese started to work on a project for a collection of travel pieces in 1952, which she then shelved, resumed and revised several times over the course of the following decades. Thanks to the philological and bibliographical work of Luca Clerici, who also has the merit of having recovered the group of reportages that now constitute the second section of the volume, the book finally came out in 1991 with the structure that it maintains to this day.[23] *La lente scura* includes pieces that were written by Ortese from the end of the 1940s to the beginning of the 1960s. While the book as a whole is taken into consideration, this chapter focuses mainly on the articles that were written and published after 1957. By this time economic growth had visibly taken off, anticipated as it was by a wave of modernization in Italian cultural life. In particular, the Hungarian uprising against the Soviet Union in 1956 and the discussions it prompted put an end to the almost totalizing influence that the Italian Communist Party had exerted over the mainstream cultural debate on the left. The new openness to sociological approaches and cultural trends such as psychoanalysis and cultural anthropology, which in Italy had until then been met with resistance, was one of the effects of this cultural renewal.[24]

Piovene's *Viaggio in Italia*, the second text to be analysed here, is a monumental endeavour to document the transformations occurring throughout the national territory as Piovene travelled from North to South, one region after the other, between 1953 and 1956. Commissioned by the RAI, *Viaggio in Italia* was originally

---

23 See Luca Clerici, 'Notizia sul testo', in Anna Maria Ortese, *La lente scura. Scritti di viaggio*, ed. by Luca Clerici (Milan: Adelphi, 2004 [1991]), pp. 467–501.

24 Crainz, *Storia del miracolo economico*, p. 50.

written for a series of radio episodes that were transmitted by Radio RAI. A member of an aristocratic family from Vicenza, Piovene was a novelist and a regular contributor to Italy's most prominent newspapers, known for his elegant writing style and lucid analyses. He displayed chameleon-like attitudes in his political views. He went from supporting the Fascist regime to sympathizing with the Communist Party after the end of the war, gaining the nickname of 'Conte Rosso' [Red Count] due to his aristocratic origins.[25] Piovene also engaged with autobiographical and introspective elements, particularly in the novels set in the childhood environment of Vicenza, *Le Furie* [*The Furies*] (1963) and *Le stelle fredde* [*The Cold Stars*] (1970). When discussing the reasons which prompted him to embark on his journey across Italy, in *Viaggio in Italia* Piovene writes: '[S]ono curioso dell'Italia, degli italiani e di me stesso' [I am curious about Italy, the Italian people and myself] (*VI*, p. 11). He therefore anticipates that travel will trigger self-exploration through the encounter with people and places. In a mirror-like effect, then, the investigative lens turns on the observer himself. Alberto Arbasino's *Fratelli d'Italia* is the third and final text to be examined here. Arbasino was one of the leading exponents of the Gruppo '63 and Neoavanguardia, which championed forms of stylistic experimentation that broke with the canon. Like Guido Ceronetti in more recent years, he belongs to a more disenchanted, cynical strand of the Italian journey, the origins of which may be traced back to Lawrence Stern's *Sentimental Journey* (1768). Elvio Guagnini argues that this tradition, which moves the subjectivity of the observer into the foreground, may be seen as a reaction to the eighteenth-century type of encyclopaedic travel writing that sought to give a comprehensive account of observed reality (of which Piovene's *Viaggio in Italia* is an emanation).[26] We shall see later that *Fratelli d'Italia* indeed offers interesting insights into the role and positioning of the writer-observer in travel literature.

This chapter explores how Ortese, Piovene and Arbasino relate to tropes and stereotypes codified in the tradition of travel writing on Italy and especially the implications of Ortese's gendered perspective against the male-connoted voice, which has been dominant in travel literature from the Grand Tour onwards and is exemplified here by Piovene's *Viaggio in Italia*. It also looks at Arbasino's *Fratelli d'Italia* as a further reinterpretation of the traditional journey to Italy. Established

---

25 See, e.g., Sandro Gerbi, *Tempi di malafede: Guido Piovene ed Eugenio Colorni. Una storia italiana tra fascismo e dopoguerra* (Milan: Hoepli, 2012), p. xi.

26 Guagnini, *Il viaggio*, pp. 5–6.

and accepted ways of seeing Italy therefore intertwine, in this chapter, with issues of gender and sexuality within the context of the post-war years, which are ripe for a critical revisiting of traditional paradigms. The writers' different approaches to travel are indicative of socially constructed notions and expectations related to gender, which in turn shape the experience of travel and its conceptualization. As in the previous chapters, the analysis here revolves around the idea of the Italian post-war period as a controversial transition. The difficulty of coming to grips with rapid changes certainly informs Ortese's and Piovene's travel writing and their very different attempts at grappling with them. A distinctive kind of underlying anxiety runs through the texts. According to Alberto Rodighiero, *Fratelli d'Italia* captures the nature of the Italian boom years as 'ultimo ballo prima della caduta nel baratro' [the last dance before falling into the abyss].[27] The characters' frantic wandering and relentless socializing betray emptiness and disorientation. Unsurprisingly, death has a prominent presence in the novel. Raimondo, one of the chief members of the intellectual circle in the book, is dying from cancer and yet continues until the end to host glamorous parties and cultural events. Ortese, for her part, openly discusses feelings of uncertainty in her personal life as well as in the country's historical phase as she sets out on her journeys. Finally, it will be argued that Piovene's *Viaggio in Italia* betrays a more hidden kind of anxiety in its very pretence of completeness.

Arguably, Italy's nation-building process was further hindered in the post-war period by the institutional failure to foster a vision of collective identity and belonging, corroborated by a critical public reckoning with the past. In the texts examined here the issue of Italy's historical fragmentation emerges, for example, through the South as the half of the country which struggles to emerge from poverty. The difficult integration process of the South within the unified nation raises the question of the geographical margins and their representation, delineating patterns of belonging and exclusion within the dominant model of modernity. David Forgacs observes that Italy's unification process involved the marginalization of certain people and places (chiefly Southern Italy) which have been defined as peripheral in relation to core social groups and locations established, by contrast, as central and important (the North as the birthplace of the political and cultural elite that led Italy's unification).[28] The

---

27   Alberto Rodighiero, 'Fratelli d'Italia', *Studi Novecenteschi*, 30 (2003), 265–81 (p. 266).

28   Forgacs, *Italy's Margins*, p. 1.

notion of margin therefore entails a way of seeing the Other, which is observed and objectified from an economically and culturally powerful centre.[29] This explains the process of 'othering' that has been inflicted on the South and that reverberates, for instance, through Piovene's superior stance in his pages dedicated to Southern Italy. As we shall see, Ortese's portrayal is more sympathetic and complex, while for Arbasino the notion of place becomes much more fleeting and less influenced by cultural assumptions.

Gendered Tropes in Travel Writing

The Undomesticated Nature of Anna Maria Ortese

In the introduction and concluding remarks to *La lente scura*, Ortese opens a window into her inner world and therefore into the interplay between travel and introspection. She evokes a time of great uncertainty when recollecting the years of her numerous journeys across Italy:

> Non auguro a nessuna persona giovane e vagamente 'dissociata' come io ero, e inoltre priva di reddito e anche di minime certezze personali e professionali – di attraversare l'Italia in un dopoguerra subito privo di unità e memoria – come io l'attraversai. C'è da uscirne spezzati. Tutto vi sembra estraneo, meraviglioso e spietato insieme: siete in casa d'altri! [...] vidi Roma, o altre città, come appunto le vidi: straniere, accese, inesplicabili! (*LS*, p. 452)

> [I do not wish any young and vaguely 'dissociated' person like I was, and also without income and with minimal personal and professional certainties – to cross Italy in a post-war period suddenly devoid of unity and memory – as I crossed it. We have to come out broken. Everything seems foreign to you, wonderful and ruthless at the same time: you are in someone else's house! [...] I saw Rome, or other cities, just as I saw them: foreign, intense, inexplicable!]

Ortese describes her younger self as vulnerable, somewhat detached from reality, without personal and economic stability. The society which she portrays and which has just come out of the war also projects a sense of lack, with its faltering memory and precarious national unity. The places she encounters in her journeying appear foreign, inexplicable

---

29   Forgacs states: 'No place is ever intrinsically marginal, peripheral or remote. It and its inhabitants are always marginal, peripheral or remote in relation to some centre elsewhere' (Forgacs, *Italy's Margins*, p. 8).

and hostile to the extent that they evoke the feeling of being in someone else's house. Ortese's travel writing is permeated by a sense of lack and non-belonging which the act of travelling is unable to heal and perhaps ultimately exacerbates. One should not forget that the vast majority of Italians had travelled very little across their country until the greater prosperity and mobility of the post-war years provided opportunities for increasing numbers of ordinary people to travel further. Ortese's perception of Italian places as foreign may, therefore, reflect the fact that knowledge of the Italian territory only began to improve with the development of adequate transport infrastructures, the amelioration of economic conditions and the advent of mass-media communication.

One may assume, however, that Ortese's hesitancy in laying claim to the places she visits and her idea of travel as a fearful, destabilizing experience are also a reflection of her being a woman travel writer. Piovene, as we shall see, lays claim to the reality that he observes in the sense that he maintains he is able to grasp it through his rational, analytical approach. Ortese's travel writing spans the years in which women's emancipation from the roles of mothers and wives was still hardly conceivable and the feminist movement had yet to develop in Italy. In her study of women's travel writing in the British colonies, Sara Mills argues that women travel writers found it more difficult to employ the 'imperialist voice' in their writings than their male counterparts for they conformed to the dominant conceptions of femininity of the time.[30] Ortese's being a female writer in the Italy of the 1950s may, therefore, explain her own apprehensive approach to travel and the travel-writing profession in the years in which more Italian women were starting to join the labour force but whose path to emancipation and empowerment had only just begun.[31] At least since the Grand Tour and before the advent of mass tourism in more recent times, travel had overwhelmingly been the prerogative of the wealthy young male.[32] Women were normally expected to be in the company of a chaperon. Even today, a woman travelling on her own is often seen as taking an unnecessary risk.

---

30 Sara Mills, *Discourses of Difference: An Analysis of Women's Travel Writing and Colonialism* (London: Routledge, 1991), p. 3.

31 Hellman points out that 'when feminism emerged in the early 1970s, it was both an outgrowth of and a response to a complex of radical social and economic changes that had already gone a long way toward transforming Italy into a modernized, industrialized and secular country much like its Western European neighbors' (Judith Adler Hellman, *Journeys Among Women: Feminism in Five Italian Cities* (Cambridge: Polity, 1987), p. 1).

32 Black, *Italy and the Grand Tour*, p. 5.

Ortese's approach to travelling is far from reconciled or conventional. It recalls more of a restless quest. Her aspiration to understand the places she visits, let alone to feel at home in any of them, remains unattainable. Ortese suggests that only when the tourist drops his or her role and identity (she fantasizes that this might happen if the tourist were to be mistaken by local people for someone else, a relative, an acquaintance or someone who belongs to their community) does it become possible for him or her to overcome the sense of estrangement and unfamiliarity conveyed by new people and places:

> In una città, come nel mare, bisogna identificarsi, per vedere realmente. Bisogna che qualcuno si dimentichi per quale motivo siete venuto, e vi confonda con un familiare. Allora, mille particolari segreti vengono alla superficie, e in quei particolari si ricompone anche per voi il volto sfaccettato della città, si ricompone in un'immagine unica. (*LS*, p. 330)

> [In a city, as in the sea, one needs to orientate oneself in order really to see. The reasons you came must be forgotten; you must be mistaken for a native. Then, a thousand secret details come to the surface and in those details the multifaceted face of the city takes shape for you, too, it takes shape in a singular and unique image.]

What Ortese says here is that one may attempt to understand a place and its inhabitants only by immersing oneself and blending in with the life of the community, a principle which also informs modern cultural anthropology, at least since it underwent a critical self-interrogation of its methodology in order to reject any involvement with colonialism.[33] Cultural relativism as one of the guiding tenets of cultural anthropology aims to avoid a superior, objectifying eye and therefore to give the observed back their voice. As for Ortese, it means setting off on her journeying without preconceived expectations. Given the power imbalance that is always involved in the relationship between the observer and observed, a certain degree of reification and cultural appropriation remains unavoidable. Nevertheless, here Ortese consciously rejects the standardized tourist experience and the acquisitive gaze that defines much of the Grand Tour tradition.

The themes of silence and incommunicability, meant as the difficulty to make oneself heard and understood, are a clear feminist element and a clue to Ortese's gendered counter-discourse. Historically, the voice of women has been silenced; their agency curtailed. In *La lente scura* the experience of travel often provides the occasion for feelings of ineffability to emerge onto the written page. In the following

---

33   Forgacs, *Italy's Margins*, p. 141.

extract, for example, Ortese describes the common occurrence of holding a conversation with fellow passengers during a train journey. After they exchange some information about themselves and their places of origin, Ortese is left baffled by the realization that places and the existences that populate them inevitably bear different meanings to different people. In other words, there is inevitably a gap in human communication, some lack of reciprocal understanding which Ortese likens to the experience of staring at a silent starry sky at night:

> Ogni volta che sono in treno, qualcuno mi racconta la sua vita; qualche volta, io racconto la mia […]. Benché le storie di questi uomini e queste donne mi spieghino stranamente i paesi da cui essi provengono, o che attraversiamo, l'impressione finale è sempre di smarrimento, come dopo aver fissato un muto cielo stellato. (*LS*, p. 347)

> [Every time I am on the train, someone tells me about their life; sometimes I tell my story [...]. Although the stories of these men and women are meant to explain to me the strange lands from which they come, or through which we pass, the final impression is always one of bewilderment, as after staring at a silent starry sky.]

The beauty of the landscapes Ortese portrays in her travel accounts, which she finds so immaculate as to almost seem unreal and intimidating, exacerbates this sense of estrangement: 'L'estraneità rimane, e trova le sue origini nell'assurdità di questa bellezza, nella sua perfezione e incomunicabilità assolutamente al di fuori dell'umano' [The feeling of 'outsideness' remains, it has its source in the absurdity of this beauty, in its absolute perfection and incommunicability that is beyond the human] (*LS*, p. 350). The contemplation of a beautiful landscape is normally experienced as pleasurable and enriching. Ortese, however, perceives it as absurd. By deeming it unknowable and not conveyable, she resists tendencies to the objectification and ultimately dominance of the natural world.

Ortese contends that a place like the Ligurian Riviera can only be contemplated from a distance and is not suitable for living. Only the rich and powerful possess enough conceit not to be afraid of manipulating and spoiling that beauty: 'Tutta questa bellezza, toccando la perfezione delle cose pensate, mi sembra inabitabile. E forse, sotto questo aspetto, è anche comprensibile perché sia diventata preda dell'infinita avidità e disponibilità dei ricchi, disponibilità di mezzi e di aggressione' [All this beauty, approaching as it does the perfection of thought, seems scarcely habitable to me. And yet, perhaps, in this respect, it is also understandable why it should have fallen prey to the infinite greed and leisure of the rich, the leisure to buy and to ravage] (*LS*, p. 337). This description has strong gendered connotations because it emphasizes the urge to dominate and possess. The final phrase, in particular, recalls the memory of war and colonization by hinting at the use of military force and technology to control what is identified as wild, natural and rich in resources that can be exploited. The chapter 'Viaggio in Liguria' [Journey to Liguria] again raises the issues of the marketization of the national territory and of the exploitation of natural resources for the purposes of economic gain. It does so through the character of Alessi, a former sailor with a heightened sensitivity and perception of reality whom Ortese meets in Santa Margherita, Liguria. From Alessi's fragmentary account, we gather that he has gone through a traumatic event while out at sea, one which is still haunting him. He lived abroad for thirty years and now that he has returned to his birthplace in Liguria he feels uprooted. He observes the recent transformations in his environment and comments: 'Hanno affittato e venduto tutto, anche le voci' [They rented and sold everything, even the voices] (*LS*, p. 357). The theme of appropriation or denial of voice adds a distinctly feminist charge to Alessi's account.

La lente scura evokes analogies between the exploitation of the environment and the exploitation of women. As eco-feminist critics point out, the connection between women and nature – a supposed archetype of the human imagination, as seen, for example, in the historical, tenacious identification of nature with a nurturing mother – may, however, reinforce the essentialist type of thinking that assigns fixed characteristics to the sexes. Similarly, Val Plumwood remarks that:

> the framework of assumptions in which the human/nature contrast has been formed in the west is one not only of *feminine* connectedness with and passivity towards nature, but also and complementarily one of exclusion and domination of the sphere of nature by a white, largely male elite.[34]

Our concept of nature therefore needs to be problematized in order to avoid perpetuating gender essentialism.[35] Ortese does so by challenging stereotypical notions of natural beauty in the dominant

---

34 Carolyn Merchant, *The Death of Nature: Women, Ecology, and the Scientific Revolution* (London: Widwood House, 1982 [1980]), p. 9; and Val Plumwood, *Feminism and the Mastery of Nature*, Opening Out: Feminism for Today (London: Routledge, 1993), pp. 22–23.

35 Stacy Alaimo, *Undomesticated Ground: Recasting Nature as Feminist Space* (Ithaca, NY: Cornell University Press, 2000), p. 10.

representations of Italy. Such notions are also central to what Pasquale Verdicchio has called the 'national unificatory discourse',[36] which has sought to depict the Italian landscape 'in terms of national treasures'[37] at least since the unification of Italy and especially through the activities of the Club Alpino Italiano (founded in 1863) and Italian Touring Club. The concept of the *Bel Paese* at the heart of such representations is re-semanticized by Ortese in opposition to both the nationalistic rhetoric and the reifying descriptions of foreign observers. She gives a disquieting representation of the natural world, presenting it as harsh and punctuating it with references to silence and death.[38] This kind of wild, uncontrollable nature articulates a resistance to domination and possession.

Piovene's Portrait of Italy as a Modern Nation

Piovene, too, distances himself from conventional modes of representation of the Italian Peninsula. The Grand Tour assigned special importance to the traditional *città d'arte* [art cities] of Rome, Venice, Florence and Naples and, like Piovene, generally followed an itineray from North to South. The encyclopaedic reach of *Viaggio in Italia* implies that all places are worthy of exploration and there is no hierarchy based on the alleged primacy of Romantic landscapes or cultural treasures. Quite the contrary: the architectural beauty of certain Italian cities is regarded by Piovene as a limitation and

---

36 Pasquale Verdicchio, 'Introduction: The Denatured Wild: Ecocritical Approaches to Italian Culture and Literature', in *Ecocritical Approaches to Italian Culture and Literature: The Denatured Wild*, ed. by Pasquale Verdicchio (London: Lexington Books, 2016), pp. vii–xvi (p. xii).

37 Verdicchio, 'Introduction', p. xi.

38 Examples include: 'Il 25 dicembre dell'anno seguente non sembrava Natale; alle due del pomeriggio ero sul treno Firenze–Pistoia. Vuoto, deserto, come tutta l'Italia che avevo attraversata. [...] Anche qui, nell'aria di primavera, un silenzio di morte' [December 25 of the following year did not feel like Christmas; at two in the afternoon I was on the Florence–Pistoia train. It was empty, deserted, like all of Italy I had crossed. [...] Even here, in the spring air, a deathly silence] (*LS*, p. 133); 'Non avevamo alcuna prevenzione, tutt'altro, verso il paesaggio toscano, ma esso, quella mattina, fosse effetto del tempo o di una nostra cattiva disposizione fisica che alterava l'esatta misura delle cose, ci parve più profondo e pericoloso e morto di quanto in realtà non fosse' [On the contrary, we had no prejudices towards the Tuscan landscape, but that morning, I don't know whether it was the effect of the weather or of my poor physical condition which altered the exact proportions of things, but it seemed to me more unfathomable and dangerous and dead than it actually was] (*LS*, pp. 142–43).

'perfezione conclusa che talvolta condanna alla sterilità' [a complete perfection that sometimes condemns a place to sterility] (*VI*, p. 74). Milan, as a city that has constantly transformed and reinvented itself, a city whose history is never concluded, embodies modern values of dynamism and innovation. Piovene praises the whole Lombardy region, which he deems beautiful, but in a more discreet and less stereotypically Italian way, 'meno esemplare, meno italiana, per lo straniero che avvicina l'Italia e la vuole conoscere nei suoi paesaggi resi tipici dalle convenzioni turistiche' [for the foreigner who approaches Italy and wants to get to know it through the landscapes rendered stereotypical by tourist conventions it is less exemplary, less Italian] (*VI*, p. 73). For this reason it has remained at the margins of the mainstream tourist circuit and, writes Piovene, one may appreciate it more authentically. The chapter on Rome opens with a similar declaration of intent as Piovene refuses, deeming it superfluous and ridiculous, to itemize all the architectural and cultural treasures of the Eternal City as so many other writers have done before him. Piovene therefore takes a clear stance against the Grand Tour and *Bel Paese* rhetoric as he openly rejects established ways of seeing and conceptualizing the Italian Peninsula (the fact that Lombardy is not typically Italian is seen as a value) and documents the complexity of the latter beyond standardized itineraries, which tended to privilege specific places, especially within the same epoch and among groups of travellers of the same nationality.[39]

The main reason why Piovene rejects romanticized views of Italy is that they clash with the image he intends to present of the country as a modern nation in the making. It is Piovene's purpose to show that Italy is bound to find its own place in the project of a unified, modern Europe together with more developed countries if the remaining obstacles to its modernization and nation-building processes are effectively tackled and overcome. The chapter dedicated to Rome – a city so often portrayed and celebrated and which arguably embodies most clearly than any other the cliché of the *Bel Paese* – provides a further example of Piovene's tendency to challenge enduring commonplaces. The chapter also contains interesting reflections on the difficulties of integrating a city with such an important history and tradition, and unique identity, into the project of the unified nation. Here, Piovene further criticizes the cult of the past, deeming it a hindrance for the modernization process, but also points out that

---

39 See, e.g., <http://grandtour.bncf.firenze.sbn.it/racconto/come-si-viaggiava/itinerari> [accessed 14 August 2017].

the end of the Second World War undermined the allure of Rome's imperial history, triggering the transformation of Rome into a modern city, 'non interamente europea, come Londra e Parigi, ma la grande metropoli con caratteri misti, tra l'Europa e il Mediterraneo' [not entirely European, like London and Paris, but a great metropolis with mixed traits, between Europe and the Mediterranean] (*VI*, p. 640). Piovene's progressive stance can also be measured against the widely shared idea of immigration as a plague for the receiving city, as seen in the following example:

> L'affluenza degli stranieri, non soltanto contemplativi, le dà un carattere cosmopolita di nuova specie; l'irruzione degli italiani da tutte le province sopravanza la vecchia società romana, popolare, borghese e aristocratica. Si compie così a Roma, con ritmo sempre più veloce, una fusione della società italiana. (*VI*, p. 640)

> [The influx of foreigners who are not only there to admire gives it a cosmopolitan character of a new kind; the irruption of Italians from all the provinces transforms old Roman society, popular, bourgeois and aristocratic. Thus, there emerges in Rome a rapidly expanding melting pot of Italian society.]

Piovene sees immigration as a resource which may boost the renewal of Rome's decadent society and accelerate the creation of a more variegated but unified Italian society. It is also interesting to note the derogatory reference to the contemplative, passive attitude of the tourist who, unlike the immigrant, does not contribute anything to the host community. Nevertheless, Piovene is not immune from some of the essentialist arguments around immigration and urbanism. For instance, he calls 'muffe' [moulds] the *borgate* [working-class suburbs] that were created in Rome during the Fascist period. He also champions a controlled transformation of Rome against what he sees as its post-war chaotic growth.

Piovene claims he is aware that, like any other 'inventory', his *Viaggio in Italia* contains omissions and gaps (*VI*, p. 5). He warns his readers that the book can only reflect the particular moment in which it was written, for the physical and social landscape of the country is changing so rapidly that it would take multiple journeys in the course of the following months and years to keep the observations up to date. It is tempting to see this rhetorical modesty as a pose, for Piovene still aims to compile a comprehensive survey of the social geography of post-war Italy. He is confident that his analytical method of observation can capture the fundamental processes at stake in post-war Italian society. These empirical observations give prominence to what Tim Youngs and Charles Forsdick identify as the analytical, objective qualities of the reportage, in which the emphasis is put on the reality described by an allegedly unbiased observer. According to Youngs and Forsdick:

> [travel writing's] modes oscillate around the usually distinct fields of autobiography and science. The former lends to travel writing its subjective qualities centred on the character of the narrator and his or her interactions with the people and landscapes that are encountered. The scientific aspect gives to travel writing its objective quality of observation and reportage. The autobiographical draws also on the construction of the protagonist in the novel (especially the picaresque and the comic), which helps introduce elements of the fictional.[40]

Youngs and Forsdick point to the varying shades of travel literature: on the one hand, the objectivity of the scientific approach to reality, which is typical of the reportage; and, on the other, the subjective involvement of the author that is usually betrayed by the presence of autobiographical or fictional elements. *Viaggio in Italia* embodies the former approach. Nevertheless, Piovene's personal involvement emerges throughout the book as his personal opinions punctuate his descriptions of the places and people he observes.

Viaggio in Italia ultimately shows that objectivity is a construct. What the book offers is an interpretation of reality, a narrative perspective, albeit an undoubtedly knowledgeable and insightful one. The kind of superior viewpoint adopted by Piovene is problematic because, while it challenges representations of Italy stemming from literary conventions and the modern tourist experience, it also creates new stereotypes in its pretence of offering a comprehensive, reassuring guide to post-war Italian society and territory. Piovene's factual, authoritative tone belongs to the tradition of travel books that rely on realist conventions, such as the reliability of the observer and the stability of travel destinations.[41] More broadly, it belongs to a certain

---

40   Tim Youngs and Charles Forsdick, 'Introduction', in *Travel Writing*, Critical Concepts in Literary and Cultural Studies, 4 vols (London: Routledge, 2012), I, *The Production of Travel Writing*, pp. 1–24 (p. 1).

41   Patrick Holland and Graham Huggan claim that 'paradoxically, it often seems that the potentially transgressive, destabilizing character of travel seeks a compensatory stability in both its subject and its destination. The typical travel book (insofar as it can ever be agreed upon such a creature exists) continues to cleave to modern realist conventions' (Patrick Holland and Graham Huggan, 'Postmodern Itineraries', in *Travel Writing*, ed. by Youngs and Forsdick, 4 vols (London: Routledge, 2012), II, *The Contexts of Travel*, pp. 489–509 (p. 490)).

type of male, self-assured and supposedly objective gaze. As an established, well-regarded male intellectual who was commissioned to undertake his reportage by RAI, Piovene arguably identifies himself with objectivity. The fact that Piovene claims for himself a privileged standpoint becomes particularly evident in the almost colonial tropes that he deploys in his treatment of the Italian South, as will be shown later. His viewpoint could not be any more different from Ortese's 'lente scura', as she calls her 'filter' on reality: a distinctive perspective on things which she describes as a blend of melancholy and protest.[42] Melancholy is the reflection of her state of mind and of the personal difficulties she was experiencing at the time. Protest may point to the rejection of ingrained ways of seeing and narrating things. Ortese's metaphor of the journey as inquiry and investigation is a means of contending with reality, not claiming to assert the truth. Piovene's methodical approach to travel and travel writing is very different from the erratic, impulsive style of Ortese as well as Arbasino. Ortese's journeys are often dictated by the contingencies of the moment and the volatility of her mood swings. Arbasino rewrites the Grand Tour, giving it an international dimension (not only Italy but Europe) and emphasizing the spontaneity of the characters' trips.

Alberto Arbasino's Inverted Grand Tour

In Arbasino's *Fratelli d'Italia* the pretext for starting the journey may resemble that of the many intellectuals who set out to explore Italy in the 1950s and 1960s, often with the support of a newspaper, a radio or a television station. It may, alternatively, even seem like the pursuit of personal (and artistic) formation, as for the Grand Tour traveller. The book features a group of four intellectual friends who are planning a journey across Italy in search of ideas for a screenplay they have been commissioned to write. The film is titled *L'Italia si chiama amore* [*Italy is Love*]. Arbasino's parodic intent is immediately evident in the film title, a satire of certain melodramatic and sentimental depictions of Italy, as it is in the title of the book itself, which echoes the opening line of Italy's national anthem with jarring effect. The values of nationalism and sentiments of unity that the brotherhood of all Italians expressed in the anthem is meant to inspire are ideals upon which Arbasino's intellectual characters can only look with condescending amusement. The main characters in the book are the first-person narrator, known by the nickname 'Elefante' [Elephant] and his friend

---

42 Ortese, *Lente*, p. 451.

Antonio (who becomes Andrea in the second edition of the book to return as Antonio in the third). Jean-Claude, who is French, and Klaus, 'un tedesco mezzo americano' [half-German, half-American] (*FI*, p. 97), flank them. The group of friends engage in frequent and rather verbose discussions, often on the subject of contemporary Italian culture, which make up large sections of the book. These conversational exchanges give us an idea of their personality. It is particularly interesting to note that three of the friends are homosexual (and Arbasino himself was openly gay), Jean-Claude and Klaus are foreigners and Elefante himself was born in Italian Switzerland. These elements arguably afford an original perspective, not least in terms of challenging the conventionally foreign, contemplative gaze on Italy. Jean-Claude, Klaus and Elefante reveal a much more disenchanted outlook on Italy than their fellow Northern Europeans who travelled to the country two centuries before them.

In fact, Arbasino is less interested in documenting the transformation of post-war Italy than in satirizing stereotypical representations of Italy. This emerges clearly, for example, in the discussions around the film project: 'La storia bisogna poi che sia estiva, assolutamente, sentimentalissima, con tanti Vesuvi e tante gondole, e colori-colori-colori' [The story must be summery then, completely, and very sentimental, with Mount Vesuvius all over the place and many gondolas and colours everywhere] (*FI*, p. 10). *L'Italia si chiama amore* turns out to be a parody which exposes romanticized images of Italy as a sunlit land of bright colours where people indulge in gondola rides and show a temperament as fiery and unpredictable as Mount Vesuvius. Arbasino aims to strip his journey to Italy of these clichéd narratives. This intention is explicitly declared by Andrea in the second edition of the book while talking about the film project that is still at an early and confused stage:

> Utilizziamo a ogni costo il gran tema del Viaggio in Italia? [...] A un patto, si capisce: questa vacanza come una trama narrativa, però in una forma che non si saprebbe davvero immaginare più dissimile dal tradizionale itinerario così geograficamente e sentimentalmente ordinato del Grand Tour.[43]

> [Shall we use the grand theme of the journey through Italy at any cost? [...] On one condition, of course: we treat this holiday as an episodic narrative, but in a form that one could scarcely imagine more dissimilar from the traditional itinerary of the Grand Tour with its customary geographic and sentimental reference points.]

---

43   Alberto Arbasino, *Fratelli d'Italia*, 2nd edn (Turin: Einaudi, 1976 [1967]), p. 19.

The idea of the screenplay is a narrative stratagem for Arbasino to engage with the Grand Tour, whose importance he does not intend to deny. On the contrary, Arbasino seems to argue that any piece of writing engaging with the theme of the Italian journey should incorporate a critical reflection on the Grand Tour.[44] That being said, *Fratelli d'Italia* appropriates tradition only to transform it through a process of dissecting the Grand Tour narrative and re-semanticizing it. The initial idea of travelling across Italy to find material and inspiration for the film is soon abandoned as the characters embark on journeys that are motivated by a whim, by erotic encounters or the occasional invitation to gatherings of intellectuals and members of the upper-middle class, to the point where the book soon turns into a portrait of this glittering world seen through Arbasino's cynical lens. The improvised itineraries represent a negation of the geographically and sentimentally organized paths of the Grand Tour, which followed predefined stages and tended to confirm one's expectations. In so doing, Arbasino inaugurates in the Italian context a spontaneous 'on the road' style that will inspire, among others, Pier Vittorio Tondelli in the 1980s.

Antonio and Elefante have extremely sophisticated tastes and are undeniably privileged, for they travel with ease and with the availability of means and money. Antonio is an established intellectual who earns well writing for Italy's foremost newspapers, while the narrator is a university student who goes on to work in finance in Zurich. In this respect they may be seen as yet another embodiment of the young male traveller of means who embarked on the Grand Tour. The extract below, which sketches a brief sociology of the types one may encounter in a motorway service area, is, however, indicative of the broader democraticization of travel brought about by the mobility of motorization, which Arbasino captures in his book:

> E che felicità le soste sull'autostrada: bere, lavarsi, verificare sulla realtà le ipotesi di studio, tra facce sempre più incredibili … Cani che saltano fuori a coppie dalle Flaminie, bambini d'una biondezza che non s'era mai vista, proletari in tuta che per la prima volta nella storia sociale d'Italia siedono a un ristorante praticamente di lusso per un buon pasto completo col loro vino e il loro caffè … anche se il contesto sociologico qui è un po' balordo, tutto di tedeschi in sandali gialli e braghe corte, con la Volkswagen fuori …. (*FI*, p. 363)

---

44   As Papotti puts it, the Grand Tour is 'quasi una definizione per antonomasia dell'esperienza itinerante in Italia' [almost the definition par excellence of the itinerant experience in Italy] (Davide Papotti, 'Il libro in valigia: eredità odeporiche nel romanzo italiano contemporaneo', in *L'Odeporica/Hodoeporics*, ed. by Monga, pp. 351–62 (p. 351)).

[And what happiness one derives from those rest stops on the highway: drinking, cleaning oneself up, testing one's hypotheses against reality, among ever more unbelievable characters ... Dogs that leap out in pairs from the Flaminie, children with blonde hair the like of which you've never seen before, proletarians in overalls who, for the first time in the social history of Italy, sit down in a practically luxurious restaurant for a good, square meal with their wine and their coffee ... even if the sociological context here is a bit silly, all those Germans in yellow sandals and shorts with the Volkswagen parked outside ....]

The service area is populated by people from different socio-cultural backgrounds and nationalities who are recreating their own modern, motorized version of journey to Italy. In *Fratelli d'Italia* the centrality of the car as the main means of transport bears witness to the widespread availability and affordability of automobiles in the boom years. The book conveys the sense of revolutionary freedom associated with cars – freedom randomly to choose where to go and to reach destinations that had never been so close at hand.[45] The above extract also suggests that, in the space of the motorway, social and cultural differences momentarily disappear. The working class, too, partake in the mobility revolution and share the sense of freedom that comes with speeding away along these long-distance routes. For the lower classes, food consumed in the service area becomes a luxury meal experience. Here, Arbasino's sarcastic portrait of incipient mass tourism indirectly laments the loss of a more elitist kind of travel. Thanks to the considerable improvement in the economic wellbeing of the Italian population in the boom years, travelling for leisure within the Peninsula is within virtually everyone's reach. The geographically and sentimentally fixed itineraries of the Grand Tour are appropriated and reinterpreted in a potentially infinite number of possibilities, no longer strictly defined by social background or economic means, although one may argue that mass tourism has ended up imposing its own dominant routes and travel experience.

The characters' wanderings are often the occasion to look at the places visited with detached irony, especially when these are iconic locations in the sentimental topography of the Italian journey. Capri,

---

45 Sidonie Smith claims that cars 'empower individuals through their own explosive mobility' (Sidonie Smith, 'On the Road: (Auto)mobility and Gendered Detours', in *Travel Writing*, ed. by Youngs and Forsdick, iii, *Modes of Travel, Types of Traveller*, pp. 98–126 (p. 99)).

for instance, is described as tedious and out of fashion: a clear example of how Arbasino challenges stereotypes associated with places:[46]

> Ma l'isola dell'amore, che stretta al cuore, col suo squallore da posto fuori moda, la gente che gira a vuoto con lo sguardo balordo: luogo di castigatezza, oltre tutto, perché le dissipazioni che fino a dieci anni fa si facevano in località eccentriche ora sappiamo benissimo che si commettono specialmente nelle grandi città industriali con più di un milione di abitanti; e qui si viene soltanto per riposarsi o per piangere. (*FI*, p. 62)

> [But the island of love, which now excites only sadness, with its old-fashioned squalor, the people wandering around aimlessly with vacant looks on their faces – a place beyond reproach above all, because the dissipations which up to ten years ago were practised in such eccentric places, we now know very well that they are committed above all in large industrial cities with more than a million inhabitants and here one now comes only to rest or to cry.]

Capri, the 'island of love' *par excellence* in the collective imagination, a celebrated and sought-after travel destination, is here a place where nothing happens, one suitable for people who content themselves with an uneventful mass leisure holiday. Arbasino mentions, by contrast, the bustling, diverse prospect of life offered by the Northern industrial cities with more than one million inhabitants, which in the transformed landscape of Italy in the 1960s have become a pole of attraction for both the working class and educated people in search of new stimuli and opportunities. Arbasino's emphasis on the present is a rejection of rhetorical celebrations of the past and the primacy assigned to certain places on the basis of their architectural and natural beauties. The following passage, which reports a commonplace conversation about the beauties of Italy between a group of old people, iterates this point:

> I vecchi sostengono che Villa d'Este invece non è bella perché è stretta, ma uno intende Villa d'Este a Tivoli, l'altro capiva invece quella sul lago di Como, e così vanno avanti un pezzo prima di passare a discutere la Ca' d'Oro e le Due Torri di Bologna. 'Eh, le bellezze d'Italia ...' ripetono ogni tanto. 'Non ce n'è da nessun'altra parte ...' (*FI*, pp. 20–21)

---

46 Similarly, Arbasino writes in relation to Naples: 'Non so cosa farmene del sole mediterraneo e dell'eredità classica e dell'architettura normanna e delle semplici gioie della vita contadina e della pizza alla pescatora' [I have no use for the Mediterranean sun and the classical heritage and the Norman architecture and the simple joys of peasant life and of pizza 'alla pescatora'] (*FI*, p. 16).

[The old ones argue that the Villa d'Este, on the other hand, is not beautiful because it is too cramped, but one means the Villa d'Este in Tivoli, the other understood the one on Lake Como; and so they go on for a while before moving on to discuss the Ca' d'Oro and the Two Towers of Bologna. 'Eh, the beauties of Italy...', they repeat every now and then. 'There's nothing like it anywhere else ....']

Arbasino's caricature portrait of those who go on repeating banalities about Italy's historical and architectural patrimony is a further indication of his intention to debunk the clichéd rhetoric of the *Bel Paese*.

Fratelli d'Italia shows a tendency to reflect on travel and on its own status of travel book (a postmodern textual practice applied to travel writing),[47] both through the revitalization of the tradition of the Grand Tour, even though turned upside down, and through Arbasino's ironic detachment. Jameson's definition of the postmodern aesthetic as a cultural dominant that incorporates and re-articulates residual models and forms of culture may be applied to Arbasino's *Fratelli d'Italia*, which appropriates the tradition of the Grand Tour in a manner that is both playful and provocative. The book comes to terms with the Grand Tour by re-codifying some of its aspects while discarding others altogether. For instance, foreign locations are assigned new prominence in a sort of inverted Grand Tour (Davide Papotti describes this as '*Grand Tour alla rovescia*'),[48] both in terms of the selected itineraries (not confined to Italy anymore, but transnational) and the unplanned nature of the trips, which are improvised and reflect the characters' volatile desires. The following passage illustrates the spontaneous, impulsive patterns of mobility in Arbasino's novel: dictated by whim or chance, deliberately unorganized ('come viene viene') and unpredictable ('un gran avanti-e-indietro'):

Stavolta si era pensato di far tutta una cosa di Europa orientale. Un giro di capitali tzigane, andando su da Vienna e toccando Budapest, Praga, Varsavia, prima l'una o l'altra, come viene viene; prendendo dentro anche un po' di Breslavie e di Cracovie; e finire a Berlino [...]. Per tornare, poi, un gran avanti-e-indietro sull'autobahn, tutto sull'imprevisto e sul caso. (*FI*, p. 8)

[This time we had thought of doing a whole Eastern European jaunt. A tour of gypsy capitals, going up to Vienna and stopping at Budapest, Prague, Warsaw, in any order at all, taking them as they

---

47   Holland and Huggan maintain that '[p]ostmodernist travel books are almost invariably metanarratives, reflecting on their own status as texts – as *theoretical* texts – on travel' (Holland and Huggan, 'Postmodern Itineraries', p. 490).

48   Papotti, 'Il libro in valigia', p. 355.

came; also taking in a little of Wroclaw and Krakow; and finishing up in Berlin [...]. Then, on the way back, a great to-and-fro on the autobahn, everything improvised and by chance.]

The novel has a strong international feel. The characters share memories of previous trips to European countries: Poland, Hungary, Greece, to name but three. The last chapter is entirely set in London. Antonio and Elefante know some of the local people and street names and can generally find their way easily in Central London, a sign that they have been in the city several times before. In their wanderings in Italy and abroad Andrea and Elefante continue more or less purposefully to run into friends and acquaintances who compose a cosmopolitan, well-educated and well-travelled society. They are perfectly at ease in the cultural milieu of the main European capital cities and have a broader perspective which allows them to question commonplace representations of Italy.

The problematization of the Grand Tour in *Fratelli d'Italia* also relies on the themes of homosexuality and liberated sexual behaviour. The motivation behind travel no longer concerns personal and artistic formation (although at the beginning of the book the reader may be bound to believe it does, as the characters are about to set out on a journey to find material for a film screenplay) but rather, somewhat more prosaically, research into sexual fulfilment or the invitation to rather vacuous gatherings of intellectuals. The erotic encounters that often initiate the characters' journeys delineate a sexual topography of places that are assigned to clandestine gay encounters. In this sense Arbasino takes a queer perspective on the Grand Tour and on Italy as nation. The notion of queerness presents a radical alternative to traditional conceptions of identity and (self-)representation defined by heteronormativity.[49] By aiming to embrace the full spectrum of differences within the non-heterosexual community, queer theory questions the idea of identity defined by social norms. Morland and Willox, for example, argue that:

> certainly the primary challenge posed by queer theory [...] is to hegemonic understandings of the relations between identity, sex, gender and sexuality. Whereas Western culture has attempted to ossify these relations in the name of patriarchy, and feminism has tended to want to reconfigure them while preserving their conventional

---

49 Lee Edelman underscores 'the appropriately perverse refusal that characterizes queer theory – of every substantialization of identity, which is always oppositionally defined, and, by extension, of history as a linear narrative (the poor man's teleology) in which meaning succeeds in revealing itself – *as itself* – through time. [...] the queer comes to figure the bar to every realization

descriptive force, queer theory politicizes sex, gender and sexuality in a way that severs the notion of identity from any stable reference points. In this way, queerness resists the regimes [...] of measuring, categorizing, and knowing the truth of sexual orientation.[50]

Arbasino's re-writing of the Grand Tour tradition, as well as the sense of belonging to a cosmopolitan, rather than national, community, are thus expressions of his non-alignment to dominant conceptions of gender and sexuality in the Italian society of the time. Alterity is central to queer (non-)identity, as it is to Arbasino's approach to travel and travel writing in *Fratelli d'Italia*.[51] The main point of view in the book is that of a narrator who challenges the heterosexual, male-centred, objective perspective on which many works of travel literature, as exemplified in this chapter by Piovene's *Viaggio in Italia*, have relied.

In this regard, too, *Fratelli d'Italia* illustrates the affinity that one may find between contemporary travel writing and postmodern aesthetics, which share some significant traits. Ian Chambers has pointed out that postmodern travel implies:

> the dislocation of the intellectual subject and his – the gender is deliberate – mastery of the word/world. The illusions of identity organized around the privileged voice and stable subjectivity of the 'external' observer are swept up and broken down into a movement that no longer permits the obvious institution of self-identity between thought and reality.[52]

This approach to travel entails a decentred perspective on observed reality, which ceases to be a means of self-affirmation. As the observer relinquishes his perceived control over reality, the latter

---

of futurity, the resistance, internal to the social, to every social structure or form' (Lee Edelman, *No Future: Queer Theory and the Death Drive* (Durham, NC: Duke University Press, 2004), p. 4).

50   Iain Morland and Annabelle Willox, 'Introduction', in *Queer Theory*, ed. by Iain Morland and Annabelle Willox (Basingstoke: Palgrave Macmillan, 2005), pp. 1–5 (p. 4).

51   Isolina Misuri Douglas argues that 'Arbasino's discourse in *Fratelli d'Italia* also predates more recent literary theories such as Queer theory. [...] It is now possible to examine the book in this light and to realize that the reviewers' ignoring (or dismissing) the theme of homosexuality in *Fratelli d'Italia* reveals that the Italian cultural establishment was not as *à la page* as it wished to think it was' (Isolina Misuri Douglas, '*Fratelli d'Italia*: Alberto Arbasino's "Great Comedy of the Sixties"', *Italian Quarterly*, 161/162 (2004), 68–81 (pp. 72–73)).

52   Iain Chambers, *Migrancy, Culture, Identity* (London: Routledge, 1993), p. 95.

also becomes less fixed. The following analysis shows precisely how, in *Fratelli d'Italia*, the notion of place is deprived of its centrality and stability and how its power always to evoke an elsewhere through resemblances and mental associations means that reality as the confirmation of one's expectations, the self-identity mentioned by Chambers, is undermined once and for all.

Regional Differentiation, Fractured Modernity

The texts differ also in their attitude to the historical diversification of Italy, particularly in the redefining post-war transition. As mentioned, a certain anxiety manifests itself in all the texts, albeit in different ways. Ortese does not hide the hesitancy and mixed feelings with which she embarks on the travel experience. Piovene aims to alleviate preoccupations about Italy's integration by presenting in his reportage a country projected towards progress and unity in line with other European nations. Arbasino's frantic mobility is a way to escape everyday reality, but the seemingly unending journeying does not provide a real alternative vision.

Ortese's Open-Ended Travel Writing

La lente scura consists of three chronological sections that include articles which were written at different periods in Ortese's life and focus on various areas of Italy, not aiming to give a systematic overview of the country. The privileging of temporality over spatiality, or at least over spatial coherence, is immediately indicative of Ortese's subjectifying of the national space. In challenging conventional understanding of regions or places within Italy as defined by their contiguities, *La lente scura* outlines a micro-historical and micro-geographical method in contrast to the codified itineraries of the Grand Tour and Piovene's macro-approach. The book conveys instead an idea of fragmentation and almost disconnection through travel pieces that are, to put it in Ortese's words, 'tanto dissimili e perfino contrastanti tra loro' [so dissimilar and even conflicting with each other] (*LS*, p. 15), traversed by lines of separation. For example, the River Po is described as 'strada schiumosa e potente che divide l'Italia in due' [a powerful, rushing waterway that divides Italy in two] (*LS*, p. 44), a boundary that can be crossed in one direction or the other, each time with the impression of entering a different country. In the chapter 'Inglese a Roma' [An Englishman in Rome], the North evokes to Ortese feelings of safety and domesticity as she crosses

190

the Po on a train heading South towards Rome. The South is instead 'agitato Mediterraneo' [restless Mediterranean] (*LS*, p. 44), chaos and unpredictability.[53] Ortese's interest in microhistory is also reflected in her approaching some of the chapters in the book from the individual perspective of emblematic post-war figures who devoted their life to a common cause. Examples are the Catholic priests Don Milani and Don Zeno Saltini, both involved in rearing and educating poor and abandoned children, and the Sicilian bandit Salvatore Giuliano, who attained notoriety after the war. Ortese seems to suggest that their endeavours offer a possible alternative to the precarious cohesiveness of post-war Italian society. The bandit Giuliano, a central figure in the Movement for the Independence of Sicily, launched a direct challenge to the Italian state.[54]

Ortese tells us that the chapter 'Viaggio in Liguria' encapsulates the themes of the book as a whole, its overarching mood. As she puts it:

E questo *Viaggio in Liguria* è proprio, per me, nella sua scrittura sbandata e ansiosa, spezzata, esitante, l'immagine dell'animo con cui cominciai a guardare l'Italia, dopo il '60: spavento e già un deluso amore della ragione; la ragione (delle cose) non la vedevo più, come quell'Alessi che parla di continuo del suo comandante che lo perseguitava, e della terra ligure tutta *comprata* dal turismo. (*LS*, p. 17)

[And this *Journey to Liguria* is precisely, for me, in its drifting and anxious, fragmented, hesitant writing, the image of the spirit with which I began to look at Italy after 1960: fearful and disillusioned. I no longer saw the reason (for things), like that Alessi who constantly speaks of his commander who persecuted him, and of the Ligurian land all *bought* up by tourism.]

The choice of adjectives to define her writing style could not be more unequivocal: drifting, anxious, fragmented and hesitant. They also denote the feelings with which Ortese relates to the historical phase of transition. Internal and external perspectives, Ortese's uncertain emotional state and the confusing field of possibility in the post-war years, mirror and blur into one another. Ortese presents post-war

---

53   Ortese believes that on this occasion her apprehension reflects the unsettling experience of any migrant who goes back temporarily to their place of origin when they feel not yet settled in a new city or country. Ortese was indeed born in Rome and later moved to the North, to which interestingly she refers in these pages as abroad.

54   See, e.g., Billy Jaynes Chandler, *King of the Mountain: The Life and Death of Giuliano the Bandit* (DeKalb, IL: Northern Illinois University Press, 1988).

Italian society as lacking a unifying principle, a sense of totality and cohesiveness. She describes a kind of fractured modernity, a transition period experienced as rupture and a loss of references. Her travel writing evokes this sense of absence. As she puts it: 'Cercavo qualcosa, strade e case, in cui riconoscermi e riposarmi; e questo qualcosa non c'era più' [I was looking for something, streets and houses, in which to recognize myself and rest; and this something was no longer there] (*LS*, p. 452). She likens the tormented figure of Alessi to her condition of a female writer trying and failing to make sense of the rapidly changing landscape which she records in her writings.

While the book is pervaded by a sense of absence, loss and the search for something that seems to be always out of reach, it is also true that Ortese does not languish in uncertainty but actively seeks to make sense of the perceived rupture through her quest and her writing. As Sharon Wood argues, for Ortese 'travelling and writing share a common function, which is to restore a sense of belonging, to minister to an irremediable sense of loss'.[55] Ortese's writings do not convey an irredeemable nihilist. There is still room for hope, which she glimpses in the renewal of Italian society:

> Non saprei dire che animo e che aspetto avessi allora. [...] L'Italia era ancora molto povera, non offriva una vita facile. Tuttavia questa vita era simile a un campo pieno di confuse, grandiose possibilità; e la speranza – e il rischio – bastavano. (*LS*, p. 15)

> [I cannot tell what mood I was in and what I looked like then. [...] Italy was still very poor; it did not offer an easy life. Yet this life was like a field full of confusing, grand possibilities; and hope – and risk – were enough.]

This is perhaps the real key to reading the book: namely, as a document of years characterized by mingled hope and anxiety. Travel becomes for Ortese a means to affirm her agency by embracing these contradictions. Her writing is more tentative and less assertive than the dominant male travel-writing tradition, but for this reason it is also more able effectively to problematize established assumptions about Italian territory and identity. In this sense Ortese takes a stance against a masculine type of knowledge that claims to be exhaustive and erases women as dissident voices. This emerges, as noted above,

---

55 Sharon Wood, 'Strange Euphorias and Promised Lands: The Travel Writing of Anna Maria Ortese', in *Literature and Travel*, ed. by Michael Hanne, Rodopi Perspectives on Modern Literature (Amsterdam: Rodopi, 1993), pp, 181–92 (p. 185).

in her representation of manipulated nature and in her connection to Alessi. The latter's position of being harassed by a dominant male authority and his experience of trauma and oppression enable Ortese to identify with his perspective.

A further example of Ortese's dismantling of stereotypes is her rejection of the simplistic opposition between the Italian North and South. The latter was arguably fully 'discovered' as a geographical and anthropological entity only in the post-war period, especially through Ernesto De Martino's famous ethnographic expeditions and thanks to efforts to reduce the economic gap to the Northern economy on the part of post-war governments. These involved initiatives such as the Cassa per il Mezzogiorno, which was set up in 1950 to stimulate growth in the South through public investment. Giuliana Minghelli observes that the concept of remorse gains prominence in the context of the post-war exploration of the national territory and specifically of its Southern margins, since 'the rush to chronicle and emancipate the South [...] emerges as an unconscious journey for the modern "north" in search of healing'.[56] The inquisitive form of travel that takes hold in the post-war years offers an opportunity to problematize the prosperity of the North as a reflection of its historical supremacy over the South and its prominence in the process of political decision-making, at least since the country's unification.

In her travel observations Ortese notices that the South, and cities like Naples in particular, are also being rapidly transformed by the accelerated pace of modernization. She detects inconsistencies in this process: while it brings undeniable benefits, it also sacrifices distinctive social and cultural features. It is an imposed model of progress that does not adequately take into account the particular socio-cultural context of the South and its peculiar history. The transformations occur so rapidly that, paradoxically, the perception is almost of immobility or, indeed, of going backwards in time:

> Era tutto più *fermo*, come se il tempo si fosse messo a correre in modo da confondersi con l'immobilità, come se la ruota si fosse messa a girare vorticosamente in avanti – o anche questa era un'apparenza, e girava invece all'indietro? (*LS*, p. 212)

> [Everything seemed somehow stiller, as if time had begun to race so quickly that it might easily be confused with immobility, as if the wheel had begun to spin forward so dizzily that one could no longer perceive the movement – or was that, too, an illusion and did it instead spin backwards?]

---

56   Minghelli, 'Icons of Remorse', p. 398.

Ortese often plays with the categories of mobility and immobility when describing the impact of modernization on the rural South, as also appears in the following extract from the chapter 'Verso Formia' [Towards Formia] describing an agricultural scene seen through the train window:

> C'era su quella campagna, non so se effetto del confronto con la corsa del treno, come un velo, un'ombra non materiale, non uscita dalle nubi del cielo, ma generata quasi dal tempo. Tutto così fermo, che si era tentati di aprire il finestrino e immettere aria su quella tenera campagna, quasi là non ve ne fosse e si trattasse di un sogno. (*LS*, p. 203)

> [There was over that countryside, I don't know if it was the effect of contrast with the train ride, a non-material shadow like a veil, not a veil made out of the clouds of the sky, but almost generated by time. Everything so still that one was tempted to open the window and let air into that tender countryside, as if there were none there and it were a dream.]

The speed of the train (a symbol of modernity and mobility) starkly contrasts with the apparent stillness of people and things outside, almost as if they were in a display cabinet or glass dome. The scene, however, is complicated by an element of doubt: Ortese wonders whether what she sees is an illusory perception and whether this part of Italy is actually frozen in time, therefore inviting the reader to question the same.

Ortese is sympathetic towards Southern customs and traditions and does not blame the Southern people for poverty or inertia. She projects instead an accusatory gaze towards the wealthy North for imposing its model of modernity on the rest of the country. As Wood has observed, Ortese shares the critical attitude towards modern urban society and abhors the dismissal of rural Italy and peasant civilization.[57] The peasant women travelling on the train are described as 'donne-mulo' [mule-women] and 'donne-bestia' [beast-women] (*LS*, p. 206). The animalization of these women's strained bodies hints at the oppression of ordinary people, and women in particular, in a traditionally patriarchal and class-divided society. These women are left alone to carry the burden of poverty while the richer half of the country turns away from them. Once again, here Ortese likens the domination of women to that of the non-human world. Elsewhere in the book she lingers on the harsh, unaccommodating natural environment of the *Mezzogiorno*. In the long description

---

57 Wood, 'Strange Euphorias and Promised Lands', p. 186.

of Montelepre, the birthplace of the bandit Giuliano in Western Sicily, and the barren mountains rising all around it, the key words *solitudine* [solitude] and *silenzio* [silence] resonate stronger than ever (*LS*, pp. 123–32). This kind of natural landscape is inhospitable and resists exploitation. Against the backdrop of this undomesticated nature as 'Other', Giuliano embodies the opportunity for the South to reclaim its power for self-determination, pointing again to the issue of breaking silence and finding a voice for all the oppressed.

La lente scura conveys an image of Italy as varied and fragmentary. It would be pointless to try and assemble the pieces of mosaic in a book that is purposefully unsystematic and unresolved, as it would be, one may argue, to force homogenization onto the different parts of the Italian Peninsula with their peculiar traits. With its fragmentary style *La lente scura* reflects Italy's strong differentiation (*LS*, p. 206). On the one hand, one has geographical boundaries, such as the North–South divide. Ortese grasps the complexity of these distinctions and does not translate them into a simplistic, static analysis. On the other hand, one has a travel experience that is often improvised and tentative, but precisely because of this relates to people and places without expectations and preconceptions. Ortese's travel writing entails exposure and vulnerability, not truth-claiming.

Piovene's Essentialist Paradox

This chapter has already shown that *Viaggio in Italia* serves a clear narrative of post-war Italy as set on the path of progress and unity. Piovene's endeavour brings to mind post-unification travel writers, whose detailed descriptions of Italy's diverse landscape betrayed their enthusiasm for the new political phase of the unified country.[58] Similarly, the post-war years, when Italy seemed on the verge of fulfilling its potential as a modern nation, were characterized by new aspirations and a desire to explore the national territory.[59] This

---

58   Clerici, *Viaggiatore*, p. xxvii.

59   As Tamiozzo Goldmann points out: 'Piovene si inserisce a pieno titolo in quel clima fervido, fatto di curiosità e di voglia di raccontare […] che aveva caratterizzato gli anni della ricostruzione, della ripresa e del boom economico nel nostro Paese' [Piovene fits right into that fervent climate, made up of curiosity and the desire to tell, [...] that had characterized the years of reconstruction, recovery and economic boom in our country] (Silvana Tamiozzo Goldmann, 'Appunti sul *Viaggio in Italia*', in *Viaggi e Paesaggi di Guido Piovene. Atti del Convegno Venezia-Padova, 24–25 gennaio 2008*, ed. by Enza Del Tedesco and Alberto Zava (Pisa: Serra, 2009), pp. 103–22 (p. 111)).

desire could be fulfilled through the wider availability of travel opportunities but also in the comfort of one's own home, tuning in to the radio or television.[60] Through travel-dedicated programmes and documentaries, radio and television partook in an educational endeavour to enhance the knowledge of the country's diverse geography, an endeavour which once again may be likened to the pedagogic contribution of post-unification writers to the newly born state and the formation of its citizens. Historically divided and separated into independent territories, in the aftermath of unification Italians were confronted with the necessity of thinking of themselves as a nation. The famous quotation, 'Abbiamo fatto l'Italia, ora dobbiamo fare gli italiani' [We have made Italy. Now we must make Italians], commonly attributed to Piedmontese stateman Massimo D'Azeglio, highlights exactly this issue. A similar educational intent imbues Piovene's *Viaggio in Italia*, which points to the need for Italians to become familiar with their own country in the renewed economic and intellectual climate, to make sense of their historical differences and to feel part of a unified nation.

Viaggio in Italia challenges contemplative and reductive views of Italy by documenting the country's differences and variations in all their complexity. At the same time, the book aims to show that, while diverse and regionalized, Italy is gradually becoming more cohesive and homogeneous.[61] In Piovene's somewhat edifying account, differences among Italian people are essentially superficial and as such cannot lead to proper conflicts and fractures. As he puts it, 'l'Italia è varia, non complessa' [Italy is varied, not complex] (*VI*, p. 661). According to Piovene, this explains why Italy has held together even though its unity has historically lacked a solid moral foundation. Such reflections are examples of how *Viaggio in Italia* seeks to challenge anxieties about Italy's constitutional fragmentation and even fears of disintegration after the disastrous outcome of

60 As Ginsborg puts it, 'no innovation of these years had a greater effect on everyday life than television. In 1954, in the first year of its introduction, there were 88,000 licence holders, a number which increased to one million in 1958. By 1965 49 per cent of Italian families owned a television set' (Ginsborg, *A History of Contemporary Italy*, p. 240).

61 Piovene claims, e.g., that 'oggi, girando per Roma, si vede come queste antitesi tra una regione e l'altra siano diventate stantie. L'Italia si sta uniformando' [today, wandering around Rome, one sees how these antitheses between one region and the other have become outdated. Italy is becoming more uniform] (*VI*, p. 641). Piovene also writes that 'con la sua grande varietà, l'Italia tende a un miscuglio uniforme' [in its great variety, Italy tends towards a homogeneous mixture] (*VI*, p. 666).

the Second World War and two years of civil war. The aim of the book to provide an authoritative and exhaustive guide to the Italian territory, as well as the fact that it was commissioned by Italy's state broadcaster RAI, point to the need to alleviate uncertainty about the integration and future of Italy at this point in history.

While *Viaggio in Italia* seeks to demonstrate that Italy's unification process has reached a significant milestone in the post-war period, it is also true that it does not support an uncritically optimistic view of the recent socio-economic developments but still presents us with a composite picture of post-war Italian society. On the one hand, the book aims to bring together the various parts that make up the Italian Peninsula and to make sense of their differences in an effort that resembles the commitment of post-Unification writers. On the other, it does not omit to highlight the controversies and issues that still remain to be solved in the creation of a truly unified, modern nation. One may also argue that Piovene's thesis of the increased uniformity and unity of Italy is partly at odds with the content of the book itself, which crystallizes the cultural identity of people and places through reifying descriptions that emphasize their peculiar, individual traits. Piovene claims, for example, that the typical Milanese 'ama l'ufficio con calore sentimentale' [loves the office with a sentimental warmth] (*VI*, p. 84). He also believes that whilst the average Turinese may at first glance appear serious and austere, he (one can assume that Piovene has mainly a male type in mind) is actually a non-conformist, inclined towards unconventional political views. His multifaceted personality perfectly embodies the city of Turin, which for Piovene is the most hybrid of Italian cities. Piovene's journeys are populated by similar types, seen and described through this objectifying eye. Another example is the figure of the clerk: the predominant professional figure in post-war Milan and Turin, according to Piovene the clerk presents distinct and unique characteristics in each of these two cities. Furthermore, he describes Roman people as 'una realtà molto concreta e irriducibile' [a very concrete and irreducible reality] (*VI*, p. 648). The Roman citizen is a contradictory individual, equally fond of and indifferent to the beauty of the 'eternal city'. He considers everything transitory except for Rome (*VI*, p. 641). Piovene therefore takes an essentialist approach to travel writing, focusing on the differences between places and their inhabitants, which are portrayed as microcosms with distinct identities and seemingly fixed anthropological traits.

The book's essentialism is particularly problematic when it comes to the depiction of the Italian South. While for some post-war intellectuals the reportage may be a way to engage critically with the historical divide between the North and South of the country, *Viaggio in Italia* takes a stand in favour of a Northern model of modernity and future for Italy. This requires, in Piovene's words, a moral migration of the old South (*VI*, p. 664). In other words, it requires the modernization of the South to bring it closer to the North. Piovene believes that a new, modern South is already emerging and is destined to prevail. The archaic Southern culture is a burden to the rest of the country and he sees its demise as inevitable. He criticizes the sentimentalism of certain journalists and writers who go to the South to document the local traditions. Such claims may once again be related to Piovene's commission by the national broadcaster RAI to produce his reportage at this particular moment, in which the Italian state has every reason to show an image of the country as unified and in the march towards progress.

The example of Sicily, which according to Piovene embodies more evidently the contradictions of the South as a whole, illustrates some recurring tropes in Piovene's discourse on the Italian South. He detects the gradual appearance, in post-war Sicily, of a dynamic, Northern-like attitude towards work and innovation, which nevertheless struggles to prevail against the ingrained habits of indolence and lack of ambition. Furthermore, when he praises the proactivity and work ethic of the younger generation, he does so in a patronizing fashion. He claims, for instance, that 'la Sicilia di oggi assomiglia a un adolescente, la cui vitalità porta l'improvvisato ed il meditato, il lavoro utile e lo sperpero, il metodo e il disordine' [present-day Sicily resembles an adolescent whose vitality engenders both the improvised and the considered, both useful work and waste, both method and disorder] (*VI*, pp. 455–56). Piovene's discourse on the South is shaped by dichotomies and oppositions such as centre–periphery and traditional–modern, as shown by the following example:

> Tutti i contrasti del Mezzogiorno italiano, in questa fase di trapasso, appaiono qui stridenti. Da un lato il sogno dell'industria, l'attivismo tecnico, l'impulso turistico ed archeologico, lo slancio verso il settentrione e l'Europa; dall'altro la città e i villaggi stipati, dove anche il palazzo del signore è ingoiato dalle casupole, le petraie deserte, la brulicante povertà di alcuni quartieri palermitani, dei paesi gialli dello zolfo, del bracciantato di Ragusa. (*VI*, p. 505)

> [All the contrasts of Southern Italy, in this phase of transition, appear here quite sharply. On the one hand, the dream of industry, technological dynamism, the tourist drive and the archaeological impulse, the effort to catch up with the North and Europe; on the other, the city and the crammed villages, where even the lord's palace is swallowed up by the hovels, the deserted cobblestone streets, the

teeming poverty of some Palermo neighborhoods, of the yellow villages of sulphur, of the Ragusa labourers.]

The opposition between emerging industrial dynamism (a quintessentially Northern value) and persistent poverty that is implicitly blamed on the Southern population shows how the South is associated by Piovene with an idea of immobilism, as if only an external force can activate those productive energies that now lie dormant.

Ongoing Journeys, Postmodern Flâneurie

With Arbasino place loses its relevance. In *Postmodern Urbanism* Nan Ellin writes that from the second half of the twentieth century onwards 'the importance of place has diminished as global flows of people, ideas, capital, mass media, and other products have accelerated'.[62] Ultimately, what matters in *Fratelli d'Italia* are the act of travelling and movement *per se*. The centrality of place in conventional travel literature is replaced by an account in which places are somehow interchangeable because nothing is as important as ongoing travel, not remaining stationary but changing perspectives on things:

> Comunque per me il posto non importa niente; glie lo ripeto, a Antonio. Purché ci sia da far tanto. Basta muoversi e non esagerare a fermarsi in una città, quando è chiaro che non va bene. [...] Ferrara o Varsavia, si capisce che per me è lo stesso. (*FI*, p. 14)

> [Anyway, for me the place doesn't matter; I'll repeat it to Antonio. As long as there's a lot to do. Just move and don't stop too long in one city when it's clear that it's not good. [...] Ferrara or Warsaw, it's all the same for me, you know.]

Papotti points out that this position may lead to a stateless ('apolide') condition of the writer, in which his or her identity is exclusively determined by the position of observer and narrator.[63] In the following extract, which illustrates an evening spent in a restaurant in Gaeta on the way to Capri at the beginning of the book, the style of the restaurant and the presence of specific objects evoke associations with different and distant places, such as the Tyrol, London and the Netherlands:

> Ma dove siamo? L'aria fuori è grigia, col cielo coperto; qui dentro sui muri ci sono degli affreschi montanari, hanno delle stelle alpine in

---

62   Ellin, *Postmodern Urbanism*, p. 1.
63   Papotti, 'Il libro in valigia', p. 356.

un vasetto davanti all'acquario. È Gaeta o è Tirolo? Quando suona l'ora, l'orologio del ristorante è a cucù, e i campanili fuori sembra che abbiano tutti un carillon tipo Westminster o tipo Olanda. (*FI*, p. 13)

[But where are we? The air outside is grey, with the sky overcast; here on the walls there are frescoes of mountains, they have edelweiss in a jar in front of the aquarium. Is it Gaeta or is it Tyrol? When the hour strikes, the restaurant clock reveals a cuckoo and the bell towers outside all seem to have a Westminster- or Holland-type bell tower.]

The ability to discern these affinities is indicative of the increased global interconnection between places in the post-World War Two world, the enhanced knowledge of and freedom in space made possible through the diffusion of modern means of transport, but also of the prominence given to the subjectivity of the observer, who is free to transcend conventional understanding of place and time.

Fratelli d'Italia is a document of the feverish mobility of the boom years. Arbasino conveys the rise in movement, for instance, through the accumulation of spatial elements, as in the following example, where the enumeration of natural and architectural features creates a frantic rhythm:

Prima che sia tardi ci si butta verso i meravigliosi odori di campagna e d'estate delle villette classiche e dei sepolcri romani, cascine del Cinquecento, ville fasciste, antenne elettriche, grotte, elicotteri, avieri, greggi di pecore, mucchi d'immondizie e in fondo la muraglia dei quartieri nuovi. (*FI*, pp. 352–53)

[Before it is too late one plunges into the wonderful countryside and the summer smells of the classic villas and Roman sepulchres, the sixteenth-century farmhouses, Fascist villas, electrical antennae, grottos, helicopters, airmen, flocks of sheep, piles of rubbish and at the end a wall of new neighbourhoods.]

The overabundance of stimuli and things seen conveys a sense of the dynamism and freedom of taking to the road, with a particular fascination for the *autostrada* that enables people to bypass provincial destinations and connects them with the rest of Europe:

Ma in principio di serata, meglio buttarsi sulle autostrade. Prendiamo quella dei laghi. Prima non si vede niente: qualche fanale giallo; e si va. Poi lumi natalizi, archi di cemento altissimi; e sotto, una costruzione cilindrica di cristallo che pare più grande e più ricca dei padiglioni americani alle esposizioni universali. Frecce, pensiline, sottopassaggi, e porte che si aprono solo in un senso, nell'altro no; cariche dei soliti divieti di sosta. (*FI*, p. 389)

[But early in the evening, it is better to hit the highways. Let's take the one by the lakes. First you cannot see anything, just a few yellow lights; and then off we go. And then Christmas lights and very high concrete arches; and below, a cylindrical crystal construction that seems larger and richer than even the American pavilions at the universal expositions. Arrows, shelters, underpasses and doors that open only in one direction, not in the other, full of the usual no-stopping zones.]

Here one has a further example of the juxtaposition of objects rolling by as if in a fast-moving film reel to create the impression of mobility. Travel is again a way of establishing associations. A glass structure on the motorway recalls the dramatic national pavilions in universal exhibitions. The imagining of being somewhere else is also a way of denying one's reality. This kind of hectic wandering is, indeed, ultimately an attempt to escape disillusionment and the *ennui* of everyday life. As it turns out, however, travel cannot offer a compensation. On the contrary, it becomes yet another source of restlessness and discontent. Travel is never a conclusive experience, as perhaps it was for the Grand Tour traveller who regarded the journey to Italy as a milestone in his (the gender is again deliberate) formation. Arbasino's characters are bound to carry on travelling in search of an ever-fleeting and short-lived sense of contentment, somewhat like Ortese.[64]

Albeit in different ways, all the authors challenge the clichéd narratives of foreign travellers in Italy. Piovene's *Viaggio in Italia* does so by rejecting the reductive rhetoric of the Grand Tour and by documenting instead the socio-cultural differentiation of the Italian territory. Ortese problematizes the dominant travel writing tradition further through her gendered perspective. The latter emerges, for instance, through the representation of unconventional natural environments that unsettle nationalistic and contemplative narratives, as well as through the theme of the denial of voice. Arbasino may seem to embrace a more hedonistic kind of travel but his sarcasm betrays a critical, self-reflective perspective and the full adaptation of clichéd representations.[65] One may, therefore, detect the emergence

64   Giulio Iacoli refers to this condition as 'postmodern flânerie' (Giulio Iacoli, *Atlante delle derive. Geografie da un'Emilia postmoderna: Gianni Celati e Pier Vittorio Tondelli* (Reggio Emilia: Diabasis, 2002), pp. 94–95).

65   Rodighiero claims that Arbasino's irony 'ha sempre un elemento di consapevolezza e di distacco metalinguistico, di riflessione divertita' [always has an element of metalinguistic awareness and detachment, of amused reflection] (Rodighiero, 'Fratelli d'Italia', p. 271).

of a new, critical voice in post-war Italian travel writing, one able to appropriate and problematize the tropes and classic themes that had long dominated travel accounts of the Italian Peninsula and thus to question established notions of national space.

The writers' specific authorial perspective has been analysed in relation to dominant notions of space, gender and sexuality within the Italian context. The idea of self-discovery bears greater implications for Ortese and Arbasino, who give prominence to the point of view and individuality of the observer as they fluctuate and evolve through the travel experience. The originality of their travel accounts lies in their non-alignment with dominant and objective ways of seeing and in their translating of feelings of unease into different ways of apprehending reality, ways which run counter to the heterosexual-male-centred viewpoint long dominant in travel writing. In so doing, Ortese and Arbasino challenge mainstream discourses not only on space, but also on gender and sexuality in post-war Italian society. Descriptions of Italy as a 'strange' place may reflect the fact that until the post-war period travel had been the prerogative of privileged sectors of the Italian population and that, therefore, the majority of Italians still had little knowledge of their country. In this sense it can be argued that Italian travel writers are motivated to adopt a foreigner's or outsider's perspective – the tradition of the *Viaggio in Italia* being largely the domain of foreign authors – to account to readers for the 'strange place' that is a modern, changing Italy. While Piovene's contribution to a better understanding of the complexity of Italian society cannot be denied, the authoritative viewpoint he claims for himself means that he is not immune to stereotyping and actually, in some cases, ends up recreating essentialist views of the places and people he encounters.

There emerges an evolution of the position of the observer: from Piovene's stable, self-assured point of view, which still relies on realist conventions, to a less secure notion of space and a more anxious relationship between the observer and the observed reality with Ortese and Arbasino. In *Fratelli d'Italia* the emphasis on the action of movement *per se* means that the actual destinations are devoid of importance: indeed, they are almost interchangeable. Arbasino's self-reflective, ironic attitude, his parodic revisioning of the traditional motif of the Italian journey and the observer's more fleeting connection with reality are all features of postmodern travel writing. With Ortese travel becomes a more introspective and destabilizing experience. The examples of Arbasino and Ortese therefore suggest that for post-war Italian travel writers travel becomes not only a means for critical exploration of the encountered realities and of themselves, as intellectuals and Italians in a peculiar moment in the country's history, but also a way to reflect on the tradition and value of travel itself in a postmodern tension towards self-reflexivity.

Conclusion

Through the analysis of an array of novels and travel accounts that take into account the two decades spanning the end of 1950s to the end of 1970s, *Mapping Post-War Italian Literature* examines how Italian writers responded to the profound social, economic and spatial transformations that were initiated by the economic boom of the late 1950s. The various literary voices that have taken centre stage across this book provide a multifaceted account of the processes at work in Italy's urbanization and modernization from the mid-1950s onwards, illuminating some of the key issues and trends in Italian society of the time. Through literary analysis two major themes have been identified, the first being the ways in which, through their specific interpretations of reality, Italian writers apprehended and conceptualized the transformations that were underway. In this sense, the diverse literary genres taken into consideration in this study are lenses through which reality (the big-city environment, a small provincial town and the changing socio-cultural landscape of the country) is observed and discursively shaped. As pointed out in the Introduction, in the process each genre and each writer reverberate with internalized views of society. Second, throughout this book space is apprehended as the locus where the anxiety that encompassed the phase of post-war transition in Italy was projected and played out. Italy's changing space is also a locus of complex intersections between past, present and future.

Each chapter offers a distinctive perspective on spatial changes over the period under scrutiny. Bianciardi and Volponi (Chapter 1) are writers on the left who see the modern city as the embodiment of capital. In their novels coercive architectures and the fabric of the urban environment impose a passive, disenfranchising experience of the city. Their urban environments have anti-social and atomizing effects. These descriptions of cities shed light on the complicity of political and economic powers and the kind of built environment that affirms it. The analysis links this stance to the reaction against enduring authoritarian tendencies in Italian society, opposed in particular by the Left. Historical research emphasizes the lines of continuity between pre- and post-war Italy, pointing to the failure to remove officials who had been involved in key positions in the state apparatus under the Fascist regime and who kept their positions in the transition to the Republic. Post-war Italian governments resorted to repressive legislation, which in some cases had been promulgated under the Fascist regime. The continuation of reactionary practices found its justification in the prospect of Communist infiltration during the Cold War. In the novels examined in this study, the threat of a revival of the past reverberates through characters who refuse to retract their Fascist ideals as well as through military metaphors that give to the burgeoning city, with its trenches of ubiquitous building sites and road works, the ambiance of a war zone.

Bianciardi and Volponi expose the connections between capitalism and the built environment by portraying a city subjugated to the economic parameters of utilitarianism and productivity (Volponi's renaming of Turin/Torino Bovino in *Le mosche del capitale* is particularly telling in this respect). One may argue that there is more to metropolitan life. With its variegated social landscape and fleeting kinship system, it may, for example, entail individual emancipation from conventional social structures and foster self-empowerment. This perspective is not completely absent from the novels of Bianciardi and Volponi. Indeed, as is argued in Chapter 1, they are informed by a dynamic of rejection–attraction towards the city, which ultimately provides the writers with the material for their succesful novels. Rejection takes the form of a withdrawal into microcosms which are perceived as protective – Brera for Luciano and the room facing the countryside for Albino – which, while still connected to the city, are also presented as counter-spaces of resistance against the urban-industrial society of Northern Italy.

The mysterious, unsettling aspects of urban life emphasized by the novels in Chapter 2 hint at the perceived loss of control over an urban environment that has been transformed beyond the comprehension of its users. The theme of the uncanny helps to illuminate how the novels examined here relate to the past as well as to the hidden, undesirable implications of the boom. Scerbanenco's Lamberti novels depict modern Milan as a hub for organized crime and illegal trafficking in which violence is commonplace. In Fruttero & Lucentini's crime fiction the shifting social landscape of Turin – a city that is portrayed as elusive and deceptive – conveys a tension between the familiar and unfamiliar. Modernity is perceived as rupture due to its neglect and denial of the past. In Freudian terms, the desire to forget and the absence of a critical public reckoning with the past give way inevitably to the return of the repressed (for instance, in the concrete possibility of a Fascist revival in the post-war Republic). In the novels the past is often conveyed as nostalgia, for example in the idealization of a traditional model of the city, allegedly more 'sociable' and harmonious. Again, at work here are socially constructed views of what constitutes a desirable urban experience.

The chapter also explores the interrelation between urbanization and the development of Italian crime fiction in the 1960s and 1970s. It discusses how the selected writings highlight a link between urbanization and the evolution of crime through criminal activities which follow the expansion of the city and the geography of industrialization (and which show the efficiency of modern industry), as well as through the socio-anthropological implications of economic development. Particular emphasis is given to the periphery as a location that is traditionally perceived and depicted as eerie and dangerous. Whilst in Scerbanenco's crime fiction all places in Milan seem equally dangerous, the more deprived areas of the urban periphery are especially linked to social isolation and violence. In Fruttero & Lucentini's *A che punto è la notte* the criminal organization carries out its activities more discreetly in an abandoned industrial area on the outskirts of the city. Hence, one may argue that Scerbanenco and Fruttero & Lucentini conform to the idea of the urban fringe as bleak and dangerous, which, in this chapter, is problematized by challenging clichés and stereotypes commonly ascribed to the modern suburbs. At the same time, Scerbanenco and Fruttero & Lucentini accord literary dignity to the periphery by giving it centre stage in their stories and, consequently, by recognizing it as a legitimate part of the city.

The remaining two chapters continue the themes of the peripheral and marginal. Chapter 3, in particular, discusses attitudes towards the province in Italian culture through the analysis of Ginzburg's *Le voci della sera*, set in a small provincial town in the Piedmont region. It explores and problematizes the notion of the provincial or smaller city as marginal and secondary to the big city. The fact that this is especially true in Italy, where the term 'provincial' is often used derogatorily, may be a way of concealing the centrality of the provinces for the Italian nation, with its long tradition of municipal autonomy and strong regional identities. In *Le voci della sera* a clue to the denied relevance of the provinces is the fact that the provincial setting acts as a magnifier of themes that reappear across Ginzburg's oeuvre, particularly her view of familial and sentimental relationships, which this tale of provincial life brings into sharper focus. Furthermore, the provinces emerge as a place where individual and apparently banal stories are emblematic of the human condition and its predicaments, thereby challenging the hierarchical distinction from the city from an aesthetic and cultural dimension.

The analysis focuses on social conventions, conservative attitudes and gender roles in the provincial microcosm described by Ginzburg and how these may compare to social and gender relations in a metropolitan environment, questioning clear-cut distinctions between the urban and provincial. These issues are explored primarily through the perspective of female characters in the novel, which brings into sharper relief questions of marginality in space. Social expectations and assumptions disproportionately affect women and their existential trajectories in Ginzburg's story as, with few exceptions that do not necessarily present an alternative model of female empowerment, they all embrace the role of wife and mother, devoting themselves to the domestic sphere. Paradoxically, however, women show more initiative than men despite their limited agency. *Le voci della sera* confirms the idea that one's kinship network is generally more stable in smaller cities than in the big-city environment, for friendships and connections often last a lifetime. While, in the novel, some characters may be comfortable with this stability and familiarity, others, especially the younger generation, feel oppressed by life prospects that seemingly allow little room for change and compromise. Nevertheless, moving away, perhaps to the big city (a possibility which only male characters may entertain), does not offer an alternative solution. Ginzburg's characters feel they would end up replicating habitual patterns, conforming to what society expects of them.

Chapter 4 is also informed by a gender perspective. It explores how Ortese's take on travel challenges the male-dominated tradition of travel writing and its implications in terms of dominant ways of seeing and representing Italy. In the post-war years domestic Italian travel accounts produced critical perspectives that increasingly called into question reifying representations of Italy, codified especially by foreign observers. Albeit in different ways, all the texts examined in the chapter complicate stereotypical views of the Italian territory and identity. Piovene documents the socio-cultural complexity of the Italian territory beyond the conventions of the Grand Tour and the stereotype of the *Bel Paese*. Ortese and Arbasino go further by challenging the ideas of gender and sexuality implicated in dominant notions of the national space. Ortese does so, for example, by rejecting comforting, domesticated images of the natural landscape. Her nature cannot be possessed, either literally or through a reductive reification. Piovene's agenda is to present Italy as steadily embarked on a path of progress towards joining other modern nations. His self-assured perspective is prone to essentialism and stereotyping. This emerges more starkly in relation to the traditionally marginalized Italian South. Piovene calls on the South to adopt a Northern-like attitude to progress in order to speed up the modernization process of the whole Peninsula. Ortese rejects the quasi-colonial juxtaposition of centre (North) and periphery (South); she is more sympathetic towards Southern people and the longstanding issues they face without falling into condescension.

By giving prominence to the gender and queer perspectives of Ortese and Arbasino, the chapter highlights an evolution in the point of view of the observer-narrator across the three texts under scrutiny: from Piovene's *Viaggio in Italia*, with its neatly separated and contained chapters that present concrete, knowable destinations; to Ortese's more tentative approach to travel, her privileging of the 'micro' and subjective in the switching and interweaving between internal and external landscapes; and, finally, the open-ended travel writing of Arbasino, in which place loses centrality and the subjectivity of the observer comes into the foreground. The confident traveller-observer who in *Viaggio in Italia* claims the authority of truth-telling is replaced by the more tentative, self-reflective viewpoint of *La lente scura* and *Fratelli d'Italia*, able to call stereotypes into question more effectively.

The heterogenous literary sources and critical approaches which inform this book help to capture the inconsistencies of Italy's post-war development, not only from a socio-economic and political point of view – as is the case with most of the existing research in the field – but also with specific reference to the interiority of individuals.[1] While there are studies and commentaries on the socio-economic changes in post-war Italy and on the Italian literary production of the time (and how they interact with one another), they are generally not based on a close analysis of the literary texts. Furthermore, existing studies on post-war Italian literature generally address a specific theme or grouping of writers, rather than providing a wider account of the Italian post-war transition, as does this study, albeit through the perspective of literary geographies.[2] Indeed, previous studies focus

---

1   See, in particular, studies on post-war Italian society such as those by historians Paul Ginsborg, Guido Crainz and John Foot.

2   Examples include Jennifer Burns's work on the idea of *impegno* in the Italian literature of the post-war period (and beyond); and Daniele Fioretti's *Utopia and Dystopia in Postwar Italian Literature*.

on particular selections of writers who share a common 'identity' or interest, such as women writers, writers of the *Neoavanguardia*, or writers from a specific region. This book addresses the complexity of a transitional period through a diversified selection of writers rather than using the traditional organizing principle based on a coherent corpus of writings. By investigating diverse perspectives and forms of literary production, this book therefore mirrors more immediately the troubled intensity of the period under examination in such a way as to bring into focus the underlying cultural patterns and anxieties in Italian society of the time.

This focus on individual internalization of post-war changes highlights the difficulty of negotiating rapid transformation. Spatial re-organization of urban and rural places, such as that witnessed in Italy from the late 1950s onwards, may be difficult to accommodate until these changes again become part of an established landscape. Jameson claims that, in contemporary globalized societies, people have yet to develop the 'perceptual equipment' that can allow them to navigate postmodern space.[3] In the present study this is seen, for example, through the periphery as an urban area that is constantly redefined and often perceived as alien and threatening. Another example is provided by the ubiquitous roadworks that, in *La vita agra* and *La donna della domenica*, bear witness to continued urban restructuring and leave the characters feeling frustrated and confused. The fact that the writers analysed in this book write in the midst of unprecedented social change may, therefore, account for their ambivalent or overtly hostile attitudes to urbanization and modernization. It may also account for the perceived fracture between the past, often connected with the values of social solidarity and simplicity of life (as can be seen, for instance, in Bianciardi's nostalgic recollection of the slow pace of life in Grosseto or Ginzburg's longing for the stability of the patriarchal family), and the puzzling reality of modern Italy. In the process the writers express the temporary loss of spatial co-ordinates, which is figured also as a loss of intellectual, emotional and psychological co-ordinates.

The emphasis on the individual perspective also exposes anxiety as defining the Italian post-war period behind the façade of progress and prosperity. In the novels analysed in Chapters 1 and 2, feelings of anxiety are projected onto changing urban spaces. By drawing on the imagery of the city as a site of alienation, these novels express the sense of estrangement and non-belonging which connect many

3 Jameson, *Postmodernism*, p. 38.

experiences of the modern city so as to become a universal trait. At the same time they document specific historical circumstances and hence their criticism of the city betrays broader discontent with the recent developments in Italian society. Chapter 3 explores how transformations play out in the Northern provincial environment portrayed in Ginzburg's *Le voci della sera*, particularly in regard to social and gender roles. Ginzburg's point of view is controversial. On the one hand, she seems, to some extent at least, sympathetic towards her (particularly female) characters' dissatisfaction with the static, conservative way of life in their provincial microcosm. On the other, her yearning for a particular patriarchal family and social order betrays her uneasiness with the modern views, particularly regarding women's emancipated role in society, which were coming to the forefront of public debate at the time thanks to the activities of the Italian feminist movement. Anxiety resurfaces in Chapter 4 as the travel accounts examined there address Italy's territorial fragmentation and problematic sense of national identity at a crucial moment in the country's history. It reverberates through Ortese's perception of the Italian landscape as ineffable and alien, Piovene's reassuring guidebook to navigating Italy's post-war transformation and Arbasino's endlessly restless travel that privileges abroad over a certain intellectual provincialism at home. In some cases anxiety triggers an interrogation of accepted modes of representation, as shown, for example, by Ortese's and Arbasino's problematizing approach to the travel-writing tradition.

As argued throughout the book, anxiety may be an indicator of the incomplete process of cultural reckoning with the past in post-war Italian society. A further thread which emerges from the analysis of literary texts is the ambivalent perception of the post-war years as a rupture with both traditional lifestyles and the political and administrative continuity with the pre-war period. The unprocessed past can, on occasion, manifest itself as a lingering totalitarian threat, the yearning for a traditional urban model, the problematic sense of national identity and, generally speaking, through the persistence of enduring issues that weigh on Italian society, especially evident in the lagging-behind of the South. Very much like the places they portray in the midst of historical transition, the examined texts may be situated at the crossroads of two epochs in the Italian literary tradition. While they retain certain concerns of the modern era, they also anticipate some of the arguments of the postmodern discourse. As seen in the Introduction, the time frame of this book coincides with the slow gestation of postmodern ideas within the somewhat fractious Italian intellectual context of the time.

Throughout this study the analysis of perceptions and representations of space highlights issues such as power and gender relations, the psychological values of the built environment and dominant narratives of Italy that were codified by a largely foreign, reifying gaze. It also foregrounds ways of challenging imposed notions of space either discursively or through concrete spatial practices, for instance the act of walking as a way of reclaiming space, as shown in *La vita agra*. These issues are explored from a variety of theoretical perspectives. Space as the locus where these tensions play out opens up multiple strands of enquiry and, in so doing, additional avenues for further research. These include, for example, exploring more closely the link between mental health and the built environment; how further social and spatial changes were conceptualized by writers in later decades; and a more comprehensive study of the provinces in Italian literature across different epochs and literary genres.

This book provides an account of the complex post-war transition in Italy as expressed by different authorial voices and their complementary narratives. By capturing some key issues and dynamics in post-war Italian society, it contributes to the study and understanding of this crucial historical shift. What has been revealed by a close analysis of the responses to the changing spaces of post-war Italy by the diverse writers who are active in this period is the intensely disruptive experience of the post-war transition, not only in terms of literary or cultural history, but also of the everyday ontological and material experience of Italians of different class, gender and professional activity across the Peninsula. Hence, the time frame and collection of writers explored in this book, perhaps conventionally regarded as anomalous, are crucial to a critical understanding of Italian culture in the post-war years and beyond. One might even say that only by re-examining the Italian post-war transition through the microscopic approach used in this book can we move towards a fuller understanding of the crises of Italian nationhood that have characterized more recent decades.

Bibliography

Primary Sources

Arbasino, Alberto, *Fratelli d'Italia* (Milan: Feltrinelli, 1963)

— *Fratelli d'Italia*, 2nd edn (Turin: Einaudi, 1976 [1967])

Bianciardi, Luciano, *L'integrazione* (Milan: Feltrinelli, 2014 [1960])

— *La vita agra* (Milan: Rizzoli, 1993 [1962])

— *L'antimeridiano. Tutte le opere*, ed. by Luciana Bianciardi, Massimo Coppola and Alberto Piccinini, 2 vols (Milan: Mondadori, 2005–08)

Calvino, Italo, *Se una notte d'inverno un viaggiatore* (Turin: Einaudi, 1979)

— *If on a Winter's Night a Traveller*, trans. by William Weaver (London: Vintage, 2002 [1981])

Fruttero, Carlo, and Franco Lucentini, *La donna della domenica* (Milan: Mondadori, 1972)

— *A che punto è la notte* (Milan: Mondadori, 1987 [1979])

Ginzburg, Natalia, *Le voci della sera*, in *Opere*, 2 vols (Milan: Mondadori, 1986–87) I (1986), 667–777

Mastronardi, Lucio, *Il maestro di Vigevano* (Turin: Einaudi, 1962)

Ortese, Anna Maria, *Silenzio a Milano* (Bari: Laterza, 1958)

— *La lente scura. Scritti di viaggio*, ed. by Luca Clerici (Milan: Adelphi, 2004 [1991])

Piovene, Guido, *Viaggio in Italia* (Milan: Mondadori, 1958)

Scerbanenco, Giorgio, *Milano calibro 9* (Milan: Garzanti, 1993 [1969])

— 'Basta col cianuro', in *Milano calibro 9* (Milan: Garzanti, 1993 [1969]), pp. 26–39

— 'Piccolo Hôtel per sadici', in *Milano calibro 9* (Milan: Garzanti, 1993 [1969]), pp. 171–86

— 'Stazione Centrale ammazzare subito', in *Milano calibro 9* (Milan: Garzanti, 1993 [1969]), pp. 93–110

— *Il Cinquecentodelitti*, ed. by Oreste del Buono (Milan: Frassinelli, 1994)

— *I milanesi ammazzano al sabato* (Milan: Garzanti, 1999 [1969])

— *I ragazzi del massacro* (Milan: Garzanti, 1999 [1968])

— *Traditori di tutti* (Milan: Garzanti, 1999 [1966])

— *Venere privata* (Milan: Garzanti, 1999 [1966])
Volponi, Paolo, *Memoriale* (Milan: Garzanti, 1991 [1962])
— *Le mosche del capitale* (Turin: Einaudi, 1991 [1989])

Films

Rocco e i suoi fratelli, dir. by Luchino Visconti (Titanus, 1960)
La notte, dir. by Michelangelo Antonioni (Dino De Laurentiis Distribuzione, 1961)
Il posto, dir. by Ermanno Olmi (Titanus, 1961)
Deserto rosso, dir. by Michelangelo Antonioni (Cineriz, 1964)

Secondary Sources

Abati, Velio, and others (eds), *Luciano Bianciardi tra neocapitalismo e contestazione* (Rome: Editori riuniti, 1992)

Agamben, Giorgio, 'What Is an Apparatus?', in *What Is an Apparatus? and Other Essays*, trans. by David Kishik and Stefan Pedatella, Meridian: Crossing Aesthetics (Stanford, CA: Stanford University Press, 2009), pp. 1–24

Alaimo, Stacy, *Undomesticated Ground: Recasting Nature as Feminist Space* (Ithaca, NY: Cornell University Press, 2000)

Amatori, Franco, and Andrea Colli, *Impresa e industria in Italia dall'Unità a oggi* (Venice: Marsilio, 1999)

Amery, Carl, 'La provincia come categoria sociologica', *L'Asino d'oro*, 1 (1990), 21–28

Amoia, Alba, *20th-Century Italian Women Writers: The Feminine Experience* (Carbondale, IL: Southern Illinois University Press, 1996)

Angelini, Maria Clotilde, *Luciano Bianciardi* (Florence: La nuova Italia, 1980)

Arnardóttir, Halldóra, 'Architecture and Modernity in Post-war Milan', in *Italian Cityscapes: Culture and Urban Change in Contemporary Italy*, ed. by Robert Lumley and John Foot (Exeter: University of Exeter Press, 2004), pp. 90–99

Baldini, Gianfranco, 'Christian Democracy: The Italian Party', in *The Oxford Handbook of Italian Politics*, ed. by Erik Jones and Gianfranco Pasquino, Oxford Handbooks (Oxford: Oxford University Press, 2015), pp. 173–83

Barański, Zygmunt G., and Robert Lumley, 'Turbulent Transitions: An Introduction', in *Culture and Conflict in Postwar Italy: Essays on Mass and Popular Culture*, ed. by Zygmunt G. Barański and Robert Lumley, University of Reading European and International Studies (London: Macmillan, 1990), pp. 1–17

Bàrberi Squarotti, Giorgio, 'La letteratura e la "nuova natura" creata dell'industria', in *Letteratura e industria: Atti del XV Congresso A.I.S.L.L.I., Torino, 15–19 maggio 1994*, ed. by Giorgio Bàrberi Squarotti and Carlo Ossola, 2 vols, Biblioteca dell'Archivum Romanicum, 276 (Florence: Olschki, 1997), I, *Dal Medioevo al primo Novecento*, pp. 25–42

— *Storia della civiltà letteraria italiana*, 6 vols (Turin: UTET, 1996), V, *Il secondo Ottocento e il Novecento*

Bàrberi Squarotti, Giorgio, and Carlo Ossola (eds), *Letteratura e industria. Atti del XV Congresso A.I.S.L.L.I., Torino, 15–19 maggio 1994*, 2 vols, Biblioteca dell'Archivum Romanicum, 276 (Florence: Olschki, 1997)

Bardazzi, Adele, and Alberica Bazzoni (eds), *Gender and Authority Across Disciplines, Space and Time* (Basingstoke: Palgrave Macmillan, 2020)

Bassnett, Susan, 'Travel Writing and Gender', in *The Cambridge Companion to Travel Writing*, ed. by Peter Hulme and Tim Youngs (Cambridge: Cambridge University Press, 2002), pp. 225–41

Bellassai, Sandro, *La legge del desiderio. Il progetto Merlin e l'Italia degli anni cinquanta* (Rome: Carocci, 2006)

Ben-Ghiat, Ruth, 'Fascism, Writing, and Memory: The Realist Aesthetic in Italy, 1930–1950', *The Journal of Modern History*, 67 (1995), 627–65

— 'Liberation: Italian Cinema and the Fascist Past, 1945–50', in *Italian Fascism: History, Memory and Representation*, ed. by R. J. B. Bosworth and Patrizia Dogliani (Basingstoke: MacMillan, 1999), pp. 83–101

Benjamin, Walter, *The Writer of Modern Life: Essays on Charles Baudelaire*, ed. by Michael W. Jennings, trans. by Howard Eiland and others (Cambridge, MA: Belknap Press, 2006)

Berardinelli, Alfonso, 'Volponi, uno scrittore "diverso"', in *Paolo Volponi. Il coraggio dell'utopia*, ed. by Massimo Raffaeli (Ancona: Transeuropa, 1997), pp. 11–18

Best, David Albert, *Ruralism in Central Italian Writers, 1927–1997: From 'Strapaese' Landscapes to the Gendering of Nature: Fabio Tombari, Paolo Volponi, Carlo Cassola, Romana Petri* (Ancona: Ancona University Press, 2010)

Bianciardi, Luciano, and Carlo Cassola, *I minatori della Maremma* (Bari: Laterza, 1956)

Biraghi, Marco, Gabriella Lo Ricco and Silvia Micheli, *Guida all'architettura di Milano, 1954–2014* (Milan: Hoepli, 2013)

Black, Jeremy, *Italy and the Grand Tour* (New Haven, CT: Yale University Press, 2003)

Bondanella, Peter, and Andrea Ciccarelli (eds), *The Cambridge Companion to the Italian Novel* (Cambridge: Cambridge University Press, 2003)

Bosworth, R. J. B., and Patrizia Dogliani (eds), *Italian Fascism: History, Memory and Representation* (Basingstoke: MacMillan, 1999)

Bracke, Maude A., *Women and the Reinvention of the Political: Feminism in Italy, 1968–1983*, Routledge Research in Gender and History (New York: Routledge, 2014)

Burdett, Charles, 'Nomos, Identity and Otherness: Ciro Poggiali's *Diario AOI 1936–1937* and the Representation of the Italian Colonial World', *Papers of the British School at Rome*, 79 (2011), 329–49

Burns, Jennifer, *Fragments of Impegno: Interpretations of Commitment in Contemporary Italian Narrative, 1980–2000* (Leeds: Northern Universities Press, 2001)

——— 'Founding Fathers: Giorgio Scerbanenco', in *Italian Crime Fiction*, ed. by Giuliana Pieri (Cardiff: University of Wales Press, 2011), pp. 27–47

Butler, Chris, *Henri Lefebvre: Spatial Politics, Everyday Life and the Right to the City*, Nomikoi: Critical Legal Thinkers (Abingdon: Routledge, 2012)

Cachey, Theodore J., 'An Italian Literary History of Travel', in *L'Odeporica/Hodoeporics: On Travel Literature*, ed. by Luigi Monga (= *Annali d'Italianistica*, 14 (1996)), pp. 55–64

Caesar, Ann Hallamore, and Michael Caesar, *Modern Italian Literature*, Cultural History of Literature (Cambridge: Polity, 2007)

Caesar, Michael, and Peter Hainsworth, 'The Transformation of Post-War Italy', in *Writers and Society in Contemporary Italy: A Collection of Essays*, ed. by Michael Caesar and Peter Hainsworth (Leamington Spa: Berg, 1984), pp. 1–34

Canosa, Romano, *Storia della criminalità in Italia dal 1946 ad oggi* (Milan: Feltrinelli, 1995)

Capozzi, Rocco, 'Dalla "Letteratura e industria" all'industria del postmoderno', *Annali d'Italianistica*, 9 (1991), 144–57

Caputo-Mayr, Maria-Luise, 'La funzione della natura e del paesaggio nei romanzi di Guido Piovene', *Italica*, 50 (1973), 53–65

Carloni, Massimo, *L'Italia in giallo. Geografia e storia del giallo italiano contemporaneo* (Reggio Emilia: Diabasis, 2006 [1994])

Ceserani, Remo, 'Dalla piccola città alla cosmopoli: Premessa: Scene di provincia', *L'Asino d'oro*, 1 (1990), 3–7

Ceserani, Remo, and Pierluigi Pellini, 'The Belated Development of a Theory of the Novel in Italian Literary Culture', in *The Cambridge Companion to the Italian Novel*, ed. by Peter Bondanella and Andrea

Ciccarelli (Cambridge: Cambridge University Press, 2003), pp. 1–19

Chandler, Billy Jaynes, *King of the Mountain: The Life and Death of Giuliano the Bandit* (DeKalb, IL: Northern Illinois University Press, 1988)

Chambers, Iain, *Migrancy, Culture, Identity* (London: Routledge, 1993)

Clementelli, Elena, *Invito alla lettura di Natalia Ginzburg* (Milan: Mursia, 1986)

Clerici, Luca, 'Alla scoperta del Bel Paese: i titoli delle testimonianze dei viaggiatori italiani in Italia, 1750–1900', in *L'Odeporica/ Hodoeporics: On Travel Literature*, ed. by Luigi Monga (= *Annali d'Italianistica*, 14 (1996)), pp. 271–303

— *Viaggiatori italiani in Italia, 1700–1998. Per una bibliografia* (Milan: Bonnard, 1999)

— 'Notizia sul testo', in Anna Maria Ortese, *La lente scura. Scritti di viaggio*, ed. by Luca Clerici (Milan: Adelphi, 2004 [1991]), pp. 467–501

— (ed.), *Il viaggiatore meravigliato. Italiani in Italia 1714–1996* (Milan: Il Saggiatore, 1999)

Clò, Clarissa, 'Visions of Italy Beyond the North/South Divide: Regional Documentaries and Global Identities', in *Negotiating Italian Identities*, ed. by Norma Bouchard (= *Annali d'Italianistica*, 24 (2006)), pp. 41–60

Coletti, Alessandro, *Mafie: Storia della criminalità organizzata nel Mezzogiorno* (Turin: Società Editrice Internazionale, 1995)

Coppola, Massimo, and Alberto Piccinini, 'Luciano Bianciardi, l'io opaco', in Luciano Bianciardi, *L'antimeridiano. Tutte le opere*, ed. by Luciana Bianciardi, Massimo Coppola and Alberto Piccinini, 2 vols (Milan: Mondadori, 2005–08), I (2005), *Saggi e romanzi, racconti, diari giovanili*, pp. v–xxxv

Corrias, Pino, *Vita agra di un anarchico. Luciano Bianciardi a Milano* (Milan: Baldini & Castoldi, 1996)

Coverley, Merlin, *Psychogeography* (Harpenden: Pocket Essentials, 2010 [2006])

Crainz, Guido, *Storia del miracolo italiano. Culture, identità, trasformazioni fra anni cinquanta e sessanta* (Rome: Donzelli, 2003 [1996])

— *Il paese mancato. Dal miracolo economico agli anni Ottanta* (Rome: Donzelli, 2003)

Crampton, Jeremy W., and Stuart Elden, 'Introduction', in *Space, Knowledge and Power*, ed. by Jeremy W. Crampton and Stuart Elden (Aldershot: Ashgate, 2007), pp. 1–16

Crovi, Luca, *Tutti i colori del giallo. Il giallo italiano da De Marchi a Scerbanenco a Camilleri* (Venice: Marsilio, 2002)

Dear, Michael J., *The Postmodern Urban Condition* (Oxford: Blackwell, 2000)

De Certeau, Michel, *The Practice of Everyday Life*, trans. by Steven F. Rendall (Berkeley, CA: University of California Press, 1984); originally published as *L'Invention du Quotidien* (Paris: Union générale d'éditions, 1980)

Dondi, Mirco, 'The Fascist Mentality after Fascism', in *Italian Fascism: History, Memory and Representation*, ed. by R. J. B. Bosworth and Patrizia Dogliani (Basingstoke: MacMillan, 1999), pp. 141–60

Duggan, Christopher, 'Italy in the Cold War Years and the Legacy of Fascism', in *Italy in the Cold War: Politics, Culture and Society, 1948–58*, ed. by Christopher Duggan and Christopher Wagstaff (Oxford: Berg, 1995), pp. 1–24

Dunnage, Jonathan, 'Conclusion: Facing the Past and Building for the Future in Postwar Italy', in *After the War: Violence, Justice, Continuity and Renewal in Italian Society*, ed. by Jonathan Dunnage (Market Harborough: Troubador, 1999), pp. 89–100

Dunnett, Jane, 'The Emergence of a New Literary Genre in Interwar Italy', in *Italian Crime Fiction*, ed. by Giuliana Pieri (Cardiff: University of Wales Press, 2011), pp. 6–26

Eco, Umberto, *Opera aperta*, 3rd edn (Milan: Bompiani, 1976 [1962])

— *Apocalittici e integrati*, 7th edn (Milan: Bompiani, 1988 [1964])

Edelman, Lee, *No Future: Queer Theory and the Death Drive* (Durham, NC: Duke University Press, 2004)

Ellin, Nan, *Postmodern Urbanism* (New York: Princeton Architectural Press, 1999 [1996])

Ferretti, Gian Carlo, *Paolo Volponi* (Florence: La nuova Italia, 1972)

Finch, Jason, Lieven Ameel and Markku Salmela, 'The Second City in Literary Urban Studies: Methods, Approaches, Key Thematics', in *Literary Second Cities*, ed. by Jason Finch, Lieven Ameel and Markku Salmela (Basingstoke: Palgrave Macmillan, 2017), pp. 3–30

Fiorentino, Francesco, 'Verso una geostoria della letteratura', in *Letteratura e geografia. Atlanti, modelli, letture*, ed. by Francesco Fiorentino and Carla Solivetti (Macerata: Quodlibet, 2012), pp. 13–44

Fioretti, Daniele, *Utopia and Dystopia in Postwar Italian Literature: Pasolini, Calvino, Sanguineti, Volponi*, Italian and Italian American Studies (Basingstoke: Palgrave Macmillan, 2017)

Fisher, Mark, *The Weird and the Eerie* (London: Repeater, 2016)

Flores, Marcello, 'La provincia come categoria storiografica', *L'Asino d'oro*, 1 (1990), 8–20

Fontanella, Luigi, 'Natalia Ginzburg Between Fiction and Memory: A Reading of *Le voci della sera* and *Lessico famigliare*', in *Natalia Ginzburg: A Voice of the Twentieth Century*, ed. by Angela M. Jeannet and Giuliana Sanguinetti Katz, Toronto Italian Studies (Toronto: University of Toronto Press, 2016), pp. 32–45

Foot, John, *Milan since the Miracle: City, Culture and Identity* (Oxford: Berg, 2001)

— 'Revisiting the *Coree*: Self-construction, Memory and Immigration on the Milanese Periphery, 1950–2000', in *Italian Cityscapes: Culture and Urban Change in Contemporary Italy*, ed. by Robert Lumley and John Foot (Exeter: University of Exeter Press, 2004), pp. 46–60

— *Modern Italy* (Basingstoke: Palgrave Macmillan, 2014)

Forgacs, David, *Italy's Margins: Social Exclusion and Nation Formation Since 1861*, Cambridge Social and Cultural Histories (Cambridge: Cambridge University Press, 2014)

Forgacs, David, and Stephen Gundle, *Mass Culture and Italian Society from Fascism to the Cold War* (Bloomington, IN: Indiana University Press, 2008)

Forti, Marco, 'Temi industriali della narrativa italiana', *Il Menabò*, 4 (1961), 213–39

Fortunati, Vita, Rita Monticelli and Maurizio Ascari, 'Introduction', in *Travel Writing and the Female Imaginary*, ed. by Vita Fortunati, Rita Monticelli and Maurizio Ascari (Bologna: Patron, 2001), pp. 5–16

Foucault, Michel, *Discipline and Punish: The Birth of the Prison*, trans. by Alan Sheridan (London: Penguin, 1995); originally published as *Surveiller et punir: Naissance de la prison* (Paris: Gallimard, 1975)

— 'The Incorporation of the Hospital into Modern Technology' [lecture 1974], trans. by Edgar Knowlton Jr., William J. King and Stuart Elden, in *Space, Knowledge and Power: Foucault and Geography*, ed. by Jeremy W. Crampton and Stuart Elden (Aldershot: Ashgate, 2007), pp. 141–51; originally published in *Hermès* (1988), 2, 30–40

Freud, Sigmund, 'The Uncanny', in *The Uncanny*, trans. by David McLintock (London: Penguin, 2003), pp. 121–62; first published as 'Das Unheimliche', *Imago*, 5 (1919), 297–324

Frisby, David, *Cityscapes of Modernity: Critical Explorations* (Cambridge: Polity, 2001)

Fyfe, Nicholas R., 'Introduction: Reading the Street', in *Images of the Street: Planning, Identity and Control in Public Space*, ed. by Nicholas R. Fyfe (London: Routledge, 1998), pp. 1–10

Gabaccia, Donna R., *Italy's Many Diasporas*, Global Diasporas (Seattle: University of Washington Press, 2000)

Gerbi, Sandro, *Tempi di malafede: Guido Piovene ed Eugenio Colorni. Una storia italiana tra fascismo e dopoguerra* (Milan: Hoepli, 2012)

Ginsborg, Paul, *A History of Contemporary Italy: Society and Politics 1943–1988* (London: Penguin, 1990)

Glaeser, Edward L., and Bruce Sacerdote, 'Why Is There More Crime in Cities?', *The Journal of Political Economy*, 107 (1999), 225–58

Gregory, Derek, *Geographical Imaginations* (Oxford: Blackwell, 1994)

Guagnini, Elvio, *Il viaggio, lo sguardo, la scrittura* (Trieste: Edizioni Università di Trieste, 2010)

Harvey, David, 'Globalization and the Spatial Fix', *Geographische Revue*, 2 (2001), 23–30

— *The Limits to Capital* (London: Verso, 2006 [1982])

Helleland, Botolv, 'Place Names and Identities', in *Names and Identities*, ed. by Botolov Helleland, Christian-Emil Ore & Solveig Wikstrøm (= *Oslo Studies in Language*, 4 (2012)), pp. 95–116 <https://www.journals.uio.no/index.php/osla/article/view/313/438> [accessed 21 September 2018]

Hellman, Judith Adler, *Journeys Among Women: Feminism in Five Italian Cities* (Cambridge: Polity, 1987)

Heynen, Hilde, *Architecture and Modernity: A Critique* (Cambridge, MA: MIT Press, 1999)

Holland, Patrick, and Graham Huggan, 'Postmodern Itineraries', in *Travel Writing*, ed. by Tim Youngs and Charles Forsdick, Critical Concepts in Literary and Cultural Studies, 4 vols (London: Routledge, 2012), II, *The Contexts of Travel*, pp. 489–509

Hollier, Denis (ed.), *Against Architecture: The Writings of Georges Bataille*, trans. by Betsy Wing (Cambridge, MA: MIT Press, 1992 [1989])

Howell, Philip, 'Crime and the City Solution: Crime Fiction, Urban Knowledge, and Radical Geography', *Antipode*, 30 (1998), 357–78

Hulme, Peter, and Tim Youngs, *The Cambridge Companion to Travel Writing* (Cambridge: Cambridge University Press, 2002)

Huskinson, Lucy, 'Introduction', in *The Urban Uncanny: A Collection of Interdisciplinary Studies*, ed. by Lucy Huskinson (London: Routledge, 2016), pp. 1–17

Iacoli, Giulio, *Atlante delle derive. Geografie da un'Emilia postmoderna: Gianni Celati e Pier Vittorio Tondelli* (Reggio Emilia: Diabasis, 2002)

Jameson, Fredric, *Postmodernism, or, the Cultural Logic of Late Capitalism*, Post-Contemporary Interventions (London: Verso, 1991)

Jansen, Monica, *Il dibattito sul postmoderno in Italia. In bilico tra dialettica e ambiguità* (Florence: Franco Cesati, 2002)

Kern, Leslie, *Feminist City: Claiming Space in a Man-Made World* (London: Verso, 2020)

Lee, Joanne, 'Alternative Urban Journeys: Italian Travel Writing and the *Contromano* Series', *Studies in Travel Writing*, 16 (2012), 203–14 <http://dx.doi.org/10.1080/13645145.2012.682820> [accessed 7 February 2017]

Lefebvre, Henri, *The Survival of Capitalism: Reproduction of the Relations of Production*, trans. by Frank Bryant (London: Allison and Busby, 1976); originally published as *La survie du capitalism. La reproduction des rapports de production* (Paris: Anthropos, 1973)

— *The Production of Space*, trans. by Donald Nicholson-Smith (Oxford: Blackwell, 1991); originally published as *La production de l'espace*, Société et urbanisme, 9 (Paris: Anthropos, 1974)

— 'Industrialization and Urbanization', in *Writings on Cities*, ed. and trans. by Eleonore Kofman and Elizabeth Lebas (Cambridge, MA: Blackwell, 1996), pp. 65–85

— 'Perspective or Prospective?', in *Writings on Cities*, ed. and trans. by Eleonore Kofman and Elizabeth Lebas (Cambridge, MA: Blackwell, 1996), pp. 160–74

— *Writings on Cities*, ed. and trans. by Eleonore Kofman and Elizabeth Lebas (Cambridge, MA: Blackwell, 1996)

Lehan, Richard, *The City in Literature: An Intellectual and Cultural History* (Berkeley, CA: University of California Press, 1998)

Levy, Carl, 'Introduction: Italian Regionalism in Context', in *Italian Regionalism: History, Identity and Politics*, ed. by Carl Levy (Oxford: Berg, 1996), pp. 1–30

Lobsinger, Mary L., 'Architectural Utopias and *La Nuova Dimensione*: Turin in the 1960s', in *Italian Cityscapes: Culture and Urban Change in Contemporary Italy*, ed. by Robert Lumley and John Foot (Exeter: University of Exeter Press, 2004), pp. 77–89

Luckhurst, Roger, 'The Contemporary London Gothic and the Limits of the Spectral Turn', *Textual Practice*, 16 (2002), 527–46

Lumley, Robert, 'Turin after Arte Povera: A New City of Art?', in *Italian Cityscapes: Culture and Urban Change in Italy*, ed. by Robert Lumley and John Foot (Exeter: University of Exeter Press, 2004), pp. 100–13

Luperini, Romano, *Controtempo. Critica e letteratura fra moderno e postmoderno: proposte, polemiche e bilanci di fine secolo* (Naples: Liguori, 1999)

Maher, Vanessa, 'Immigration and Social Identities', in *Italian Cultural Studies: An Introduction*, ed. by David Forgacs and Robert Lumley (Oxford: Oxford University Press, 1996), pp. 160–77

Manai, Franco, '*La donna della domenica* and the Italian Detective Novel of the 1970s', in *Differences, Deceits and Desires: Murder and Mayhem in Italian Crime Fiction*, ed. by Mirna Cicioni and Nicoletta Di Ciolla (Newark, DE: University of Delaware Press, 2008), pp. 83–98

Martignoni, Clelia, Cinzia Lucchelli and Elisabetta Cammarata (eds), *La scrittura infinita di Alberto Arbasino. Studi su 'Fratelli d'Italia'*, Biblioteca di Autografo, 4 (Novara: Interlinea, 1999)

Massey, Doreen, *Space, Place and Gender* (Cambridge: Polity, 1994)

Mastrogianakos, John, 'Embedded Narratives of Subversion in Luciano Bianciardi's *La vita agra'*, *Forum Italicum*, 37 (2003), 121–46

Mazzola, Alessandro, 'Giorgio Scerbanenco e Duca Lamberti: note su un incontro fatale', *Delitti di carta*, 6 (2006), 37–47

Merchant, Carolyn, *The Death of Nature: Women, Ecology, and the Scientific Revolution* (London: Widwood House, 1982 [1980])

Mills, Sara, *Discourses of Difference: An Analysis of Women's Travel Writing and Colonialism* (London: Routledge, 1991)

Minghelli, Giuliana, 'Icons of Remorse: Photography, Anthropology and the Erasure of History in 1950s Italy', *Modern Italy*, 21 (2016), 383–407

Misuri Douglas, Isolina, '*Fratelli d'Italia*: Alberto Arbasino's "Great Comedy of the Sixties"', *Italian Quarterly*, 161/162 (2004), 68–81

Mondello, Elisabetta, 'Il "*noir* italiano". Appunti sul romanzo nero contemporaneo', in *Noir de Noir. Un'indagine pluridisciplinare*, ed. by Dieter Vermandere, Monica Jansen and Inge Lanslots, Moving Texts/Testi mobili, 2 (Brussels: Lang, 2010), pp. 23–31

Mori, Piergiorgio, *Scrittori nel boom. Il romanzo industriale negli anni del miracolo italiano* (Rome: EdiLet-Edilazio, 2011)

Morland, Iain, and Annabelle Willox, 'Introduction', in *Queer Theory*, ed. by Iain Morland and Annabelle Willox (Basingstoke: Palgrave Macmillan, 2005), pp. 1–5

Muraca, Giuseppe, *Utopisti ed eretici nella letteratura italiana contemporanea. Saggi su Silone, Bilenchi, Fortini, Pasolini, Bianciardi, Roversi e Bellocchio* (Soveria Mannelli: Rubbettino, 2000)

— *Luciano Bianciardi. Uno scrittore fuori dal coro* (Pistoia: Centro di Documentazione, 2012)

Murakami Wood, David, 'Beyond the Panopticon? Foucault and Surveillance Studies', in *Space, Knowledge and Power: Foucault and Geography*, ed. by Jeremy W. Crampton and Stuart Elden (Aldershot: Ashgate, 2007), pp. 245–63

Ogborn, Miles, *Spaces of Modernity: London's Geographies, 1680–1780* (New York: Guilford, 1998)

Olivetti, Adriano, *Città dell'uomo* (Milan: Edizioni di Comunità, 1960)

Ouditt, Sharon, and Loredana Polezzi, 'Introduction: Italy as Place and Space', *Studies in Travel Writing*, 16 (2012), 97–105 <http://dx.doi. org/10.1080/13645145.2012.682807> [accessed 7 February 2017]

Paoli, Marco, *Giorgio Scerbanenco: Urban Space, Violence and Gender Identity in Post-War Italian Crime Fiction*, Moving Texts/Testi mobili, 8 (Brussels: Lang, 2016)

Papotti, Davide, 'Il libro in valigia: eredità odeporiche nel romanzo italiano contemporaneo', in *L'Odeporica/Hodoeporics: On Travel Literature*, ed. by Luigi Monga (= *Annali d'Italianistica*, 14 (1996)), pp. 351–62

Pastore, Judith L., 'The Personal is Political: Gender, Generation, and Memory in Natalia Ginzburg's *Caro Michele*', in *Natalia Ginzburg: A Voice of the Twentieth Century*, ed. by Angela M. Jeannet and Giuliana Sanguinetti Katz, Toronto Italian Studies (Toronto: University of Toronto Press, 2016), pp. 89–98

Pavone, Claudio, 'La continuità dello stato: istituzioni e uomini', in *Italia 1945–48: le origini della Repubblica*, ed. by Enzo Piscitelli and others (Turin: Giappichelli, 1974), pp. 137–289

— *Alle origini della Repubblica. Scritti su fascismo, antifascismo e continuità dello Stato* (Turin: Bollati Boringhieri, 1995)

Pedullà, Walter, 'Vita e opere di Paolo Volponi', in *Paolo Volponi* (= *L'Illuminista*, 24 (2008)), pp. 25–36

Petrillo, Gianfranco, 'The Two Waves: Milan as a City of Immigration, 1955–1995', in *Italian Cityscapes: Culture and Urban Change in Contemporary Italy*, ed. by Robert Lumley and John Foot (Exeter: University of Exeter Press, 2004), pp. 31–45

Pezzotti, Barbara, *The Importance of Place in Italian Contemporary Crime Fiction: A Bloody Journey*, The Farleigh Dickinson University Press Series in Italian Studies (Madison, WI: Farleigh Dickinson University Press, 2012)

— *Politics and Society in Italian Crime Fiction: An Historical Overview* (Jefferson, NC: McFarland, 2014)

Pieri, Giuliana, 'Crime and the City in the Detective Fiction of Giorgio Scerbanenco', in *Italian Cityscapes: Culture and Urban Change in Contemporary Italy*, ed. by Robert Lumley and John Foot (Exeter: University of Exeter Press, 2004), pp. 144–55

— 'Introduction', in *Italian Crime Fiction*, ed. by Giuliana Pieri (Cardiff: University of Wales Press, 2011), pp. 1–5

— 'Milano nera: Representing and Imagining Milan in Italian *Noir* and Crime Fiction', in *Italian Crime Fiction*, ed. by Giuliana Pieri (Cardiff: University of Wales Press, 2011), pp. 132–50

Pistelli, Maurizio, *Un secolo in giallo. Storia del poliziesco italiano (1860–1960)* (Rome: Donzelli, 2006)

Plumwood, Val, *Feminism and the Mastery of Nature*, Opening Out: Feminism for Today (London: Routledge, 1993)

Pombeni, Paolo, 'Christian Democracy in Power, 1946–63', in *The Oxford Handbook of Italian Politics*, ed. by Erik Jones and Gianfranco Pasquino, Oxford Handbooks (Oxford: Oxford University Press, 2015), pp. 255–67

Provost, Claire, and Simone Lai, 'Story of Cities #21: Olivetti tries to build the ideal "human city" for its workers', *The Guardian*, 13 April 2016 <https://www.theguardian.com/cities/2016/apr/13/story-cities-21-adriano-olivetti-ivrea-italy-typewriter-factory-human-city> [accessed 8 March 2022]

Raffaeli, Massimo (ed.), *Paolo Volponi. Il coraggio dell'utopia* (Ancona: Transeuropa, 1997)

Randoing, Chantal, 'Il plurilinguismo del romanzo-conversazione in *Fratelli d'Italia* di Alberto Arbasino', *Collection de l'ÉCRIT*, 11 (2007), 359–75

Rhodes, John David, *Stupendous, Miserable City: Pasolini's Rome* (Minneapolis, MN: University of Minnesota Press, 2007)

— 'Antonioni and the Development of Style', in *Antonioni: Centenary Essays*, ed. by Laura Rascaroli and John David Rhodes (London: Palgrave Macmillan, 2011), pp. 276–300

Riccobono, Rossella, 'Introduction', in *The Poetics of the Margins: Mapping Europe from the Interstices*, ed. by Rossella Riccobono, Cultural Identity Studies (Oxford: Lang, 2010), pp. 1–16

Righini, Michele, 'Città degli incubi', in *Luoghi della letteratura italiana*, ed. by Gian Mario Anselmi and Gino Ruozzi (Milan: Mondadori, 2003), pp. 142–52

Ritrovato, Salvatore, and Donatella Marchi, 'Nota', in *Pianeta Volponi. Saggi interventi testimonianze*, ed. by Salvatore Ritrovato and Donatella Marchi (Pesaro: Metauro, 2007), pp. 7–8

Rodighiero, Alberto, 'Fratelli d'Italia', *Studi Novecenteschi*, 30 (2003), 265–81

Ross, Silvia, *Tuscan Spaces: Literary Constructions of Place*, Toronto Italian Studies (Toronto: Toronto University Press, 2010)

Ruggiero, Vincenzo, and Nigel South, *Eurodrugs: Drug Use, Markets and Trafficking in Europe* (London: Routledge, 2016 [1995])

Schoonover, Karl, 'Antonioni's Waste Management', in *Antonioni: Centenary Essays*, ed. by Laura Rascaroli and John David Rhodes (London: Palgrave Macmillan, 2011), pp. 235–53

Scrivano, Fabrizio, 'Individuo, società e territorio nei romanzi di Paolo Volponi. Le soluzioni narrative di *Memoriale* e *La strada per Roma*', *Esperienze letterarie*, 25 (2000), 88–104

Sechi, Mario, 'Centri e periferie di città in Pier Paolo Pasolini e Paolo Volponi', *Urbanistica*, 125 (2004), 90–96

Self, Will, 'Will Self on the Meaning of Skyscrapers: From the Tower of Babel to the Shard', *The Guardian*, 27 March 2015 <http://www.theguardian.com/books/2015/mar/27/will-self-on-the-meaning-of-skyscrapers> [accessed 20 May 2015]

Serino, Gian Paolo, *Luciano Bianciardi. Il precario esistenziale* (Florence: Clichy, 2015)

Smith, Sidonie, 'On the Road: (Auto)mobility and Gendered Detours', in *Travel Writing*, ed. by Tim Youngs and Charles Forsdick, Critical Concepts in Literary and Cultural Studies, 4 vols (London: Routledge, 2012), iii, *Modes of Travel, Types of Traveller*, pp. 98–126

Spunta, Marina, 'Escaping the World and Returning to the "Province" in Claudio Piersanti's Fiction', in *The Poetics of the Margins: Mapping Europe from the Interstices*, ed. by Rossella Riccobono, Cultural Identity Studies (Oxford: Lang, 2010), pp. 33–53

Stoner, Jill, *Toward a Minor Architecture* (Cambridge, MA: MIT Press, 2012)

Tambor, Molly, 'Prostitutes and Politicians: The Women's Rights Movement in the Legge Merlin Debates', in *Women in Italy, 1945–1960: An Interdisciplinary Study*, ed. by Penelope Morris (New York: Palgrave Macmillan, 2006), pp. 131–46

Tamiozzo Goldmann, Silvana, 'Appunti sul *Viaggio in Italia*', in *Viaggi e Paesaggi di Guido Piovene. Atti del Convegno Venezia-Padova, 24–25 gennaio 2008*, ed. by Enza Del Tedesco and Alberto Zava (Pisa: Serra, 2009), pp. 103–22

Terrosi, Mario, and Alberto Gessani, *L'intellettuale disintegrato. Luciano Bianciardi*, Bibliotheca Ianua, 9 (Rome: Ianua, 1985)

Thompson, Kristin, 'The Concept of Cinematic Excess', in *Narrative, Apparatus, Ideology: A Film Theory Reader*, ed. by Philip Rosen (New York: Columbia University Press, 1986), pp. 130–42

Torriglia, Anna Maria, *Broken Time, Fragmented Space: A Cultural Map for Postwar Italy*, Toronto Italian Studies (Toronto: University of Toronto Press, 2002)

Valtorta, Roberta, Sarah Patricia Hill and Giuliana Minghelli, 'Photography and the Construction of Italian National Identity', in *Stillness in Motion: Italy, Photography and the Meanings of Modernity* (Toronto: Toronto University Press, 2014), pp. 27–56

Varese, Federico, *Mafias on the Move: How Organized Crime Conquers New Territories* (Princeton, NJ: Princeton University Press, 2011)

Varotti, Carlo, 'Fabbrica', in *Luoghi della letteratura italiana*, ed. by Gian Mario Anselmi and Gino Ruozzi (Milan: Mondadori, 2003), pp. 180–90

Verdicchio, Pasquale, 'Introduction: The Denatured Wild: Ecocritical Approaches to Italian Culture and Literature', in *Ecocritical Approaches to Italian Culture and Literature: The Denatured Wild*, ed. by Pasquale Verdicchio (London: Lexington Books, 2016), pp. vi–xvi

Vermandere, Dieter, Monica Jansen and Inge Lanslots, 'Introduzione', in *Noir de Noir. Un'indagine pluridisciplinare*, ed. by Dieter Vermandere, Monica Jansen and Inge Lanslots (Brussels: Lang, 2010), pp. 9–19

Vidler, Anthony, *The Architectural Uncanny: Essays in The Modern Unhomely* (London: The MIT Press, 1992)

Virdia, Ferdinando, 'Il tema è sempre l'utopia', *La fiera letteraria*, 12 (1974), 18–19

West, Rebecca, 'Introduction', in *Natalia Ginzburg: A Voice of the Twentieth Century*, ed. by Angela M. Jeannet and Giuliana Sanguinetti Katz, Toronto Italian Studies (Toronto: University of Toronto Press, 2016), pp. 3–9

Williams, Raymond, *The Country and the City* (Oxford: Oxford University Press, 1973)

Williams, Richard J., *The Anxious City: English Urbanism in the Late Twentieth Century* (London: Routledge, 2004)

Willson, Perry, *Women in Twentieth-Century Italy*, Gender and History (Basingstoke: Palgrave Macmillan, 2009)

Wood, Sharon, 'Strange Euphorias and Promised Lands: The Travel Writing of Anna Maria Ortese', in *Literature and Travel*, ed. by Michael Hanne, Rodopi Perspectives on Modern Literature (Amsterdam: Rodopi, 1993), pp. 181–92

— *Italian Women's Writing 1860–1994*, Women in Context (London: Athlone, 1995)

Youngs, Tim, and Charles Forsdick (eds), *Travel Writing*, Critical Concepts in Literary and Cultural Studies, 4 vols (London: Routledge, 2012)

— 'Introduction', in *Travel Writing*, ed. by Tim Youngs and Charles Forsdick, Critical Concepts in Literary and Cultural Studies, 4 vols (London: Routledge, 2012), i, *The Production of Travel Writing*, pp. 1–24

Zinato, Emanuele, 'Paolo Volponi: letteratura e industria', *Doppiozero*, 27 August 2012 <http://www.doppiozero.com/materiali/made-in/paolo-volponi-letteratura-e-industria> [accessed 20 February 2018]

Index

Milton Keynes UK
Ingram Content Group UK Ltd.
UKHW020658180124
436254UK00016B/791